*Anne
Boleyn*

Anne
Boleyn

BY EVELYN ANTHONY

THOMAS Y. CROWELL COMPANY, NEW YORK

*Anne
Boleyn*

1

I T WAS A STILL AND LOVELY SUMMER AFTERNOON WHEN THE TRAIN
of riders, headed by the King, turned into Hever Castle. He rode a
head taller than the others and, after setting a grueling pace from
London, he was still fresh. At thirty-four Henry VIII was in his
physical prime. He was tall and massively built; he still wrestled
and maintained his reputation as the most formidable sportsman
in the country.

He had called his gentlemen and ridden out of Greenwich Palace
on an impulse to visit his new comptroller, see the Kentish countryside, and rest for a few hours at Hever before returning to London.
The King had made the Lord of Hever a peer when he gave him
the post of comptroller a short time before, and Sir Thomas Boleyn,
grandson of a London merchant, had become Viscount Rochford.
As the cavalcade trotted into the castle courtyard, two flustered
servants ran inside with news of the King's arrival, which brought
the new Lord Rochford hurrying to Henry's stirrup after a volley
of orders to his wife to get everything prepared.

He kissed the King's hand; and Henry dismounted and smacked
him on the shoulder, grinning at the comptroller's confusion and
delight. It was pleasant to feel welcome, a relief to arrive like any
private gentleman on a visit to a friend's house, and stop for wine
and talk before returning to London and the problems he had
ridden away from so abruptly that afternoon.

"Your Grace . . . This is a great honor! I fear you find us unprepared. . ."

Henry laughed; he had the gift of putting people at their ease.
He had only to throw his arm around a man's neck and speak a few
friendly words to him to make that man his servant for life. He

1

liked Rochford. Even if the man was a parvenu and a place seeker, he was able and clever in his dealing with the King and that was all that mattered.

"No ceremony, Rochford, no ceremony this time. I've come to spend an hour or two in your fine house and take some simple hospitality from you."

Rochford made a deep bow.

"I'm overwhelmed, Your Grace. My house and everything in it is yours."

"Then take me inside, out of the heat. Come, gentlemen!"

Lady Rochford met him on the steps, curtsying to the ground; immediately he was surrounded and led away into Rochford's best apartments, while servants ran to take care of the horses and his suite split up in search of drink and shade.

Hever had very fine rooms, the King thought, noticing the magnificent tapestries on the walls and the gold plate set out on the sideboard. He had an eye that noticed everything. Rochford had certainly profited by his favor. . . . The first hour passed pleasantly enough; they discussed the affairs of the Household and Rochford's duties as comptroller, while his wife sat nervously on the edge of her chair and moved only to offer the King more wine or some of the ripe fruit which, she explained, grew in their own walled gardens.

Elizabeth Rochford was a dull, rather plain woman, obviously afraid of her husband. Looking at her, Henry found it difficult to believe that she was the Duke of Norfolk's sister and one of that fierce breed of Howards who had been the scourge of so many Kings of England. Not his ancestors, he thought, and grinned to himself. His wily old father, Henry VII, was the descendant of Henry V's widow, Katherine of France, born of a liaison between her and a certain Owen Tudor, who had been clerk of her wardrobe. The Tudors were bastard stock but they married the right women, like the Boleyns. Their wives were of the blood royal, and the first Tudor laid claim to the throne of the ancient Plantagenet kings through the distaff side.

After a time he felt cool and rested, but the company began to jar and his thoughts were straying back to Greenwich and Catherine, his wife. Wolsey, his Cardinal Minister and closest friend, was urging him to have his marriage to Catherine of Aragon annulled, and cement the new alliance with France by marrying the French Princess Renée. Catherine's nephew the Emperor Charles was emerging as a great power in Europe, and Wolsey wanted to side with France and put a check on imperial ambitions. Politics were Wolsey's especial genius, the King thought moodily, and in the last twelve years the Cardinal had taught his young master a great deal.

But politics alone would never have made him agree to Wolsey's approaching the Pope over an annulment, an agreement which sent him hurrying out of the palace, shouting for horses to ride down to Hever and forget what he had done. Catherine was gentle and affectionate; her husband had an almost filial awe of her good qualities. But every child born to them had died and the rest had miscarried, all except the little Princess Mary. And now there would be no more children. As only Wolsey had dared point out, the world was saying that there wasn't a son in the loins of King Henry.

Rochford was talking about something; he had a rather foxy face with shrewd light eyes and usually displayed a keen wit, but now the conversation dragged, and Henry looked beyond him to the open windows. The sun was shining outside and the birds were singing noisily in the trees. The novelty of the visit was wearing off. Rochford at court, where he was quick and amusing, was one thing; Rochford in his own home, weightily playing host, was quite another.

Henry was bored. He stifled a yawn, which Rochford noticed, hastily changing the subject, but Henry stood up and stretched in the middle of his sentence, bowed to his hostess and asked permission to see the castle gardens.

"With pleasure, Sire." Rochford moved to the door at once and opened it. "If you'll allow me to show them to you . . ."

The King smiled and shook his head.

"There'd be no novelty in it for you, my Lord. I have a mind to see them on my own. You offered me the freedom of your house— Madam your wife has been such a good hostess that I feel it's

3

mine already—now I'll make free with your gardens and your fresh air, before I leave for London."

He walked out alone and turned out of the courtyard, watched by two gaping stable boys, and opened a little wrought-iron gate in the side wall. A smooth lawn stretched out in front of him, leading to a sunken garden, a garden cut in a deep hollow out of the ground and paved with soft gray stones. A flight of shallow steps led down to it and he stood at the top of them, looking down. It was one of the loveliest gardens of its kind that he had ever seen, a rose garden, where the rich, sensual flowers bloomed in profusion in their beds of Kentish clay, and a little stone faun stood on a pedestal in the center of the sea of pinks and reds and whites and yellows, piping a soundless tune into the scented air. And there, as she stood cutting a crimson rose, Henry saw Anne Boleyn again.

He had forgotten all about her till that moment. He had forgotten that he had ever seen a woman move so gracefully, or blend so well with her surroundings. She wore a plain dress of green, and her black hair was plaited simply around her head; it shone like polished ebony. In that moment when he saw her, he remembered instantly who she was and what had happened—why, it must be months ago that she'd been sent from court . . . Months, and he'd forgotten her existence.

It was always the same with him where women were concerned. Out of sight, out of mind. He had slept with Boleyn's other daughter, Mary, a year or so before. She was plump and fair and very stupid, and Henry had sent her off with a nominal pension and a plain country squire for a husband, promptly forgetting about her, as he did with all the others. Like them, she had proved a disappointment. . . .

Then one day he had seen this one, dancing in the great hall at Greenwich, as dark as a Spaniard among the English ladies, and her feline grace had caught his fancy. He was surprised to learn she was Thomas Boleyn's elder daughter, now returned to England after years at the French court. He had signaled his interest, but the minx ignored it. He mentioned the matter to Wolsey, to whom he confided everything, and his fancy turned to a burst of jealous pique when he discovered that the girl preferred another

4

suitor to the King. An intrigue existed between her and Henry Percy, heir of the Earl of Northumberland. He had snapped at the Cardinal to make an end of the affair and see both participants properly punished. How dared Percy try to marry some little court nobody without the King's permission. How dared the nobody angle for a great noble and ignore that other beckoning finger.

Percy was sent home, he remembered, after a rating from Wolsey which took place in public, and his fierce old father had forced the unhappy young man into marriage with the Lady Mary Talbot. Boleyn's daughter—Anne, that was it—was banished and disgraced. And forgotten until now. He'd forgotten that a narrow, supple figure had voluptuous charm, but Henry was ready to acknowledge it again as he saw her straighten up, holding the long-stemmed rose in her hand. Slowly he came down the steps, swinging his feathered cap, and at the sound of his step on the flagged path, Anne turned.

It was more than a year since she had seen him; more than a year since she had left the court and lost her chance of marriage, parted from Henry Percy by the Cardinal's orders without the chance to say good-by. Her father had smacked her face and cursed her for jeopardizing his favor with the King and bundled her down to Hever Castle, and threatened to beat her unconscious if he found her with child as a result of it all.

But she had not been Percy's mistress. That was the irony which lay like a stone at the bottom of her unhappiness. Dozens of men in France and England had pursued her dishonorably, but the scion of the mighty house of Northumberland had stammered his love and his wish to marry her before he asked to touch her lips. And whatever her furious father had said, Anne had loved him for that and not for the high position he had offered her. Gangling and awkward, Percy stuttered badly; he was as shy and graceless as she was poised, but she loved him and every instinct urged her toward the marriage. It was the first offer and the last, and she knew it. Whether her mother was a Howard or not, Anne was still the daughter of the parvenu Sir Thomas Boleyn whose grandfather had been a mercer, and the great families of England did not take such women for wives. The Norfolks had been under

5

a cloud of treason, their dukedom suspended and estates forfeited, when they allowed Elizabeth Howard to marry so far beneath her.

All that was over. Percy was married, and the months of her exile dragged by without hope of recall. It was less than a year since she had let her persistent Cousin Tom Wyatt into her room and surrendered the virginity she had been keeping for a husband. More than a year and less than a year and her whole life had changed on account of that twice-damned priest and the man who now suddenly appeared in front of her, smiling and looking up and down at her as if nothing had happened. She had forgotten his height and his splendid build; forgotten too, or never noticed, that he carried himself so royally. The color rushed up into her olive skin, and one hand flew to her breast like a startled bird.

"Your Grace . . ."

She sank down in a low curtsy, her green skirts spreading around her.

He came close to her and held out his hand. It was a heavy hand, with coarse red hairs on the back and a big gold ring set with a diamond on the index finger.

She kissed it, and he caught her fingers and drew her to her feet. The top of her head only reached his shoulder. Henry smiled, and his pale eyes were quite warm. Then to her surprise he bent and picked up the long, freshly cut rose which she had let fall in her confusion.

"Mistress, your flower."

"I thank you, Sire." He noted with pleasure that her voice was rather low-pitched; she was still suitably flushed; feminine confusion always pleased his vanity, but her brilliant dark eyes were smiling back at him.

"Were you avoiding the King, that I find you here?" he asked.

She laughed then; she had recovered her composure. Years of living in the sophisticated French court had taught her that a King was still a man. And this was the King who stood and ogled and picked up her flower. The King, but still a man.

"I'd no idea we were to be honored by a visit from you, Sire. My father said nothing about it."

"It was a surprise," Henry said genially.

6

"And a noisy one," she retorted mischievously. "I'll swear my father strutted like a cock with apoplexy, and my mother banged her nose on the floor like any kitchen maid making a curtsy!"

The description was so apt that he roared with laughter.

"You're a disrespectful baggage," he reproved, grinning. "A cock with apoplexy . . . God's death, I've a mind to tell him!"

"Your Grace is too kind to do that; think of my poor head aching from a box on the ear."

"That would be a pity," Henry admitted. "It's a pretty head, and a prettier ear. We'll say nothing to Thomas, then. Come, show me the rose garden, if you want me to be silent."

Together they turned down the path, and Anne laid her flowers on a little seat set into the wall. They walked through the massed beds, pausing, as she pointed out some special bloom; he found her very knowledgeable about flowers, and at last she led him to the statue of the faun.

"I've often wondered what tune he plays," Anne said.

The King looked at her; she had a trick of calling attention to her breasts by placing one hand on the neck of her dress. It was cut low and straight across, and the shape of her bosom was firm and perfect.

"Do you like music, Mistress?"

"Very much, Sire. I pass much of my time here playing. And my lute is well acquainted with Your Grace's melodies."

He was immediately pleased.

"You like them, then?"

She turned to him smiling. "If you hadn't been King, you'd surely have been the first musician at your own court. I think, 'Come Love, sweet Love,' is my favorite."

"It's mine too," he said eagerly. "But 'In Winter Mine Heart,' do you play that too?"

She shook her head. "It's too sad, Sire. The words make me weep." They often had the same effect on Henry; he had composed the tune and the verses one afternoon when it was too wet to go hunting and his spirits were low.

"You have a fine perception," he remarked. "If your musicianship is good, then you must play for me."

7

"It's no match for yours," Anne answered. "But for a woman, I play quite well."

They were walking side by side, nearing the end of the garden, where more steps led up to the main lawns; the King touched her elbow.

"There's a pleasant seat there in the wall. Come, sit with me."

She obeyed, drawing her skirts aside to make room for him; she had a curious feeling of suspension. The King, the sunny garden, their conversation, the whole scene was almost unreal. And running through it was a sensation of racing excitement.

She glanced quickly at him; he had a noble head. He was more kingly in bearing as he sat beside her like any country squire, dallying on a lovely afternoon, than when he walked among his court at Greenwich. Their silence was natural as their talk. Henry leaned back against the wall. The odd strain of informality that loved to serve himself from his own sideboard and to relax in genial company was more satisfied in those moments than he had ever known it. His experience with women, certainly with his Queen, had convinced him that silence and women equalled boredom; worse still, their chatter was the end of peace. But this woman had the art of tranquillity; yet she had made him laugh, and laughed herself with sparkling vivacity. He wondered if she really played well, for his Welsh heritage rejoiced in music. How pleasant it would be sometimes to sit and listen to her, and to watch her. While Wolsey wrested his divorce from the Pope, he could revert to his old whim and make this one his mistress. He congratulated himself on the soundness of his first impression. The whim, so quickly forgotten once she left the court, reasserted itself as a positive wish.

He turned and smiled at her, considering the beautiful face framed in glistening black hair, the delicate neck, and again her breasts; the narrow waist and the line of her thighs under the folds of her skirt. Suddenly his whole body heated with the idea of pressing upon her until she cried out under his weight.

She stood up as if she had read his thoughts, and drew away from him with a movement that made him long to reach out and pull her down over his knees.

8

"My father will be angry if I keep you from him any longer, Sire."

They walked down the little paved path, and she stood back to let him mount the steps before her. Some moments later they entered the castle, where the anxious Lord Rochford hurried forward. In a few seconds the King was surrounded, and Anne drew back into the shadows of the castle hall.

When Henry turned to look for her, she had gone. The evening came and his good temper began to fray as he sat in front of a fire specially lighted for him in the open grate of Thomas Rochford's apartments, and drank wine, hardly listening to the efforts being made to entertain him.

He had already informed them that he was going to stay at Hever that night instead of riding back to London. That was after meeting Anne, who had promised to play for him, but as soon as she vanished he missed her and became irritable. He asked what time his host dined, and was told that the hour had been fixed in accordance with custom at court.

His Grace would be entertained by a fine band of musicians playing from the gallery above the dining hall; Mistress Anne had an excellent ear for music and she had helped select them some months earlier. It gave him the opportunity to ask where Mistress Anne was, and her mother went out to find her. She returned alone. Her daughter had a headache, she explained, and begged to be excused. The King walked down to dinner in the great hall, and began to eat in bad-tempered silence.

In the musicians' gallery above, minstrels played during the magnificent meal, and one of them sang several songs in a fine tenor voice. The King ate hungrily, but for most part he was silent. He enjoyed feminine company, but the presence of Mary Boleyn, his former mistress, awakened anything but tender feelings, while his hostess was so self-effacing under her husband's eye that she might as well not have been there. He had looked forward to seeing the other daughter again, but she hadn't come, and now he was bored and disappointed. His visit was spoiled. . . . Rochford talked during a ballad that Henry especially liked; Henry was leaning back in his chair between two courses, listening and thinking that he

9

might ask Rochford to send the tenor into his service, when his host interrupted for the second or third time, and the King turned and glared at him with an expression that closed Thomas Rochford's mouth long past the end of the song.

Upstairs Anne had her supper in her room, and fed Tom Wyatt's little dog with tidbits from her plate. She could hear the music drifting up from the dining hall below, and had slipped out once to the gallery above the staircase to look at the scene. The old hall was lit by dozens of wax candles, and torches blazed in the walls, setting fire to the gold plate on the raised table where her family and their royal guests were sitting. Scullions and kitchen maids hurried backward and forward from the kitchen, bringing elaborately decorated dishes and flagons of wine. The gentlemen who had ridden out with him dined at tables further down; some of them were openly bored, because the whole visit was impromptu and no ladies had been invited to amuse them. And the King would be bored too, Anne thought as she slipped back into her own room. He was already bored earlier in the evening, when he sent for her, and she had refused flatly to obey her mother and come down.

By the time the second message came, she had sent for her maid-servant to undress her. Her father opened the door, slammed it behind him and stood in front of her. He was furious; one gesture sent the frightened country girl scurrying out of the way, and then he faced his daughter.

"What game is this you're playing, in God's name?"

"Game?" She stood quite calmly in her long green satin petticoat with her unbound hair hanging straight to her knees.

"Don't jest with me," Rochford snapped. "The King has sent to ask that you come and play for him. Get that wench back here and be dressed and in his presence in the next ten minutes!"

He turned to go; his authority over her had weakened in the last months, she was more intractable than ever, and for the first time in his long reign of tyranny over his family, he preferred not to argue with his daughter because he feared he might not win. Anne didn't move.

"I have a headache," she said coolly. "Make my excuses to His Grace and say that I have gone to bed."

Rochford swung on her, one hand raised to smack her face, but she didn't recoil. Instead she tensed like a cat and her black eyes narrowed with hatred. In a corner, her little dog growled. "Strike me," she said softly, "and I'll go down as I am and show him the mark."

He hesitated. The King fancied her, and for the moment that was her protection. There was a vein of fierce hysteria in her nature which would make her carry out that threat, and he knew it.

"You black bitch!" he said. "You're no child of mine!" The door crashed behind him; and Anne stood waiting, listening to his footsteps turning down the corridor. She laughed; of one thing she was sure: her pale, spiritless mother had never had the courage to betray her husband or anyone else. . . .

Later she lay in bed with the curtains drawn, and let herself think of Henry Percy for the first time that summer. The King had a mind for her again. The first time she had lost a husband; now she had a lover at least and she was happy at Hever. The King's favor brought no fortune to women. She had suffered on account of it already, and if the King's visit was marred on her account, then she was glad.

She twisted sensuously and sighed, remembering that Wyatt had promised to ride over within the next two days. Would to God he had been with the King; he might have slipped away that night and come to her. . . . Sometimes he was away at court for a week or more, and the absence whipped her nerves. He was gay and he was passionate and he was handsome. When they weren't making love, shut up in her cavernous bed, they were laughing and making up verse, which she had loved. He was married, but Anne had long ceased regretting that; marriage, as Tom often told her, only soured love instead of sweetening it. Witness his own wife, whom he had loved before he married her. . . . He scarcely thought about her now.

He thought of no one and wanted nothing but his Cousin Anne. . . . She fell asleep at last and though Wyatt's was the

11

last image on her conscious mind, she dreamed of no one but the King.

Early the next morning Henry mounted to return to London. It was a clear, lovely morning and he was looking forward to a strenuous ride; he thanked Lord and Lady Rochford graciously, his quick eyes noting that the one he was looking for was not among the family grouped on the steps, and for a moment he felt an extraordinary pang of disappointment. His gentlemen were mounted, waiting for his sign to leave, when he looked up suddenly with the instinct of someone who knows he is being watched.

She was standing in a window above the courtyard, still in her white nightgown, with her black hair hanging loose. The moment lengthened as he waited, one heavy hand on his bridle, looking up. She smiled and lowered her head, and then stepped out of sight.

It was a picture that was to torment him for the next seven years.

"The thing I love most about you is your hair."

Anne turned her head on the pillow, smiling toward the man lying beside her; she put out her hand and stroked his face.

"Dear Tom, I'll wear it loose if you like. I kept it hanging down my back the other day and George laughed and said I looked like a gypsy."

Wyatt moved till his lips touched her neck.

"George's only a brother—I know better."

She lay with her eyes closed while his mouth traveled to her ear and his fingers turned her chin till he reached her mouth and kissed it. He pulled her body into his arms and began the slow, hot caresses that she knew so well and never tired of; suddenly she wrenched free of him and laughed.

"No," she whispered. "No, Tom, not again."

He let her go and she sat up away from him, pushing the long strands of black hair over her bare shoulders. In the soft summer light he watched her, and his desire was tempered with the warmth of his love for her.

12

"I love you, Anne," he said.

"And I love you," she answered gently. "You've made me very happy, Tom."

"We have little enough time together," Wyatt complained. "I come to you as often as I can, but lately the King's always finding some court duty to keep me with him."

She smiled.

"He's heard rumors, I suppose. You'll need to be careful."

"I'm careful enough, but I'm not afraid of him or anyone else."

"I know that," she answered. "And nor am I. Do you know he sent a message to my father, suggesting that I come to court?"

"It's common gossip that he stayed the night with you at Hever." She looked at him then.

"Gossip lies," she said. "You believe that?"

He nodded; she was too fiercely independent to deny such a thing if it had happened, but even the rumors had made him afraid that beside the power and personality of the King he might lose her. He couldn't lose her, he thought, and he wouldn't; whether the King wanted her or not, she had a right to stay with him if she wished. . . .

"I love you, Anne," he whispered again.

"That's why I can't come to court to be near you. If I go, you know what it would mean, even more, what it would mean if I refused him for you."

"I know," Wyatt agreed. "He's as cruel as Lucifer if he's crossed. But most women wouldn't hesitate between being the King's mistress and being mine. . . . Are you sure, Anne?"

"I'm sure. I'll never submit to him. I'm not Mary, and I've told my father so. He'd play the pander with his own mother if he'd gain by it! Oh, Tom, enough of it!" And she leaned over and kissed him fiercely, her hands on his chest, caught in the chain of the gold locket he wore round his neck. The locket was her love token, his was a ring which glittered on her right hand. The little finger of that hand was deformed by a double nail and she was clever at disguising it in a long flowing sleeve of her own design.

The shadows lengthened in the room, and the last of the late autumn sun sank out of sight behind the towers of Hever Castle. It was dark when Wyatt left her, and she stood fastening her dress, listening to the sound of his horse trotting across the courtyard and out of the castle gate. She was brushing and plaiting her hair when another horseman rode across the cobbled yard outside her window, and a woman came to light the candles in her room.

A few moments later George Boleyn opened the door and came in. He was as fair as his sister was dark, but they shared the same fine features. Of all her family, he was the only one Anne loved.

"A courier from Richmond," he said. "There's a letter for you, Nan."

She opened it, breaking the royal seal.

Anne looked up at George at last; her expression was strange and her eyes had narrowed as they always did when she was excited or alarmed.

"It's from the King. Here, read it."

"He offers you an appointment as lady in waiting to the Queen!" he exclaimed. " 'My heart is sore, and I wish for the music you promised me at Hever and for the sight of yourself again . . .' Christ's blood, Nan, there's no refusing this!"

"And why not?" she demanded. "Have I no freedom? He can't make me go!"

George folded the letter and held it out to her.

"None of us are free. You've been at Hever too long to realize what it means when the King says, 'Come,' however well it's worded. It's Tom keeping you here, isn't it?"

"I can't have Tom at court," she answered. "I at least know that."

"Sister, you can't have him anyway," he answered gently. "The King's marked you out for himself, and he's heard about Wyatt."

"Tom knows," she said defiantly. "And he's not afraid."

"Tom's mad and in love," he retorted. "He'll lose his head,

14

Nan. Nan, listen to me! I've been at Richmond for the last three weeks and the King's sighing and playing melancholy music and acting the lover when he isn't losing his temper twenty times a day. Whatever you've done to him, it's lasted through the summer and he's getting impatient—impatient with Father and with me. And he looks at Wyatt in a way that sends most men to the block. If you love Tom, sister, love him enough not to bring the King's spite on him, for God's own sake!"

Wyatt's words came back to her as she stood there with Henry's letter in her hand. "He's cruel as Lucifer when he's crossed . . ." She opened it and read it again slowly. The post of maid of honor to the Queen was a coveted honor, one assigned only to the highest born. She looked at her brother for a long moment.

"I'll never be his mistress, George. That I've sworn, so he'll be just as vengeful in the end."

"Decide on that when it comes," her brother urged. "He's notoriously fickle, Nan, and likely enough he'll tire of the idea when he sees you again."

"You underestimate me," she said softly. "He hasn't tired in the last three months, you said so yourself. Suppose he finds me even more agreeable, what then?"

"I don't know," George answered. "Before God. But I do know this. He's not a safe man to defy; this letter, and this offer —it's more than he's conceded to any other woman. And you dare not refuse it, for Tom's sake apart from your own."

"Too many women have yielded too easily," Anne said. She was folding the letter into small, neat squares. "But I shan't, brother. If it weren't for our Cousin Wyatt, I'd tell him to go to the devil."

He put his hands on her shoulders. "I know him, Nan, better than you do. I've seen behind that knightly grace of his . . . don't play with him or he'll make you suffer for it. That's what I'm afraid of, and I love you well enough to tell you, go to court, for a time at least, or you'll see Wyatt in the Tower."

"And you too, my George," she said gently. "You and Tom,

15

the only two people in the world I love. So His Grace the King has another fancy for me! And this time I lose Tom, as before I lost Henry Percy!"

George Boleyn started; it was the first time in months that she had mentioned Percy's name.

"Do you still remember that?" he asked. "I thought you'd forgotten him."

She turned to him suddenly and the fury in her face shocked him. Alike though they were, Anne's emotional capacity was deeper and fiercer than his, and there were times when it startled him.

"Forgotten! As long as I live, I'll remember." She leaned toward him, one hand on the oak marriage chest at the end of her bed. "How d'you suppose I felt, hearing he was wretched, married to that Talbot heifer—that's what she looks like and that's what she is . . . Do you think I didn't feel? He's pale, you said, and he never smiles, and his wife and his father rant at him together . . . George, George, did you think it meant nothing to me that he was suffering? And he always will, he's not like me, to find a Wyatt and forget for days on end."

"But I thought you loved Tom," her brother interrupted. "Now you tell me you're still heartsore for Henry Percy."

"Heartsore describes it," she admitted slowly. "Not in love with him any longer—I'm Wyatt's now—but there's an ache still when I think of him and me and what I might have been, and what I am. I dubbed him my gentle knight, George, and by God that's what he was!"

She sat down on the edge of an old chest.

"We have our friend Wolsey to thank for it all," Anne said at last. "Percy for his marriage and I for my great accomplishment—the mistress of my own cousin! By God, I'll pay that debt if it takes me till the last years of my life!"

Her brother shrugged and shook his head at her. "Nan, I don't understand you. I thought you were happy here—you seemed so."

She half smiled at him. "Don't shake your head and look perplexed; I've learned to take my pleasures where I find them, and they've been sweet enough. But no woman likes to play the

16

whore rather than the wife, even the worst. . . . Allow me my regrets, brother."

He came and put his arms around her. "Banish them, Nan. Life's short enough. Had Percy been a man, he'd have defied his father."

"And the Cardinal?" she shot at him. "You forget him."

He laughed angrily. "Small chance of that. He's greater than ever; believe me, the court bows as low to him as to the King himself. Don't tilt with him, Nan, I beg you."

"I'll tilt when I'm ready," she answered. "A woman may succeed where men fail, just because she is a woman. . . . It seems there's another reason why I should obey the King's command and come to court."

She was calm and mocking again, fanning herself with Henry's letter.

"You needn't, Nan," he said quickly. "Forget what I said, excuse yourself to the King, and give up Wyatt quickly, that's all you need do. Father and I can keep in his favor. . . ."

"Don't lie to me, George; you'll all be in danger if I refuse, you admitted as much till I talked of the Cardinal and paying off that trifling debt. You needn't fear for me, brother. No harm will come to me. No harm ever comes to the Queen's maids of honor," and she laughed.

She walked to the bell rope hanging beside her bed and pulled it sharply. A few moments later her country-bred maid appeared, bobbing in the doorway, her mouth a little open as usual. She was terrified of her mistress, who boxed her ears if she was clumsy or misunderstood an order, and then gave her a piece of velvet or a pair of slippers twinkling with embroidery when she cried.

"Bring paper and a fresh quill and ink. And don't dawdle!"

Anne kissed her brother's cheek. "Don't look so, George. There's no need to frown and fret. Now I've two letters to write which must go by morning. One to Tom and one to the King."

"I'll ride to London with them," he said. "The King's at Greenwich now, and Wyatt's been given another duty among

17

the gentlemen which'll keep him at court for a month at least."

"He was here today," she said.

"I know, I saw him. What answer will you give the King?"

"While deeming myself unworthy of the great honor of serving Her Grace Queen Catherine, I yet presume to accept, being moved by a great longing to see the King's Grace but once again, his presence being the source of all happiness to his most obedient subject, Anne Boleyn."

She wrote that letter first, phrasing it in the most modest terms, signed it and sprinkled it with sand to dry.

And then she wrote to Wyatt, that for his safety and for hers, they must wait on the King's will.

Catherine, Princess of the Kingdoms of Castile and Aragon, and Queen of England, was kneeling praying in her oratory. The furnishings for the little chapel had come with her from Spain; the velvet prie-dieu had belonged to her mother, the great Isabella of Castile, the gold and ivory crucifix was an heirloom of the house of Aragon, and in the tiny room, Catherine came more and more often to pray for peace of mind and remember the country she had left more than twenty years ago.

She was a tall woman, big-boned and fair, with strong features and very fine gray eyes, but at forty she was lined and the hair drawn back to the edge of her cap was turning gray. She dressed very richly, with the Spaniard's passion for fine clothes, and took a pleasure in jewels that her confessor had once said was sinful; she had brought a casket of magnificent pieces as part of her dowry, and sometimes changed her ornaments two or three times a day. Even as a girl, these innocent vanities were her only vices; she expiated them by constant charity to the poor of her husband's city, and by sheer kindness won the affections of everyone who served her.

She was a naturally motherly woman, and as each child died, her devotion to her splendid husband became more maternal in expression. The love he had awakened in her as a Prince of eighteen had faded gently from passion to steadfast devotion which neither his infidelities nor neglect had been able to shake.

18

She bore both patiently for the sake of the times when he returned; whether for comfort, advice, or in the hope of a living heir. After seven years the infant Princess Mary was born, and of all Catherine's children, the frail girl lived.

But there would be no more children now. She was nearly past the age of child bearing, and Henry saw her less and less. He was always hunting or jousting, surrounded by a crowd of courtiers and women, most of whom Catherine disliked. Many of the King's intimates were parvenus like the Boleyns, risen because he had slept with one of the daughters, and Catherine's stiff upbringing revolted against such company.

Everything of which she disapproved at court was typified by Cardinal Wolsey; luxury, immorality and worldliness even under the mantle of the priesthood. And now Wolsey and what he represented were trying to separate her from the King. Her nephew the Emperor Charles V had sent her a warning through the imperial Ambassador, that the Cardinal was urging the King to petition for annulment in order to effect an alliance with France and marry Henry to a French Princess. The excuse Wolsey meant to put forward to Rome was Catherine's youthful marriage to Henry's brother Arthur, who had died after a few months. After sixteen years of marriage, that first, unconsummated union was being brought against her. The Emperor advised his aunt that when the time came she must resist at all costs. The shock had prostrated the Queen; her first impulse was to go to Henry and implore a denial, but wisely she restrained it. She had a child, and Henry loved his daughter Mary. Whatever Wolsey advised, he would not injure Mary and deprive her of the crown which was her right. Catherine prayed and calmed herself and nothing was said by the King or the Cardinal.

She raised her head from her hands and gazed at the crucifix, her lips moving in a prayer for protection. She was aging and her child was delicate.

There was a movement behind her and she turned; one of her ladies stood in the entrance to the alcove, holding the Princess Mary's hand.

"Her Highness has come to say good night to Your Grace."

19

Catherine rose, and the child curtsied; she held out her arms and the little girl ran into them, hugging her mother.

The princess was small for her age, pale and redheaded like the King, with a round, pretty face and Catherine's gray eyes. The Queen kissed her and gently turned her to the altar.

"Kneel with me, and pray before you go to bed," she said.

The child looked up at her. "I pray every night for the King my father and for you," she answered primly. "What shall I pray for now?"

"Just for that, Mary; for the King your father and for me."

Later Catherine walked to the door with her, where the Princess' own ladies were waiting to take her to her rooms, and kissed her fondly good night. Then she took up her sewing and sat down; most of her evenings were passed embroidering while one of her ladies read aloud. Unlike the King, she had no ear or liking for music. But that evening they were interrupted by one of Henry's household, a young knight called William Bryant, whose bad reputation and careless manners had always distressed the Queen.

He bowed; the King had sent to ask a favor of Her Grace. Catherine nodded; whatever it was, she had to comply.

The King wished her, Bryant said, to take a noble and worthy lady under her protection, and appoint her a maid of honor.

"My household is at His Grace's command," Catherine said. "Who is this person?"

"My Lord Rochford's daughter, Madame, Mistress Anne Boleyn," came the reply.

Henry was lonely and in low spirits. He sat in the window of his room in Greenwich, staring moodily out over the river. Already it was growing dark, and the nights depressed him as they lengthened, closing out the sunshine and the crisp autumn days. He had been alone for almost two hours, having suddenly roared at his gentlemen to go away, and then picked irritably at his lute, till that too was pushed aside.

He was restless and angry, because Catherine had spoiled his enjoyment of the bear-baiting that afternoon. They had gone to the royal pits with a large company of courtiers and the Queen's ladies to watch Henry's favorite sport, and he'd settled into his seat with Catherine beside him, leaning forward eagerly as the bear shuffled round the post, shaking the chain which tethered him. He was a good bear, he had been starved to make him fierce and the King looked forward to a good afternoon's sport. Part of his enjoyment was the presence of his wife's new lady in waiting, Anne Boleyn.

She had been at court a week, but he had only spoken to her twice, and then in the presence of the Queen. Catherine did not like her, he could tell by the way she looked at her and turned away to talk to someone else whenever Anne was near. He had heard that Catherine had reproved her angrily for laughing in the maids of honor's rooms.

But she came to the bear-baiting that afternoon, brilliant in a scarlet dress and a tiny scarlet cap that framed her dark hair and enhanced her olive skin; and like him, she was excited, smiling and commenting to the other ladies in a whisper which he strained to hear.

When the dogs were released into the pit, he forgot about her in his enthusiasm, and shouted his approval when the first of them crouched and then sprang like an arrow at the bear's throat. The second and third followed, and the pit became a bedlam of snarls and the yelps of a wounded dog, its chest scored open by the bear's claws, and the deep, furious growls of defiance and pain from the bear as it plunged on the end of the chain, fighting off its attackers. One of the dogs hung from its leg, its teeth clamped into the fur and flesh, its eyes red with hate. They were a magnificent breed, Henry remarked joyfully, the best in England. Look, the wounded dog had jumped like a stag to the attack again. . . . It was bleeding profusely, spattering great crimson stains on the floor of the pit, but it fought on. Now the bear was bleeding too from several savage bites; maddened by pain, it slashed and snapped and staggered like a drunken man. The King and most of the court roared with laughter at the spectacle.

One of the dogs was dead, its skull crushed by a bite; only two were left, and the second was weakening from loss of blood. Quickly he signaled, and two more dogs were released into the pit and leaped onto the bear's back and chest, encouraged by roars from the spectators. The bear overbalanced and came to his knees; at the same moment Catherine touched his arm, and he turned angrily; the kill was near and he didn't want to miss it. Now he was down, one of the dogs would get his throat . . .

"With Your Grace's permission, I wish to retire," she said; she was terribly pale, and to his annoyance he saw that her eyes were full of tears. "'Tis too cruel. The poor bear . . . I can't watch it . . ."

She was out of her seat, beckoning to her ladies, and the whole finale of the fight was disrupted while they moved. The last to go was Anne; one of the ladies touched her shoulder and whispered urgently before she rose to follow, and for a moment she looked into Henry's face. She was flushed and excitement had made her brilliantly beautiful; she waited to curtsy to him, and her eyes expressed disappointment. Then she was gone. By the time he settled down again, the bear was dead on the floor of the pit and the dogs were tearing it to pieces.

They suggested another bear and another fight, but he refused and stamped back to his apartments in a savage temper. Why had she come, he demanded furiously, and no one dared to answer him. He knew she was squeamish, always petting her cursed lap dogs and feeding her tame birds; why did she ask to come and then spoil his pleasure? His voice rose to a bellow, while his gentlemen stood about awkwardly. Was it part of her policy to force herself on him, he shouted, knowing her presence embarrassed him, thinking perhaps he was too kindhearted to forbid her?

From that moment he *would* forbid her! Was there no one to protect him from the Queen's pestering? He stood straddled like an angry bull, his pale eyes reddening like his own breed of pit dogs.

"Are you all dumb?" he roared. God's blood, where was Wolsey . . . Wolsey would have found something to say, Wolsey would probably have stopped her attending. But Wolsey was at York House, working on the problem of the divorce. He ordered

22

them out and sat by himself, brooding and vindictive and as usual when he was depressed or angry, his thoughts turned to the divorce and his grievances against his wife. How many children had Henry fathered in the Queen, the Cardinal asked, and how many had survived? One; the sickly ten-year-old Princess Mary; the rest had died. He knew the kindness of the King, but such a mortality surely betokened the anger of God and his punishment for a union which was incestuous. . . .

They had discussed it so often that the King had begun to believe it; he was profoundly superstitious, the religion of form and ritual was a passion with him, and theology a hobby with which he sharpened his intellect, in common with most brilliant men of his time. But the seat of his religion was within himself; he held the same beliefs as the rest of Christendom until that time, because the beliefs had never conflicted with his own will. The possibility that the two might differ never seriously occurred to him; once he believed that Catherine had deceived him, that he had committed incest and been punished by the deaths of all but one of his children, then the belief became an unshakable truth. And he had Wolsey to assure him that the Pope would share the conviction.

The Cardinal never missed an opportunity to praise the Princess Renée; he was shrewd enough to know that sixteen years of marriage to the admirable Catherine had predisposed his master toward a congenial union as well as a political one. The Princess was intelligent, graceful and very womanly, and as eager to marry Henry as her modesty allowed. He would find her an excellent wife, and the French royal family were notoriously prolific; her brother Francis had bastards in every corner of the Kingdom.

Then he stressed the need for the French alliance. The Emperor Charles was too powerful for the safety of Europe; he was expanding his dominions at the expense of the Italian states, and his armies ringed the Vatican. His dominions in the New World had made Spain fabulously rich, and the great trading center of the Netherlands had been added to his inheritance by his father, Philip of Burgundy.

At this point, Henry had surprised his Minister by remarking that the English people, whose principal trade was the export of wool to the Netherlands, would hardly welcome the loss of their best market in exchange for an alliance with their hereditary enemy, France.

The point irritated Wolsey, whose interest lay with politics rather than economics, and he brushed it aside a little too quickly. The King's vanity was touched and for a moment he watched his Minister with dislike; he interrupted again, to say shortly that the poverty resulting from a break with the Netherlands might well prove a greater danger to the security of his throne than all the might of the Emperor, mustered thousands of miles away.

The Cardinal had recovered himself, within seconds he was humbly admitting that the King was right and he was wrong, and that whether Henry married the French Princess or not, the trade in wool must be maintained. But he made the mistake of confounding Henry's argument, by pointing out that it was in the Emperor's interest to keep the Netherlands market open; he was too realistic to avenge the divorce of his Aunt Catherine at the expense of his dominion's prosperity. Either way, there was nothing to lose.

Henry had listened in sullen silence. There were times when Wolsey's opinions carried him too far, when he forgot that the young inexperienced King of former years was now a man and a ruler. The Cardinal had retired from that audience, unaware that his very plausibility had cooled Henry's enthusiasm for Princess Renée or any other candidate he might put forward.

The King moved restlessly in his chair, and his foot kicked the lute; the strings quivered and the sound suddenly drove his thoughts into another channel. He forgot his anger with Catherine and the scene at the bear-baiting; he forgot Wolsey and the divorce and the difficulties which harried him.

The lute reminded him of Anne Boleyn. He remembered her letter and his excitement when he read her acceptance of the post at court. God, but she was beautiful that afternoon, and as keen on the sport as he was himself. . . . He remembered the lively atmosphere in the group where she was sitting, and the looks of some of his gentlemen as she took her place. Wyatt had been among them, but he knew that she had never seen Wyatt alone since she came to Greenwich. That was over, then; his vanity suggested that it had never really begun. He wondered if she was a virgin, and then rejected the idea; the only certain virgin at court was his own daughter Mary . . . his thoughts shied away from her and returned to Anne.

It was odd how Anne's image heated his imagination. A week passed already, and Catherine had kept her so occupied that she might as well have been buried in Kent for all the good it did him! Three months of thinking about her, driving out of his mind that memory of the figure in the window in a white nightgown because it made him sick with desire; remembering her wit in the rose garden, and the ease he felt in her company, and then suffering jealousy for the first time in his life when he heard that Tom Wyatt was her lover. . . .

He sighed and stretched; his bad temper had gone, only his loneliness remained, and there was a remedy for that. He bent and picked up his lute and struck a few chords; the sweet tones echoed in the quiet room. A boatman called out on the river below, and he looked out of the window.

The red and gold barge of Cardinal Wolsey was drifting into the jetty and he could see the figure under the rich canopy, the Cardinal's boatmen drawing in their oars. He suddenly resented Wolsey's state; the barge was too big and too splendid; he had too many attendants with him, and his musicians played a fanfare when he landed; for some time that ostentation had annoyed the King. He frowned, watching the long graceful boat edging into the landing steps, and the noise as people came running. A crowd always gathered round Wolsey, self-seekers hoping to be noticed.

The King raised his voice for his page, and the boy hurried in from his post outside the door.

"Go to the Queen," Henry ordered him. "Request her to send Mistress Anne Boleyn to me; I have a mind for music, and command her to play to me."

2

ANNE DID NOT BECOME THE KING'S MISTRESS THAT NIGHT AT Greenwich, nor on any of the other occasions when he sent for her that winter.

They supped together and rode together, and he ordered her place at the maid of honor's table to be moved higher, so that he could see her when he dined publicly with the Queen. But she refused as firmly each time he approached her as she had done on their first evening alone. No one even considered the possibility that Henry's relationship with her was still technically innocent, certainly not Wolsey, who viewed it with dislike but a certain complacency. He knew his King too well to fear Anne's ascendancy would be of long duration. Henry hungered quickly and was quickly appeased; the new mistress would be retired like all the others—better provided for, perhaps, as the King was unusually generous to her. He began sending her little sentimental gifts; a gold pomander filled with French perfume, a well-bound book of love poems, gloves and small trinkets, and presents of delicacies for her table. He sent for her at all hours on some pretext; attendants used to hear them laughing as soon as they were alone; sometimes they played and sang duets, Henry's baritone blending with her clear voice.

The King was in love, but only Anne and her brother George knew that his love was unfulfilled.

The first night he had come up behind her and caught her in his arms, and been abashed when she begged him to let her go. Completely unused to resistance, for a moment he was angry. But she stood before him meekly, all vivacity and impudence forgotten, and asked him gently not to attempt anything against her honor.

She was virtuous, she said, and by God's grace she hoped to

remain so. After a moment she asked him if he wanted her to leave. Moodily he turned from her but swung round as she went to the door, telling her to stay where she was. That evening, like the bear-baiting, threatened to be spoiled, and his disappointment changed to irritation with himself. The harmony between them was disrupted; he supposed he had better dismiss her. . . . But Anne had gone to the window and picked up the lute. She began to play one of his compositions; and by the time it was finished, the King was standing by her, listening, and they were perfectly at ease again.

When she left, he kissed her on the cheek according to court custom, and his desire leaped like a flame, but she withdrew before he could make a move. The urge to touch, to kiss and fondle was so strong he sweated when she came near him, and though the form of his desire was the same with Anne as with all other women who aroused his fancy, the intensity was not. The violence of it bewildered and goaded him, and when she did surrender, he thought hotly—and she would in time—he might well find the satisfaction neither wife nor mistresses had ever given him.

The King gave a masque and a ball before Christmas, and Anne spent days choosing her costume and headdress. She ordered a dress of scarlet velvet, with a collar and long sleeves lined with cloth of gold, and a mask of black satin, sparkling with gold embroidery. The theme of the masque was the elements, and she asked Catherine's permission to symbolize Fire. The Queen assented coldly; thanks to the King's brutal display of preference, her natural dislike of Anne had become hatred. Once she had gone so far as to order Anne to stay upstairs and mind her dogs at one court function, because her nerves were quivering at the insult offered her so publicly. Furious, Henry had turned to his wife and ordered her loudly to send for Mistress Anne, and after dancing several measures with her he kept her by him for the rest of the evening.

She made him laugh, Catherine thought bitterly, which she had never been able to do; she was witty and scintillating and impertinent, and the unhappy Queen used to pray earnestly for grace not to feel so jealous of her. But she never dared try to keep her from the King again, and when she asked to choose her costume for the masque Catherine wearily gave permission. Fire would suit her, she thought, watching her as she moved round the room. There was an aura of sensuousness about her which made the Queen uncomfortable. Standing, kneeling or sitting on a stool at her mistress' feet sewing, she seemed to emanate seduction like a poison, and she reminded Catherine of a serpent when she walked. Often she ordered Anne out of the room, and then hurried into her oratory to weep and pray for help before the Blessed Sacrament.

The day before the masque, Anne was in the maid of honor's room alone, dressed in her red costume. She stood in front of a polished steel mirror, the headdress of scarlet points simulating flames, in her hand, the glittering mask sewn below it. She wondered whether he would recognize her quickly; originally, she planned to wear the gold pomander round her waist and then rejected it; the ruse was obvious, and the King loved subtlety. She smiled, thinking of him; he was a challenge that she never tired of meeting. His brilliance challenged hers when he was in a learned mood, and she delighted in trying to match it; his wit was keen and his sense of humor uproarious once it was aroused, and she knew instinctively what made him laugh.

She loved her life at court, apart from her duties with the Queen—God, how could such a woman hope to keep a man of Henry's make! She loved the admiration of the first personage in the kingdom, and the looks of friends and enemies watching them together; life was exciting and full of some strange promise which she sensed rather than understood. She lived from day to day, playing her extraordinary gamble with the King without knowing either the outcome or how long she could expect to win. But she had played the right moves, she thought triumphantly; had she yielded, he would have taken her for granted in a few weeks. Like this, he was fascinated. In her high spirits, she laughed aloud. God's death, this was better than living at Hever, better even than Tom Wyatt and all his love.

She put on the headdress and adjusted the elegant little mask; it was a striking costume, and the effect of the scarlet points suggested darting tongues of fire that rose round her head.

But she frowned, considering for a moment. She was too well disguised; it might take even Henry a long time to recognize her, and her purpose was to catch and keep his eye in competition with the loveliest women at court. Then slowly she smiled; an idea had formed in the last seconds while she looked at her reflection. It was a breach of etiquette and might well cause trouble with the Queen. But it was worth it. A few moments later she had taken off her costume and was answering Catherine's bell from the next room.

The great hall at Greenwich had been decorated for the masque; wreaths of holly and ivy hung from the beamed roof, with the mistletoe plant, relic of pagan England, to ward off evil spirits from the feast.

The tall bronze candleholders had been filled with thick wax tapers, as the King complained that the wall sconces smoked and would hide his view of the dancers. A gold and scarlet canopy was stretched above the royal dais, and pikemen of the King's Guard stood beside the dais in their crimson doublets and polished breastplates. The King's fool sat on the lowest step, his rattle held like the scepter. In their chairs of state, Henry and his Queen sat side by side waiting for the masque to begin.

The great hall was filled with courtiers of every rank and office; the bright red robes of Cardinal Wolsey and the purple and black of his clerical entourage mingled with the rich colors and jeweled costumes of the great lords and their wives. In the minstrels' gallery the King's musicians played softly; one of them prefaced the dancing with a song. Henry listened and smiled. The singer was Rochford's minstrel, the same whose voice he had admired that night he stayed at Hever, waiting for a second sight of Anne Boleyn.

He had the same feeling at that moment, the same irritable expectancy, as if he were about to see her for the first time, while the minutes lagged like hours. Was that her secret, he wondered, that gift of variety; never to do or say exactly the same things, to change from one mood to the next like quicksilver. To be gay and witty and sophisticated, and suddenly melt into gentle simplicity. . . . From one day to the next, he never knew what to expect, whether she would respond to his mood, or force him to change his to suit her own. He had soon discovered that he even indulged her faults; his critical faculty, so sharp where others were concerned, and so blunt with regard to himself, was equally kind to Anne.

She was inordinately vain; Catherine had remarked on it before she realized the position. The girl spent hours arranging her hair and experimenting with cosmetics; she was casual in her religious duties and incurably light-minded, and at the same time, she had a violent temper and an unbridled will above all. Catherine complained that she was openly restless in the company of women, a trait which the Queen especially disliked. Haughty, worldly, self-willed and vain . . . vain, yes. But Anne was easily the most striking woman at court, and even if she lacked the milkmaid skin and golden coloring of the acknowledged English beauties, she defied the convention of beauty. She was thin and supple, rather than voluptuous, dark and black-eyed and high-spirited instead of pale and meek, and she went to Henry's head like a very strong wine.

At times she had surprised him with stable-boy language, a habit he disliked in women, because like most dissolutes, he was a prude at heart, but that too he forgave her.

It was the stimulus of her companionship that held him, and he admitted it; also admitting that his passion had increased under restraint. No woman had ever refused him before. They had all surrendered, and the excitement of pursuit was spoiled by the possession. Within a week or so he had grown used to them and restless—always restless and disappointed. But the more he thought of Anne and wanted her in vain, the more desirable she became. And his uncertainty about her body was matched by uncertainty about her feelings. He loved her, he insisted. This was no passing lust, but he had never wrung the admission from her which fell so easily from the lips of other women. And there was still the sight of Thomas Wyatt to torment him.

The music composed for the masque was beginning; there

was a fanfare and a troupe of dancers entered from the other end of the hall.

Earth came toward him first, in a brown costume trailing with green silk leaves and a headdress decorated with real ivy; her four attendants held garlands of artificial flowers and corn, and the group swayed in front of the dais, curtsying.

He stared at the figure in brown for a moment, and then looked away; the face was half hidden by a mask, but he knew by the height and plumpness that it was not Anne. He signaled his pleasure and then Air approached with her maids, and immediately he leaned forward.

She was tall and slim enough to be Anne, and dressed in delicate shades of blue and white, with a headdress of silver stars topped by a crescent moon; a veil of palest blue floated from her shoulders. There was a murmur of admiration from the spectators as Air and her attendants, each symbolizing a planet, curtsied to the King and Queen. He watched the woman in the blue dress as she made way for the third figure in the masque, undecided because she didn't move like Anne. A look assured him that Water, dressed from head to foot in green and silver, with a silver triton in her hand, was too big-boned and half a head too short. Catherine leaned toward him to ask if he were pleased with the costumes, and he nodded impatiently.

Then, from the farthest part of the hall the last troupe of ladies were coming, four attendants dressed in yellows and orange, with Fire in vivid scarlet. He knew her at once, in spite of the mask which covered her face; there was a general hum of comment as she came nearer, and he heard Catherine draw in her breath. There was no fear of his mistaking her and dancing in ignorance with anyone else, because she had let down her magnificent hair and it hung to her knees.

The Cardinal had turned to watch, his attention called to the scene by one of his secretaries, and from the curtsying figure in the blazing dress, his eyes moved quickly to the King. Henry was on the edge of his chair, leaning forward, and there was a look on his face that made Wolsey ask sharply who the woman was.

31

"The Queen's maid, Boleyn," his secretary answered. "Look at her hair; no one else would have dared."

"A whore's trick," the Cardinal said slowly. Then he shrugged slightly and quieted his fear. The King would tire. He had once said to Wolsey that women were like dishes; all had different flavors and only a fool contented himself with the taste of one.

The masquers danced a ballet, specially composed by the Master of the King's Musick, and it was spoiled for Henry because Anne's part ended early, as Fire was extinguished by Water in the course of the mime. She stood at the side, and he could see her laughing and flirting with a little court of men; his eyes almost closed with rage when he saw Wyatt among them, pushing close to her. The length of the ballet seemed interminable as he sat there, unable to leave his chair and scatter her admirers by his presence. At the end he applauded loudly and briefly and stood up; the masque was over and the general dancing began. No one could begin until the King chose a partner and led them out. Catherine had risen and stood beside Henry, waiting to take his arm in accordance with custom, but he turned suddenly to her and bowed.

"His Grace the Duke of Norfolk shall have the honor, Madame." The next moment Norfolk was standing before her, offering his arm, and the King had left the dais and was hurrying to Anne.

"I'm overwhelmed, Madame," Norfolk said. He was a tall, ugly man with a savage squint, and Catherine had never felt at ease with him. He was one of that fierce breed of the old English nobility, whose struggles for power had sent many of them to the block. He was also the uncle of Anne Boleyn.

The King and Anne were dancing, and he kept up the required pretense of not knowing her identity. She moved with the grace and lightness of the deer he hunted, turning, curtsying and leaping in the difficult figures of the sarabande. The King, an expert himself, excelled in dancing as he did in sport and he delighted in a partner whose skill complimented his own.

At the end he led her to a corner, where wine and sweetmeats were served from a long table; those standing near moved to a discreet distance so that they could speak without being overheard.

He swallowed a glass of wine and refilled it.

"Now, Mistress, I shall guess who hides under that mask," he said playfully.

She smiled at him. "Well, Sire, who am I?"

He hesitated and then slapped his side.

"Donna Maria de Feria Gonzalez!" he declared, naming the most gaunt and gloomy of Catherine's Spanish ladies.

Anne laughed. "No, Sire, and I'm not Friar Pedro, either!" she retorted, naming the Queen's Confessor.

"I know there's no monk under your skirts, Mistress Anne," he said mockingly. "I pierced that disguise when you first entered."

"I'd prayed God you would," she responded.

"Why?" he said eagerly.

"What woman in England would want to be recognized by anyone else?" she said.

As usual, it was a flattering answer, but not the one he wanted. She smiled up at him, her eyes bright through the slits in the mask; everyone was watching them. She could see her uncle, Norfolk, staring from the other side of the room where he paid unwilling attendance on the Queen; the squint became exaggerated as he tried to focus. And there was Tom Wyatt, pulling at his beard. She knew that gesture well. He was as much in love with her as ever, and reckless enough to wear the locket she'd given him outside his doublet. She looked at the big bearded King standing over her, his face alight with expectation, and drove the thought of Tom out of her mind. George was right when he warned her that night at Hever; there was no room now for anyone but the King. Sooner or later she would have to give in; her excuses were wearing thin, and the situation was slipping out of her control.

"Come with me, Anne, I'm weary of this," Henry urged suddenly. "Come, walk in the gallery with me."

She followed him, knowing, by the way he looked and his haste, what must happen as soon as they were alone. She had held him off before, teasing and serious by turns; he had kissed her once and she'd nearly succumbed to his rough insistence. It would

33

have been so easy and it was what he wanted; she was afraid every time she refused, and then exhilarated when he came back to her, more eager than before.

Outside the hall she stopped; they were alone in the long cold passage, and only the wintry moonlight streamed thinly through the windows overlooking the river.

"We should go back, Sire," she said. "Think of the scandal . . ."

"The devil take the scandal," he retorted. "Can't the King ever be alone? Give me your hand, Anne."

Still she hesitated. "The Queen will be angry with me."

He laughed unpleasantly. "The Queen knows better than to show it if she is. Take off your mask; it's the penalty for being recognized."

She was helpless then; he was poised on the line between passion and rage, and his rage was something no woman had ever aroused with impunity.

She put her hand out to him. "Let us walk down to the end of the gallery; I'm hot from dancing, Sire. Then I'll unmask."

He stopped her by the far window, turning her so that the soft light fell on her face, and obediently she took off her headdress.

"I saw you in the window at Hever," he muttered, "standing just so, with your hair all round you. Oh, Anne, Anne . . ."

He was tremendously strong, and she gave way at once; he had lifted her off her feet without noticing and was kissing her face, her mouth and eyes, and down, reaching for her throat. With a great effort she pulled away from him, gasping. Another moment and he would have pulled her into the window seat.

"I beg you, don't dishonor me."

"Dishonor . . . the King's love, is that dishonor?"

He set her down, but he still held her shoulders.

"I owe the Queen allegiance," she said desperately. "How can I betray her, even to please you? Or myself," she added quickly. He seized on her last words.

"Would it please you? Would it? Say so, Nan, say it would . . ."
She was caught in the trap of her own flattery, but she was quick enough to turn the slip to her advantage.

34

"More than anything in the world." She moved farther from him till she stood nearly at arm's length. "But a light woman isn't worthy of your love, Sire. And I'm not light in love.

"I serve the Queen," she continued, her voice a whisper, "and the Queen is your wife. . . ."

"By the living God, I'm not so sure of that!" he burst out. "I'm so little sure, I've had no peace of mind for nearly sixteen years!" The lie escaped him easily, and within seconds it seemed as if it had always been the truth. Catherine again; Catherine, his brother's widow. . . . He let her go suddenly and for some moments there was silence between them.

"I've ordered the Cardinal to see into it," he said at last. She answered almost by instinct, still playing for time, trembling on the edge of an idea so tremendous she hardly dared formulate it to herself.

"If Your Grace's marriage is unlawful . . . what would it mean?"

"That my daughter's a bastard," he said brutally, "that I've no wife and am free to take another."

As he spoke he was thinking of the French Princess. Then she suddenly came close to him and put her arms round his neck. He felt her shivering; she seemed suddenly small and gentle.

"If Your Grace were really free," she murmured, "then I might dare to think of you without hurt to your honor or to mine." And with those words she left him, her light footsteps pattering down the stone corridor until the echo of them died away.

That night she lay awake, listening to the snores of Catherine's other ladies, the masque costume thrown on the floor, never to be worn again. The game was still to be played out, but for the first time, Anne saw the stake. The rumors were true; he did want a divorce and a new wife. He and Wolsey were determined to remove the Queen, and Anne knew she had not a chance against them. Everything was in their favor, and nothing in Catherine's, she thought coldly. Catherine was old, looked more than her years, was past child-bearing, and had nothing to show the King for his years of marriage but that sickly red-headed brat. Anne disliked the little Princess Mary, a pious, solemn child, who sensed her mother's antipathy to the new maid of honor, and treated Anne with stiff reserve. The Queen was too serious-minded to offer Henry much companionship; her prayers and her readings and her ordered life bored Anne to screaming pitch. God's death, what charm would they hold for a young and lusty man! No, Catherine had no weapons. . . .

Anne moved, resting her head in the crook of her arms, and thought quite clearly that if she could keep the King's love and continue to withstand him, she might become Queen of England.

Queen of England. She stared at the ceiling, trying to imagine it; Catherine divorced, herself standing beside Henry at the head of the court; herself married, and by the Cardinal! she thought viciously, the Cardinal who'd prevented her marriage to Percy because she was too low-born. . . . What a magnificent revenge!

For a moment her excitement was swamped by a tide of hatred.

"Don't tilt with the Cardinal, I beg of you," her brother had pleaded, and she remembered her answer. "I'll tilt when I'm ready; sometimes a woman can succeed where men fail. . . ."

What did Wolsey think of her success with the King? Did he realize how Henry was besotted? He had spoken to her several times, his manner slightly condescending, and then passed on with his head held as high as if he were the King himself. A man with many enemies, she thought fiercely, her uncle, Norfolk, among them. In fact, he was surrounded by men who were only looking for a means of poisoning the King against him.

She smiled slowly. What better means than a woman; declare herself Wolsey's enemy, and she'd find supporters among the most powerful faction at court. She was sure of her uncle; Norfolk had always treated the Boleyns with contempt, as too parvenu to be redeemed by his sister's infusion of Howard blood, but he had spoken to her father and to George on several occasions since she came under the King's notice. Norfolk was a squint-eyed fox, but he was ambitious enough to help one of his own blood to the throne. No Howard had ever been able to resist intrigue; Anne had studied them and she knew the long history of wars

36

and treachery in the family's struggle to increase their power. And she was one of them. She had their skill and their ambition, and their pride; she also possessed the shrewdness of her merchant ancestors.

Norfolk must be approached and tactfully sounded out. Her father was the man to do that, Anne decided; much as she hated him, she acknowledged his subtlety. She almost laughed, imagining her father's face when she told him her intentions. He'd be afraid; he'd shout and bluster at her for not making the utmost of the King's favor while it lasted instead of wasting her opportunities in pursuit of an insane ambition. She knew exactly what he'd say, but in the end his greed would get the better of him. He'd go to his dread brother-in-law the Duke of Norfolk, and propound the idea of his kinswoman becoming Queen of England and ruining the hated Cardinal in the process. Norfolk would find other allies as powerful as himself.

It was only a beginning, she reminded herself, checking her thoughts as they outstripped the difficulties. An idea born of that moment in the corridor when the frantic King had answered her excuse by forswearing his wife and his own child. Of course there were other candidates for the crown matrimonial; he and Wolsey must have some foreign Princess in mind to step into Catherine's place when she was forced out of it. But the political rival was far away; likely enough the King had never even seen her. He had seen Anne and fallen in love with her, though he still saw her as a mistress. In time, he might see her as a wife . . .

It was dawn when Anne fell asleep, and she was wakened in less than an hour to help the Queen dress and attend morning Mass.

"As you may have noticed, My Lord, the King's Grace has become much attached to my daughter Anne."

Thomas Rochford chose his words carefully; he was never at ease with his grim, black brother-in-law, and the vicious cast when Norfolk looked at him distracted his attention. They were alone in the gentlemen's antechamber.

"What of it?" the Duke demanded. He rubbed his long nose

with one finger, wondering what this shifty little tradesman wanted of him. Viscount Rochford! Ha, there were more like him everywhere, with their ridiculous titles, protegés of the King, who cared nothing for the niceties of birth provided they hunted well and could amuse him.

Rochford shifted awkwardly. His mission had sounded simple enough when Anne explained it, so simple that his imagination had been fired into a wild enthusiasm for her impossible dream.

"As head of my wife's family, I wanted to ask your advice on the matter," he hedged.

"I don't see what advice is needed," Norfolk said. "If the King beds my niece, what the devil have I got to do with it?"

"That's just the point, My Lord. He hasn't. Yet."

Norfolk stared, his untidy eyebrows raised.

"She's not his mistress? Then what's the meaning of this great wooing for the last months? Don't tell me the King's content to admire from a distance!"

"The distance is imposed by my daughter," Rochford said. "And in his respect for her honor, the King may well be considering a more virtuous relationship."

The Duke swung fully around and glared into the sly, bearded face of Anne's father.

"In Christ's name, what are you suggesting? Out with it, and stop haggling with me like an old woman!"

Rochford flushed at the insult, but he managed to smile and bow slightly.

"A divorce from the Queen is being considered by the Cardinal. If and when the King's marriage is dissolved, he intends to take another wife."

"That's been rumored for months," Norfolk interrupted.

"The King assured my daughter of it," Rochford answered.

The Duke stared at him in disbelief, but Rochford met his eye for once and something told the Duke that he seemed very sure.

"And the cunning baggage sees herself with the chance of being Queen, is that what you've come to tell me?"

"I've come to ask your opinion; supposing the King's Grace decided to marry a subject, would you approve, My Lord?"

"If the commoner were my own niece? By God, man, d'you think I'm witless? I'd expect her to remember her uncle and her allegiance to her family—being a cunning baggage as I said, I'll swear she'd take care to advance her own. Approve of it? Of course I'll approve, you fool, and so will you and so will all her relatives . . . that's supposing the girl's not gone mad and imagined a chance where none exists. . . . I trust you to be sure of that. But who else will want it besides us? What of the daughters of the other great houses, how many enemies d'you think Mistress Nan will have at court when any whisper of this gets out? And how many enemies among the people when they learn their good Queen Catherine is being put away to make room for her own maid of honor. . . . Ah, Rochford, where's your merchant's cunning? The thing's impossible!"

"And how many enemies has the Lord Cardinal got at court and among the people?" Rochford shot at him.

The Duke scowled. "No one could count them. I'd give my good eye to see that puff adder with his neck broken. What's he to do with this?"

"His influence with the King is very strong," Rochford said softly. "But so is Anne's. It might be that the King will listen to her and see the truth of what she says about the Lord Cardinal where he might suspect the motives of such men as myself, and even you."

"Ah, by God, you're a cunning villain," Norfolk said, his finger rubbing his nose again. "You'd offer my niece as a weapon against Wolsey, would you . . . in that case she'll draw men to her side as if she carried the Banner of the Holy Ghost . . ."

"Anne hates the Cardinal," Rochford went on. "She bears him an old grudge and you know the venom of women, My Lord."

"I know the venom of your daughter," Norfolk answered shortly, "but she'd do well to hide it from the King."

"I fancy she's proved she knows His Grace's moods in these last months," her father answered.

The Duke nodded. "No one's denying it, but what do you want of me in this?"

"Your promise to speak well of Anne to the King, and to urge on the Queen's divorce."

"You have it, and I'll make you the promise you haven't yet asked; I'll inform my Lord Suffolk and some others that the rise of Mistress Nan may be the fall of Master Wolsey."

Three weeks after the masque, Anne received the Queen's permission to retire to Hever Castle for a short rest. She left the court in a comfortable litter with an escort of her father's servants, and halfway a messenger from the King halted the procession.

He brought her a letter and a gift. She opened the gift first, having thanked the King's Grace and promised to send a courier from Hever with an answer as soon as she arrived. Inside a finely tooled leather case, she found a little Book of Hours in a cover of most beautifully worked gold; the prayers were exquisitely illuminated. She fastened the book to the chain on her girdle, and settled back in the swaying litter to open the King's letter.

"Mine own sweetheart,
    This by the hand of him who is heavy through your absence . . ."

Two nights before when she told him she was leaving Greenwich, he had almost wept, then blazed into anger, accusing the Queen of driving her away. Gently, Anne refuted it, at the same time leaving the suspicion that her life in Catherine's service had not been altogether happy. She was leaving because her conscience insisted, she explained, leaning her cheek against his hand. She was in a state of sin and temptation where she was, and she was determined to take refuge at Hever. What sin, he implored her, what temptation? Did she mean his love and the brief kisses he took from her now and then . . .

The same, admitted Anne. His love for her threatened her

soul's salvation, and his kisses weakened the defenses of her poor flesh.

She was one of those rare women who can invest even their pieties with eroticism. Her description of her struggle against yielding to his temptations only roused his passion till he seized her again, crushing and bruising in the agony of his desire. When he released her his eyes were full of tears, and he bowed his great shaven head against her shoulder. Think of his loneliness, he murmured, think how he would miss her sweet company and her laughter to cheer him when he was sad . . .

Immediately she comforted him, kneeling with her arms round his waist, stroking him as if he were a child, hiding her triumph and her smile at the same time. If he went hunting near Hever, perhaps he might honor them with a visit. . . .

The day she left he was already making plans to ride to Kent, and the letter she read during the journey spoke of the absence as being made short by his impatience to take horse and hunt the wild sweet hart of Hever. It prayed her to accept the Book of Hours, and with it the assurance that he who loved her well besought God to protect and cherish her, since she refused to allow him to perform the office himself.

She folded it up and hid it in her dress, and took out the little gold book to look at it again. It was very beautiful, and much more valuable than the pomander.

She had left the court in spite of her father, in spite of her Uncle Norfolk, who had sent for her and demanded fiercely what she meant by abandoning the King when so many were now interested in her advancement. Her answer, short and impertinent, was also ill-advised, for it turned the Duke's indifference to her to real dislike. She had managed the King well enough without the advice of either well-wishers or those who sought to profit by her; she would continue as she had begun.

Nothing sharpened Henry's interest like uncertainty, as Anne knew; nothing made the pleasure of reunion keener than a short absence at a time when she would be most missed. The weather had been wet and unsuitable for hunting; he would be confined to his palace and indoor sports like wrestling and tennis, and he would miss her more than if she left him in the spring. In any case, she was far too clever to stay away too long, and in spite of her calculation, the exile was a strain on her.

She did not love the King but she dearly loved the life at court, the glamour and increasing notoriety of her position, and the fantastic goal of marriage drew her like a magnet. And the man fascinated her. He was a bewildering mixture and it taxed all her ingenuity to keep up with him; he was bored in a second with something that had once amused him, and he liked to play at chivalry although the least sign of open defiance revealed the nature of a tyrant. He was a gross sensualist; his superficial attempts at lovemaking had proved that the refinements did not appeal to him, and at the same time he censured others for the things he did himself. He was deceitful, Anne had discovered that by watching him with the Queen. In general he treated her with courtesy and respect, while he discussed her repudiation and disgrace behind her back. He was a man of free emotions; he wept as grandly as he laughed; his rage was a hurricane and his favor extravagant, but he was quite capable of deciding on a man's ruin and keeping the victim in complete ignorance of his displeasure until the order for exile or arrest was carried out. He was enormously vain, mentally as well as physically; the friend who bested him in argument was never forgiven, nor was the man who outdid him at sports. His brother-in-law the Duke of Suffolk had somehow managed to win over Henry in the lists and outshoot him at archery without losing his favor, but Suffolk was a fierce, blunt man of remarkable character, daring enough to marry the King's sister Mary against royal wishes, and yet bluff his way back to court.

Suffolk had been enlisted by her Uncle Norfolk; she had spoken to him several times and been antagonized by his contemptuous appraisal. Here was the tool that might lever Wolsey out of his position, if used properly, and as a tool he judged her. In return Anne quipped maliciously at his expense and was dismissed with the observation that the King had no liking for shrews. Suffolk's atttude was typical of the men who suddenly took an interest in her; they were arrogant and ruthless and they conveyed to the

42

uneasy Lord Rochford and his daughter that their patronage was a high honor.

If Rochford was quelled, Anne was not. But she swallowed her resentment for she needed the Suffolks and Norfolks at court on her side and not on Catherine's; she needed them to influence Henry politically while she achieved a stranglehold on his heart. When she was Henry's wife the time would come to remind them of their condescension in the past.

Henry's wife. She lay back in the litter with her eyes closed, her thoughts back to him again. He was the one man who could never wound her sensitive pride; he was the King and any contact with him could only elevate her. Had the situation been different, she would have become his mistress in spite of her vow to the contrary, and treasured the experience of walking in his shadow even for a few months. No wonder women yielded, no wonder her silly sister Mary had gone open-mouthed into his bed and left it almost empty-handed, with nothing but the memories to reward her.

Anne understood now. The power and personality of the man enhanced his kingship, whereas usually the crown gilded the man. If Catherine's place had been secure, the litter would never have started for Hever; there would have been no intrigue. She would have become his mistress, and fought to remain so as fiercely as she was going to fight to be his wife. She did not love him, no; there was no tenderness, such as she'd felt for Tom, no thickening of her blood at the thought of Henry's arms. And nothing like the feeling, more distant, but still painful, that was aroused by Henry Percy. She'd seen him at court that winter, taller and thinner than before, with his wife at his side. They'd spoken and passed on politely, then caught each other looking back. Nothing of the past was left to them but a regret and a debt to Thomas Wolsey which she intended to repay.

Those two men who had once entered his life had no rival in the King; though the King had driven them both out, he could never touch her as they had done, but he'd spoiled her for any man now but himself. They had infected each other with the fever to possess the unattainable; his was the simple desire of a man who relished the pursuit above the capture; hers was the passion for prominence which would only be satisfied now by the highest role open to a woman.

Wife to the King and mother of a Prince of Wales.

She stayed at Hever Castle for nearly two months. The King rode from London three times to see her, and he wrote to her daily.

She answered irregularly with letters shorter than Henry liked, and rather formal. But his disappointment in them was forgotten in his anxiety when she didn't write at all. Their meetings were as tantalizing as ever. Once she allowed him the liberty of kissing her breasts when they were alone, and then pulled away and ran out of the room. To his intense rage, he thought she was laughing. She had a trick of rousing his passions with a deliberate skill that made a mockery of her virtue, and another trick of placating his temper with a disarming show of gentle innocence. In mingled longing and exasperation he wrote to her at Hever.

"Once again I await some word from you, and have received none, wherefore my heart is heavy considering whether the love I bear you is returned or no. For a year now I have been wounded by the dart of love, and such is my despair that I determine upon learning whether you look upon me with a like feeling, or not knowing, then doubtless time will abate my great folly.

"Sweet mistress, Henry your King kneels at your feet and offers you the first place in his heart, swearing that if you return to court and to him who desires you above life itself, he will renounce all other mistresses and remain faithful only unto you before any who may have held his affections or have designs thereon.

"Send news to him who waits with eagerness and wishes only that he may long remain your humble servant, Henry R."

He was at Hampton Court when he received her answer, a long letter describing in such detail her health and pursuits since his last visit that he swore with impatience. Then she thanked him for offering her the post of his official mistress; she was filled with gratitude and humility that she had awakened such a regard in the heart of her lord. Encouraged by his declaration, she laid aside her maidenly modesty to admit that the dart which had struck him had dealt her a mortal wound of love. But she could not do violence to her conscience, though she risked His Grace's anger, by coming to him until he was as free in the eyes of men as he had convinced her he was in the eyes of God. On that most blessed day she would lay her heart and herself at his feet. For this scruple she begged his indulgence and prayed that he might not withdraw his love from her, believing her ever his devoted and humble subject until death.

Slowly Henry got out of his chair, one hand resting on the oak table in front of him, the other holding the letter. He stood in a circle of pale February sunshine which streamed through the tall windows and made patterns on the polished wood floor. The insanitary rushes which harbored fleas and dirt at Greenwich and some of the country palaces like Hunsdon were being replaced by fine rugs from Persia. It was a luxury that he learned from Wolsey, like covering the paneled walls with hangings of Spanish leather, beautifully painted and embossed.

With the letter in his hand he walked to one of the windows; the room was originally Wolsey's own study, and it was one of the most elegant and luxurious in the whole of that splendid palace. The ceiling was high and gilded; the Cardinal's coat of arms had been replaced by the arms of the King; the walls were paneled in pale polished wood and the floor was laid in a pattern. There was a heavy chair of state set against one wall with crimson velvet hangings, because the King sometimes granted audience there, and there were tables and chairs covered with elaborate carving, cushioned in velvet. A harp stood by the window, set to catch the best of the light, and he often played on it or took up his lute and sang the songs which reminded him of Anne.

So she refused to be his mistress. He looked out of the window onto the Clock Court, that most striking feature of Wolsey's creation. Henry loved the chiming clock set up above the archway which led out to the main courtyard. She had rejected what had really been an ultimatum, and presented him with another. He began to reread the last part, "A mortal wound of love." It was the first time she had ever plainly admitted that she loved him and suddenly his pleasure was so intense it was very near to pain.

45

But she would not yield to him, accept the promise that she would be his wife in everything but name, with all the honors and advantages he'd promised her. She could not come to him till he was free, the words said gently. As free before men as he was before God.

The heavy gilt hands of the Court Clock moved to the hour; it was three in the afternoon. The preliminary chimes rang out over the red roofs and twisted chimneys in a delicate harmony before the first resonant stroke echoed over the courtyard, sending dozens of dozing pigeons to flight. He remembered that Catherine refused to stay on that side of the palace, preferring the rooms overlooking the Base Court, because she could never sleep within sound of the clock chimes.

If he wanted Anne, he would have to marry her. That's what the letter meant; that's what she herself meant when she left him that night after the masque at Greenwich. Never, even in the extremes of passion and despair, had Henry thought of marriage. But he stood by his window on that sharp, sunny February afternoon, and thought of it then. His marriage was going to be annulled. It was incestuous, sinful, barren. . . . He was defiled in soul and body by living with Catherine, Wolsey had said so over and over again. She must go, so he could marry again. Not again, he corrected himself, marry, lawfully and with God's blessing, and produce at least one son.

It was taken for granted that he would marry the sister of the King of France, or some other Princess with an alliance as part of her dowry. After one hideous mistake, undertaken at the command of his father because he wished to keep the friendship of Spain and Catherine's bridal portion at the same time, after damning his soul for sixteen years, he must embark on marriage with another woman chosen by someone else. . . . Why not a woman he chose for himself? Why should the King be denied domestic happiness while his subjects enjoyed it. What power was that, he asked angrily, if a King's will was fettered while a peasant's was free?

Anne was young and beautiful and healthy, Anne could bear him the sons he needed. And he loved her, he thought hotly. He wanted her by his side every day and in his bed at night. And if

46

he wished to marry her, by God, who had the right to question it?

She would carry her position well, he knew that, not with the stately poise of Catherine, who had been born royal, but with spirit and grace. He thought of her bearing a child, and bit his thin lips, imagining the cries of the London crowd, the bonfires blazing up and down the countryside, the pealing church bells and saluting cannon, and himself with the new Prince of Wales in his arms. . . .

The last of the clock chimes died away and the birds drifted back to their perches on the carved parapet of the red roofs and the window sills and alighted on the stone unicorns and prancing lions keeping watch from the four corners over the court.

Henry closed the window and folded the letter in his doublet. He had made up his mind to marry Anne.

3

IN THE SUMMER OF 1527, THE CARDINAL WAS BUSY PREPARING FOR a second journey to France. He was more confident and more sure of his favor with the King than at any time in his career, in spite of the occasional clashes of opinion which arose between them. Henry's temper was smiling and affectionate toward him; he made a great display of walking among the court with his arm round the Cardinal's shoulders and invited him to his table several times a week. He had become as eager as Wolsey to secure the divorce. Now the scruples of conscience which he complained of so bitterly were related to his doubts about his marriage instead of the injury impending to the Queen. His softness for Catherine had given place to a stubborn wish to be rid of her as soon as possible, and the Cardinal rejoiced at his determination.

The King's favorite, Anne Boleyn, had returned to court and taken up her post with Catherine again; Henry was still besotted, but Wolsey saw no harm to his plans or himself in the association. Anne kept the King in a good humor and though her powerful relative the Duke of Norfolk had taken her and her family under his patronage, Wolsey shrugged in contempt. No woman, and no one connected with a woman, had ever had the slightest influence upon Henry or profited through the association. Even Anne's father, Rochford, had risen only because the King liked him and enjoyed his flattery; the charms of his two daughters would have brought him nothing on their own merit. And Henry hated Norfolk. The time to deal with the pretensions of the Boleyn family, and indeed the Norfolks, was when he returned from France. A few words to the King regarding the lady's virtue, for instance. . . . The Cardinal knew that terrible mixture of pride and prudery in his master. A hint that her relations were ambitious and trying to use the King for their own ends . . . No, he was content to leave the situation as it was. By the time he returned, Anne would probably be out of favor; she had lasted a year already.

There was no secrecy about his mission to France, because the whole issue of what was now known as the King's Secret Matter had leaked out after the first deceitful move he and Henry had made to have the marriage annulled in England. He had been surprised by Henry's sudden impatience to get the sentence of divorce pronounced, but he tried to meet the King's wishes with a proposal of typical cunning.

Wolsey and Warham, Archbishop of Canterbury, held a secret court at Westminster Palace and charged the King with marrying his brother's widow and living in incest for eighteen years. Counsel for Henry was appointed to offer a faint plea against the indictment, while Catherine was neither told of the proceedings nor represented. After three sessions, Wolsey advised that a question should be put to the English bishops: was it lawful to marry a brother's widow? There could be only one answer and the self-appointed court could use the opinion of the hierarchy as the instrument of annulment without reference to the Pope.

It was the easiest way and the quickest, and the Pope, harried by war and invasion from the forces of the Emperor Charles V, would be glad to acknowledge it.

But the Cardinal, so long accustomed to humoring the King himself, had misjudged the bishops of his Church. Their answer was simple and disastrous. Such a marriage was valid if granted Papal dispensation. Their reply went further, instigated no doubt by Fisher, Bishop of Rochester, a godly, outspoken man whom Wolsey had always disliked. Under any circumstances, the Queen had the right to appeal directly to the Pope against any decision annulling her marriage.

The court at Westminster never sat again, but its failure had the effect of hardening Henry against his unhappy wife, where success might well have made him merciful.

So much was at stake, as Wolsey pointed out; not only the condition of his soul, which was blackened with sin, but the plan for a French alliance against the Emperor must be cemented by Henry's marriage to the French Princess, and every time the King risked his limbs jousting and hunting, he left his kingdom at the mercy of civil war with only an eleven-year-old girl as his successor. The time for tact was past.

Henry agreed so readily Wolsey was surprised. He decided he'd nursed the Queen's feelings long enough and ordered the Cardinal to proceed openly against her. News of the impending divorce burst like a thunderbolt over the country.

In his first rage and disappointment, Henry went to his wife, informed her that he considered himself living in incest, and asked her to leave the court. The brutality of the action should have warned her. A more timid woman might have been driven to exile and confessing what Wolsey and the King wanted, but Catherine only cried wretchedly, refusing to admit anything unlawful. With great dignity she also refused to leave her husband unless he drove her out. The angry storm between them passed, but the Cardinal made his preparations to go to France. A new contingency had arisen, and Wolsey seized on it to turn the circumstances to his purpose. The Emperor's troops had invaded Rome and sacked it with appalling ferocity; they had captured the Pope and shut him up in the imperial Castle of St. Angelo.

Christendom was leaderless, and Wolsey issued a summons to the remaining Cardinals to meet at Avignon and assume the Papal authority. At the same time he promised Henry that one of the first actions of the commission would be to annul his marriage. He urged him to avoid the Queen and publicly lament his conscience because the opinion of the bishops was also the opinion of the people. Catherine was kind and her charity had made her loved; even at court she had no enemies, since the powerful lords had nothing to gain by her dismissal. Their power depended upon the weakness of the Crown, and a new Queen was likely to strengthen it with male heirs.

The day before Wolsey sailed for France he received a summons from the Queen. The court was at Richmond and the Cardinal left York House and came by barge down the Thames. Catherine received him in her private apartments, which always had the stillness and solemnity of a church; the contrast between them and his own luxurious lodgings angered him by the implied reproach, but the false smile widened as he approached her.

"Your Grace," he said.

The Queen was taller than he by half a head, and the stiff three-cornered headdress made her seem taller still. She wore a gown of dark brown velvet, in spite of the heat, and an enormous cross of pearls and rubies hung from a gold chain round her neck. The dull color didn't suit her—she looked tired and her eyes were red-rimmed as if she had been crying.

She gave him her hand to kiss and he noticed that it was trembling. "It was good of you to come, my Lord Cardinal." There was still a trace of her Spanish origin in her voice after more than twenty-five years in England. Several of her ladies were standing near her and she turned to them.

"Leave us, if you please."

When they were alone, Catherine sat in the window seat and gestured for the Cardinal to sit down. The action surprised him; in previous encounters, she had kept him standing.

"You must wonder why I sent for you," she said suddenly.

"I seldom have such an honor from you, Madame," Wolsey answered.

She looked at him. "We have never been friends, my Lord, as we both know, so let there be no deceit between us. It's said that you first put doubts into the King's mind about his marriage; it's also said that you are going to France to get it annulled. Is this so?"

"I am not responsible for His Grace's conscience, Madame. And my mission to France is in obedience to his will."

"You are a priest," Catherine said slowly. "And as a priest I speak to you now. The marriage is valid and I've sent for you to prove it, so that you can convince the King."

"I will willingly convince him. I only wish for His Grace's happiness, and for yours, Madame."

"Then if I go to the altar and swear before the Sacrament, will you at least believe me?"

Wolsey folded his hands in his sleeves; there was no danger. She had no proof.

"Swear what?"

"That my marriage with the King's brother was never consummated!" she said desperately. "I've sworn to His Grace, I've gone on my knees to him, but he turns away from me . . ." She stood up, gripping her hands in agitation. "All my life I've lived in obedience to the law of God and the Church; do you think I'd have lied and damned my soul, just to be Queen of England?"

"I'm quite sure Your Grace never lied," Wolsey said. She swung round to him and he saw that her face was wet with tears.

"Then you believe me? You believe that my marriage is lawful?"

He looked up at her. "I believe you may have been mistaken. You were very young, Madame, and innocent. It's understandable."

"Oh, God!" She almost cried out the words.

He made room for her by the window. "Don't be distressed," he said. "Sit down, Madame, and listen to me. Now I will speak to you, not as a priest, but a friend."

"He tried to send me away," she muttered. "I've borne his infidelities, God knows, but he still came back to me; I was his wife. Now he denies that, he says my daughter is the child of incest . . . My Lord, you know it isn't true!"

"Nobody knows," Wolsey answered. "You say you've been obedient to God and the Church. And obedient to the King. Well, now I counsel you; obey in this. The King is troubled; his love and respect for you are unchanged, but if you try to keep him in mortal sin, Madame, I can't judge what he may feel toward you. . . . Why don't you submit, why don't you place yourself in his hands and mine?"

"How can I, when you want me to admit to a lie? If it were only his happiness, I'd do what he wanted. If he's tired of me, I'll bear it and I'll never trouble him—he knows that—but I won't deny my conscience and make a bastard of my only child! My Lord, you have great influence with him . . ." She moved and suddenly she knelt before him, her face pale and swollen with tears. He had never seen her look so old.

"Help me, I beg of you! Persuade him to abandon this mission to the Cardinals in France; at least wait till the Holy Father is free and can hear my petition too!"

That, Wolsey said to himself, was the last thing he or Henry wanted to do.

"My influence with the King is not that great," he said. "And it may be that the commission in France will support the marriage. But think how much could be saved if you would only listen, Madame. Why not show your good will to the King by retiring from court till the hearing is over? A little pliancy would earn his affection more than all your tears."

Catherine wiped her eyes and slowly raised herself up.

"Don't hide your meaning behind words. You are telling me to submit and confess that we have been living in mortal sin."

"The King would provide handsomely for you," Wolsey said smoothly. "You could have what title you wished and even live at court."

"That's all you have to say—submit? You refuse to help me, as a priest of Christ, you tell me to perjure myself, to submit?" she repeated.

Wolsey rose. "I do. Submit of your own free will, before the King finds a way to compel you."

She faced him, one hand pulling the jeweled cross on its chain. One more agitated tug, the Cardinal thought coldly, and it will break.

"In my wretchedness, I hoped to find some pity in you," Catherine said bitterly. "I should have known better. You made your journey to Richmond for nothing, my Lord Cardinal. Nothing but my death can dissolve the King's marriage to me."

Wolsey bowed. "That, too, is not impossible."

The King had moved to Hunsdon in Hertfordshire in August, and Anne was with him. There was no longer any pretense that she was Catherine's maid-of-honor; the post was nominal and no duties were allowed to keep her from the King though she still slept in the communal rooms with Catherine's other ladies and accompanied the Queen to Mass; she even performed a few services for her, but she spent the best part of the day and every evening in Henry's apartments. When he rode, she went with him riding well for a woman, and hawking with equal enthusiasm. She gambled with him and won large sums, until she realized that Henry hated losing; then very skillfully she allowed herself to be beaten. She was the wittiest, most stimulating companion he had ever known, and she allowed him every physical liberty but consummation, once she knew that he was going to marry her.

The knowledge had changed their relationship and charged it with a tremendous intimacy; opposition only strengthened their resolve and turned them to each other. As the situation appealed to the King's love of self-dramatization; he played the part of the heroic lover to his heart's content, and Anne encouraged him.

Hunsdon House had been redecorated for the King's visit. At the first outbreak of summer sickness in London he had left Hampton Court and retired to the lovely red brick country mansion with a chosen nucleus of the court. Anne loved Hunsdon; it was furnished in imitation of the elegance of Wolsey's magnificent palace, with rich hangings and rugs and fine oak furniture. The sprawling building was set in a large park, with a steep green lawn running down to a rose garden almost as beautiful as the one at Hever, and Henry had ordered a special walled garden to be built to the south, where the sun could nourish the rock flowers and climbing plants.

Hunsdon was peaceful and rural and comparatively free from

court etiquette, and there, with Anne, the King lived in the role of country gentleman.

He had been hunting that afternoon in late August and returned to his own rooms, hot and hungry, to find Anne waiting for him. Sweating and dusty as he was, he caught her in his arms, his mouth searching avidly for those torturing kisses that were her special talent. At last he set her down and went in search of water and fresh linen.

A few moments later he came into the room, dressed in a clean white shirt and velvet breeches. His face was still flushed from the exercise, and his cropped red head was damp where his servant had sluiced it with water to cool him. The collar of his shirt was unfastened, showing the thick neck and powerful, hairy chest. He smiled at her and held out his arms.

"A good day's sport, sweetheart! Have you been lonely?"

"Bitterly," she replied, stroking his cheek. "I would I'd been the deer, that you might have hunted *me* . . ."

"I've hunted you for nearly two long years, my Nan," he answered, his face against her hair. "Christ's blood, take off that damnable headpiece, so I can kiss your hair."

She removed it, smiling, and flung it across the room to a chair. Then she twisted her arms round his neck and pressed close to him, her brain calculating, watching the impulses of her body, determining exactly when to draw away from him. . . .

"Oh, God, Nan, why wait till we're married?" he burst out at last. "We're contracted now, why torture me with waiting?"

She had her answer ready. "And would you have your son a bastard, Sire?"

"You're right enough," he admitted, releasing her. "But it's hard when I love you so, Nan."

"As I love you," she said. "And perhaps it won't be long now. If My Lord Cardinal's plan succeeds . . ."

Henry shrugged and flung himself back into a chair, his arms locked above his head. "I've tried to make assurance doubly sure," he said.

Her skirts whipped the floor as she turned round. "How? What have you done that you haven't told me?"

"Wolsey's negotiating for a marriage with Renée of France," he answered. "I've sent Master Secretary Knight to Rome itself to gain two dispensations which enable me to marry *you*; when he's successful, 'twill be all the easier to convince our friend Thomas that an English Queen is better than a French one."

"What points are these?"

"Permission to marry within the forbidden degrees of relationship, and to take another wife while the matter of Catherine's divorce is still pending," Henry announced triumphantly.

"The last I understand but not the first. Why forbidden degrees? There's no blood tie between us."

"There's the tie of my indiscretion with your sister Mary, my love," he retorted. "That's enough to invalidate a marriage between us if no permission were given by the Pope. I've sent Knight to see him in prison and secure these grants in return for a promise of English support."

Anne looked at him narrowly. "And what will the Lord Cardinal say when he learns you've dispatched him to France and sent another messenger ahead of him to Rome? If he learns that you wish to marry me instead of his French candidate, d'you suppose he'll work as hard for the divorce as before?"

"For that reason I kept him in ignorance," Henry admitted. He checked her with a movement. "Stay your reproaches; it's policy, not weakness that makes me humor him. When I tell him my desire, he'll obey in that as in everything else."

"I've heard it said that he obeys only where it suits himself," she said quietly. "Sire, what kind of minister is he, that you must keep things from him and send messengers about your own business behind his back?"

He moved irritably. Why was she always implying that he bent to Wolsey? In the last few weeks he was hearing a chorus of complaints and innuendoes about the Cardinal from men like Norfolk and Suffolk, and he listened in spite of himself because Anne's subtle taunting had roused his suspicions. They all hated Wolsey; they envied him for his favor and they hated him because he symbolized the power and immunity of the Church. He had been aware of that for years and paid no attention because it had never occurred to him seriously that Wolsey's position might shadow his own.

"Why couldn't you trust him to place your wishes above his own design?" she went on. "If he loved you without self-interest, he'd welcome a marriage that would bring you happiness. What right had he to suggest the Princess Renée as a wife for you? Did he think whether she'd please you, or whether the alliance would further his own plans?"

"Nan, Nan, for Jesu's sake, the choice seemed well enough before I met you. . . ."

"A poor choice indeed, if you permit me," she said. "A means of continuing his foreign policy, and God knows the failure that's been!" Norfolk had coached her what to say and she had learned the outline of the attack by heart.

"We've meddled in the affairs of Europe for the past twelve years; we've had wars that have sucked the last ducat out of your treasury and taxes that cripple the people. First he sets out to humble France; and Your Grace won the battle for him and achieved the peace at the Field of Cloth of Gold. France is laid waste, and the reason he gives is the safety of the Pope because France was at war with him. . . . Oh, the Cardinal knows how to take advantage of a truly Christian Prince!"

He tried to stop her but she pretended not to hear.

"In ruining France to support his own glory and strengthen the Church, he wires the crossbow of the Emperor! Look at the power of the Emperor now, with France too weak to withstand him. . . . And the folly of shedding English blood for the sake of Rome. Let's see how the Pope shows his gratitude to Your Grace in this matter of the marriage! Let's see the mighty Cardinal persuade him to divorce you from the Emperor's aunt while the Emperor holds him prisoner!"

"But Nan, that's why he's gone to France, to summon the Cardinals and assume the Pope's authority until he's free," the King protested. Her vehemence distressed him; he refuted her words, but he was unable to forget them afterward.

"He's a good servant," he insisted; "a poor priest, perhaps, but a good servant to me."

"One poor priest among many," Anne retorted. "Poor in virtue but mightily rich in the things of this world!"

Again the words were not her own; they were Suffolk's, repeated to her by her father, who reported that the Duke was bitterly anticlerical. Suffolk's views were quickly becoming Rochford's as he copied the Duke's dress and mannerisms and echoed his opinions, flattered because he was admitted to his counsels. Suffolk and Norfolk found him easier to influence than Anne.

Henry frowned.

"That's Catherine's complaint against him. I'll admit some of his display is unseemly."

He was thinking of that magnificent barge and the quasi-royal fanfare that preceded Wolsey's arrivals and departures. And the liveried servants who overran York House. He thought of York House too. Wolsey had rebuilt on a lavish scale after giving Hampton Court to the King; his treasures of plate and jewels were reputed to be the finest in England.

"It's unseemly in a servant to try to rival his master," Anne said quietly. "God knows what impression he creates abroad."

Henry didn't answer; he sat there tipping his chair backward and forward, watching her and thinking.

All his life he had hated carping women; even his wife, whose opinion he respected and who never offended his pride by persisting in advice, even Catherine had never abused Wolsey like this. But then Catherine had never had the wit to see through him as Anne did, to recognize affronts to his dignity and resent them for his sake. Catherine only criticized because she disapproved of him as a Minister of Christ while Anne's concern was for the honor of the King.

"I'll see to these matters when he returns," he said, "but spare me your complaints till then. I hear enough of them from my brother-in-law Suffolk and your good uncle and Christ's wisdom knows who else! Enough of Wolsey now! I balance his mistakes against his twelve years' service, and no one shall persuade me to do otherwise."

"Your Grace mistakes mercy for justice," Anne went on.

He raised his head and looked at her.

"Enough, I said," he repeated quietly. She curtsied. "As you command," she said softly. She went to him and sat on his knee, her arms round his neck.

"I beg you, don't be angry," she whispered. "It's only my great love for you that speaks . . ."

The King's chair came to rest on all four legs and stayed firmly on the floor. There was silence in the room.

Wolsey returned to England on the twenty-fourth of September and he arrived at Richmond Palace on the last day of the month. He came back to report failure, his mind ready with excuses and new plans. The Cardinals had refused to meet and arrogate the Papal authority to themselves; the Pope was negotiating with the Emperor for his freedom at the same time, and Wolsey had been forced to give up his plan. And at Compiègne he had met the King's secretary Knight and found that Henry had decided to go straight to Rome over his head.

For the first time in his career Wolsey was uneasy when he came back to the court; new influences were at work and the King's urgency for the divorce was out of all proportion to his proposed marriage to the French Princess.

Wolsey journeyed from Dover to London in three days, in spite of mud-logged roads and driving rain, and he hurried to his first audience with the King as soon as he was robed. He always saw the King in private and they talked informally. Informality was part of the secret of his influence with Henry and they were accustomed to sit and talk as two men together, while the Cardinal exercised his great gifts of flattery and persuasion uninterrupted. This time, he thought as he waited for word to come, this time he had a great deal to say, and a great deal to find out. . . . Why had the King sent Knight to Rome behind his back? Why was he suddenly so impatient to get rid of Catherine?

Both his questions were answered that night. Not in private, conversing with the King, but by a command to appear before Henry in the great hall at Richmond and be received in public for the first time in twelve years. He knew then that his friendship with the King was finished. And when he reached the dais he knew why Knight had gone to Rome and why Henry wanted the divorce. He knew it suddenly and finally, as he saw the King's eyes, pale and unsmiling while they watched him, and as he saw Anne Boleyn, her neck and head blazing with diamonds, standing by the King's chair of state with her hand on Henry's arm.

4

"I should never have left England for so long," Wolsey said. It was unlike him to repeat himself, but he had said the same thing over and over again that morning. He was living in York House, trying to work on the state papers as usual, and he had sent for a member of his staff to assist him. But they had done little work; instead, the Cardinal pushed the documents aside and sat hunched in his chair, waving his secretary to be seated with him. The secretary had not been long in his service, and Wolsey had chosen him because his abilities as a lawyer had come to his notice. He was a short, ugly man with flat plebeian features and an unexpected gift of oratory. Like his master, he was of humble origin but unlike Wolsey, he made no attempt in dress or manner to disguise it. His name was Thomas Cromwell.

"Her influence with the King is all-powerful now," he remarked. "She can say and do no wrong in his eyes."

Wolsey struck the arm of his chair with his fist.

"I must have been blind not to see it! But Christ's death, I thought I knew the King. I've lived in his shadow and served him for nearly thirteen years and I'd have staked my head that no woman would bring him to this pass . . ."

"No man ever knows the King, my Lord."

"You're a shrewd fellow, Thomas, too shrewd for your years," Wolsey said slowly. "I think well of your opinion. Now listen to me. I've had audience of the King since that night at Richmond; he's been putting his arm round my neck and calling me Thomas,

59

but I know he cares nothing for me any more. Once he did and now he's friendly to me from habit, or because he's not quite ready to throw me to my enemies. And that woman is the cause. I tried him out the other day when we were alone talking of Europe and the Emperor, and he was listening to me in the way that he has when he mistrusts the words and the speaker. So I spoke of Mistress Anne. I praised her, Thomas, I said what a fair and worthy lady she was and how devoted to His Grace. And before God, his face lit up and his tongue wagged like a lovesick boy's, bragging about her wit and her musicianship and her virtue. Her great virtue, he said." Wolsey snorted. "Virtue! I longed to remind him that she was Wyatt's strumpet before he took her for himself. I sat there and listened and I knew before he blurted it out to me that he was mad to marry her."

"What did you say to the proposal?" Cromwell questioned.

Wolsey raised his head; under the line of his scarlet skullcap his face was terribly gray.

"There was no proposal. The King who once said, 'Thomas, I've a mind to do this or that, what do you think? . . .' is gone forever. No, he looked at me with his mouth drawn so tight it nearly vanished in his beard, and said it was his will to marry the lady, and to secure his divorce as soon as possible. I was bidden to make haste about it."

"If I may suggest something, my Lord," Cromwell interposed, and Wolsey nodded. "It seems the King's been won away from you. Even though you bend immediately to his will, you'll get no thanks for that, and probably little mercy in the end. Don't try to win the King back; win the woman instead."

"Wise words," the Cardinal answered. "I've already told them to myself. Doubtless I'm expected to oppose the marriage, to argue with the King and anger him further. There's more than Anne Boleyn involved in this, my friend for behind her are my real enemies, Norfolk, Suffolk and the rest. And behind them are Parliament, and the lawyers and men like Thomas More."

"More is very able," Cromwell conceded. "But he's not of the stamp of the others you mention. More is devoutly religious; Lord Suffolk and many of the nobles are not; as for the Parliament, you know how fiercely they resent some of the Church's privileges. The attack is not only upon you, but upon the power of the Church itself."

Wolsey watched him; some of the despair had left his face, he was alert again, his mind darting and twisting ahead, exploring possibilities.

"As a layman and a lawyer with experience in Parliament," Cromwell continued, "I can speak with assurance of the temper of the professional classes. It is essential that you make your peace with the King, and not only to save yourself, but to prevent an attack on the security of the Church itself."

"Suffolk would do it," the Cardinal muttered quickly. "He'd have the support of the nobility; they've long resented a priest holding the first place in the governing of the country after the King. Office has always been their privilege; so has civil war. Norfolk feels the same; it's too long since one of the great Lords had the chance to play Warwick the Kingmaker again, and they blame me for that. And they're right!"

He raised himself on the crossed arms of his oak chair and stood up, a short heavy figure in his scarlet cassock, the gold and diamond cross hung round his neck gleaming in the light as he moved. He turned to Cromwell, still sitting, small and ungainly in his black doublet and hose, almost blending with the oak paneling and black shadows.

"I've curbed their power whenever I could," Wolsey said fiercely. "I've known them for what they were, ruthless and self-seeking, without love for their land or their King. I made them disband their private armies, so that the game of marching on the sovereign couldn't be played at the first whim . . . I've devised taxes for them and taught the King to keep them at court under his eye rather than let them live like monarchs on their estates and pass the time plotting against the Crown! We've suffered enough in England through the great lords and their ways; for thirty years in the Wars of the Roses, one house sworn against another, bloodshed and pillage and murder up and down the country . . . The first Tudor put an end to that, and I've lived and worked to build up the power of his son Henry. The power of the

61

Church, you say—how well that sounds, Master Cromwell. . . . No, rather the power of the King, for King and Church are one in England; one against the nobility, and the Parliament and its parent, the City of London!"

Cromwell crossed one thick leg over the other.

"The King and the Church may be one as you say, my Lord. But will they remain so, if the divorce is not granted?"

Wolsey stepped toward him. "It will be granted," he said, "it must, for I'll tell the Pope what you've told me; the safety of the Church itself depends upon my keeping the good will of the King. The Pope values England; he values Henry's friendship and wishes him well, I know that. And when he hears of the situation he'll give his decision in the King's favor. And none but I can approach him properly, as even that black strumpet must realize!"

He was calmer now, biting his lower lip and talking fast as he thought aloud.

"I've confidence, Tom, however evil things appear. They need me to get the divorce for them, and once Madame sees that without me her hopes of marrying the King will come to nothing, then I feel she'll abandon her Uncle Norfolk and the rest of the conspirators. She'll accept me as her ally. And if I've got to destroy the plan for a matrimonial alliance with France, then God's death, I'll destroy it but I'll keep my place with the King!"

"One point," Cromwell interrupted quietly. "You're presuming on the lady's gratitude, my Lord."

The Cardinal looked at him. "On what else can I rely?"

"Nothing," Cromwell shook his head, "and she should be grateful if you bring the marriage about. She should turn the King toward you as she turned him away; she should side with you against her own kin when she's Queen, forgetting everything but the great debt she owes you . . ."

"You've little faith in human nature," Wolsey said slowly.

Cromwell smiled amiably.

"I have none at all," he answered. "So I beg you to proceed in her interests for as long as they coincide with yours, my Lord. If you can gain her over, you have won the King. Then it may be that you'll regain the influence you lost during that trip to France.

Forgive me if I quibble, but it's a failing with lawyers. All the same, don't rely too much on the gratitude of women."

"She's not as clever as you think," Wolsey said. "I've watched her carefully in the last weeks, and if the King tires of her before they marry, it'll go hard with her as well as me. She's dealing with dangerous men, Tom; men like Suffolk and her uncle at the top and many others not less powerful. It's taken all my skill to keep my heel on them for nearly thirteen years, and I've never antagonized them openly as she does. She's clever with the King, but she's a fool with them, by God! I've heard her insult Suffolk and make a mock of him in front of the whole court, and she snubs her Aunt Norfolk and great ladies as if she were already Queen. Such people have long memories, Tom, and no mercy; at this pace she'll have no one to befriend her but the King and the day may come when he abandons her as he's abandoned me."

"I've heard many comparing her with the Queen," Cromwell remarked. "And she's made more partisans for Catherine in her trouble than the Queen ever had when she was safe at Henry's side.

"Catherine is doomed," Wolsey said. "That at least is certain. Those who cling to that barque will certainly sink with it, whoever sails in her place. Come, Tom, take your pens and paper; when this morning's business is finished, I'm going to pay my respects to Mistress Anne."

In the royal apartments of the Tower, Anne and Henry were alone in his bedroom. The King was never disturbed in his chamber, and the other rooms, all leading into one another, were always filled with courtiers. The door was closed, and the windows tightly shut, for a cold wind was blowing in from the Thames. The King's huge tester bed stood in the center of the room, hung with curtains of velvet; the rugs newly imported from Persia were spread over the tables and covered the bed itself. The floor was covered with rushes and scented herbs to keep the room warm in winter, and the King sat in a wide oak chair before the fire, with Anne on his knee.

There was no danger in intimacy with him now, no need to deny him and hold him off. They made love fiercely and without restraint, but he never tried to take her, or urged her to give way. The heir they both talked about must be born in wedlock; that was Anne's weapon and excuse, and he agreed with it. Her arms were round his neck, and he caressed her blindly, greedy for the abortive pleasures their relations allowed. He had unpinned her hair and the long plaits hung to the ground. She held his head and kissed him slowly on the mouth, feeling his heart pounding against her breast. Then she drew back, and caught his strong hands in her own.

"The Cardinal came to me today," she said.

"Nan, Nan sweetheart," he muttered, not listening, and laid one finger gently on her mouth. She kissed it, and moved her head free.

"Harry, beloved, this is important. He talked about the divorce."

The interlude was over, and Henry knew it; he relaxed and leaned back, shifting her so that she rested comfortably on his knees.

"He spoke of it to me, at his last audience."

She stiffened. "You never told me! What did he say?"

Henry sighed. "Ah, Nan, I didn't want to vex you with it. He failed to convene the Cardinals in France and take the Pope's authority, you knew that. Well, now there's nothing for it but to go direct to Rome. The Emperor's set Clement free, and he must give the authority for the divorce to be tried. It'll take time, my love, but Wolsey swears he'll use his influence to hurry it."

"That's what he said to me," Anne interrupted. "That and how anxious he was to serve me. I didn't believe one word!"

Henry stared at her. "How, and why not?"

"Because a serpent doesn't grow legs overnight," she retorted. "He hates me, and I'll swear he's clinging to his idea of a French marriage. And you've received him with favor again," she accused. "So he thinks he'll rule you as he did before. In the meantime he makes false promises to lull me so that he can work against me."

The King flushed with anger. "He went on his knees and vowed he'd spend his last drop of blood to hurry the divorce and marry us himself!" he said. "Now you tell me it's deceit. Rule me again,

64

you say . . . By the living God above, if I thought he'd such a thing in his head I'd cut it off!"

He pushed her off his knees and stood up, towering over her. She began winding her plaits round her head; she knew his anger was directed against Wolsey. The private audiences hadn't altered Henry after all.

"Naturally I don't trust him," she said. "He's had his own way too long to submit so easily. That's all I say, don't trust him . . ."

"Then who am I to trust?" Henry demanded. "Who is to deal with Rome if he does not?"

"He'll deal with Rome," she said. "He'll dally and make difficulties in the hope you'll sicken of me in time and come round to his way again."

Then Henry smiled at her, a triumphant smile. She was sometimes right too often and it irritated him, but now he had her. His temper was soothed at once.

"You think too fast and too crookedly, sweet," he said mockingly. "And you underestimate the Cardinal. If he dallies and makes difficulties, he'll lose his head and he knows it. He knows my mind and he's wise enough not to balk me. You've said often enough that he ruled me, and you know how that angers me. Say it no more, for I've proved it's a lie. Wolsey himself suggested sending Bishop Gardiner and Dr. Foxe to Rome to see Clement and obtain a commission from him to try the divorce in England. Now tell me he's trying to thwart my will!"

She retorted with a mock curtsy, pinning her plaits into place with a jeweled pin, and then she came close to him and put her arms round his waist and her head against his chest.

"I thank God," she said gently. "And I pray him to help us, with Wolsey or without. But to please you, Harry, I won't speak against him till we see how he conducts this matter and keeps his promises. It may be that he's true at last; he said the fairest words on his tongue to me today."

Perhaps Wolsey *was* genuine, she mused; perhaps he was so afraid of her and so alarmed by the King's change of attitude that he was prepared to alter his whole policy and follow theirs . . . Henry believed so, and she knew that he was seldom mistaken. If it was true, the anticlerical party who supported her would be furious; they were hoping for Wolsey's dismissal within the next few months. Well, they would have to wait, she decided. The devil take them. If she needed Wolsey to become Queen, Wolsey must remain till his turn was served. Afterward . . . afterward they should have their victim and so would she. And so would Henry Percy, who was reputed to be living so unhappily with his wife that they were separated. He was subject to fits of epilepsy. . . . His marriage—as Agnes Throgmorton, one of Catherine's ladies, said in her hearing—his marriage to that shrew Mary Talbot had broken his health.

It was a long time ago, Anne thought, with her cheek against Henry's silk doublet and her eyes closed; a very long time since the days Percy had held her in his arms and begged her to marry him, and now an unbridgeable gulf separated them. They had nothing to say to each other. He was a wreck of a man, nervous and violent and near to feeble-mindedness at times, while she was the most powerful woman in England, who was expected to marry the King.

There was nothing left but some tiny core of regret which throbbed when they met; he would flush and stammer and his hands would shake, and she would smile and say something and pass on. Though there was no future for them with each other any more, the memory of the past remained. There were times when the past seemed sweeter than the present, when she remembered her early years in France with a gay and brilliant court, and her return to England, ready for marriage and children, like her friends.

Percy had offered her both; he was the only one who had, besides the King, she thought suddenly. He could have made her happy then, but now it was too late. Now marriage and domesticity were impossible. If she had changed Henry, as her enemies said, then Henry had changed her. She was suspicious and on edge, and the struggle to keep her position had made her fierce and ruthless. Sexually the King was coarse and brutal, so in that too she had become debased. The Cardinal had set her life on its present course and there was no turning back.

"Why are you laughing, Nan?"

Henry could feel her shaking against him. Sometimes she

laughed for no reason, and like her father, the King was disconcerted by it. He was frowning. "Come, tell me the joke."

She looked up at him, giggling, with her eyes full of tears.

"The joke, Harry . . . why it's just that I was thinking that I couldn't live without you now. Isn't it comical? Before God, I really couldn't . . ."

On January twenty-second the heralds of England and France declared war on Emperor Charles V. The pattern of the Cardinal's foreign policy was taking shape for the last time, as the French King prepared to launch a new attack against the power of the Empire with the help of English money and a force of Englishmen. Heavy taxes had been levied on the English people for the purpose of another unpopular war abroad and the enclosure of common lands by the great nobles had deprived large numbers of peasants of pasture for their flocks. Poverty began to spread, so soon after the prosperity of Henry VII's thrifty reign, and the Cardinal's splendid barge was greeted with yells and handfuls of filth whenever it sailed too close to the banks of the Thames. Wolsey was blamed for everything, because it was commonly accepted that he directed the King's policy. He, and the Church with him, were joined to the greedy, hated nobility who had tyrannized for centuries over the common people, and became the focus of their resentment. By contrast the King's popularity increased while Wolsey was bitterly accused of trying to remove their good Queen Catherine and there were growing rumors of a conspiracy between the hated Cardinal and some court lady to have her put away.

Dispossessed peasantry roamed the countryside, begging and robbing, so that the roads were unsafe without an armed escort, and the wool merchants and the townspeople waited anxiously for the effect of the Cardinal's war on the Netherlands' trade. In Europe the armies of France had penetrated deeply into the imperial kingdom of Naples under the leadership of the Sieur de Lautrec, and the emissaries of the King of England had their audience with the Pope on April third to open the petition for the annulment of his marriage.

67

At the Vatican Dr. Reginald Foxe and Dr. Stephen Gardiner were announced at the door of the Papal audience chamber, guarded by the halberdiers of the Swiss Guard in their scarlet doublets and breastplates, emblazoned with the arms of the Vicar of Christ. The chamber was high-ceilinged and lit by torches set into the walls; it was hung with magnificent tapestries depicting episodes from the New Testament, and the Pope's throne stood at the far end of the room, under a white and gold canopy.

Clement VII seemed like an old man; his shoulders were bent and his hands knotted with rheumatism; he withdrew them from his scarlet sleeves and made the sign of the cross over the two Englishmen as they bowed before him, and came forward to kiss his ring. He looked delicate and tired, but his dark eyes were alive with intelligence. The face was very Italian with its aquiline nose and sallow skin.

"I give you a hearty welcome, gentlemen. Please sit down. You had a good journey, I trust?"

Clement looked from one to the other and smiled gently. He knew how fast they had traveled, gathering speed as the French armies drove further into imperial territory, and he knew that their insistence on the point at issue would have gained by the Emperor's weakness. The day before, he had given an audience to the imperial Ambassador and listened to *his* pleas not to yield to English pressure and injure the Emperor's aunt. He had said as little to Charles's emissary as he meant to say to Henry's. Until he knew the outcome of the war, he dared not give a decision either way.

"We come to Your Holiness on the matter of the King's Grace and his marriage to Catherine of Aragon," Gardiner began. He had been told to avoid calling Catherine "Queen." "May I present this letter from your Legate Cardinal Wolsey?" Clement thanked him and opened the paper. There was silence for some moments while he read, holding the letter close to his eyes.

The situation in England was very dangerous, Wolsey had written. The anticlerical party was using the King's wish for a divorce as a lever with which to dislodge him and strike a blow at the independence of the Church in the Kingdom . . . Clement frowned.

The English Church was well known for its independence of Rome anyway; the management was left entirely to the English Cardinal and the English bishops, all the Holy See received was the friendship of the King and a few revenues. Clement read on.

Feeling against Wolsey was high in the country, and his enemies at court had a powerful advocate in the woman whom the King had determined to marry. In order to safeguard the Church's interests in England, it was vital that he should retain the favor of the King and remain in office, and he begged the Holy Father to take all these factors into consideration when listening to the petition of Foxe and Gardiner.

In other words, Wolsey was in mortal danger unless he got for Henry and the woman what they wanted; and as he said, the interests of the Church in England were probably in danger too Clement nodded to himself. He understood how Wolsey felt.

But the danger of the Church in England was nothing compared to the danger of the Church on the continent. Rome, the heartbeat of the Christian faith, was only a city built on seven hills, ringed by the nationalistic designs of the Italian Princes and the dictatorial might of France and the Empire.

Europe was in a religious ferment; the whole structure of medieval society had been changing for years, as the power of the monarch superceded that of the feudal nobility. With the centralization of power, the Papacy faced its first challenge; and with the spread of learning and the founding of lay universities, it faced the deadlier challenge of heresy.

Clement still held the letter, apparently reading, while his mind ran on. He and his Church were paying for the sins of previous Popes, for the worldliness and power politics of the Borgias, who had transformed the mighty spiritual power of the Papacy into an armed political force. Once already the Church had been threatened by the laxity of its members in medieval times, and the great army of Franciscans roamed Europe, preaching and purging into the heart of Rome itself. Now the reformers were attacking not only the human abuses but the spiritual structure of Christianity itself. The Church of God was held in contempt, Clement said to himself, concentrating on the scrawl of Wolsey's signature at the end of the page; she was despised by even those who professed her doctrines and drove merciless bargains in return for their protection. And the wave of austerity sweeping from Lutheran Germany was turning many away from the forms and rituals which were part of her worship.

The Church in England was in danger; if he wished to preserve it, he had better grant the King his freedom. And risk the fury of the Catholic Emperor, who had already permitted his troops to sack Rome.

He looked up at Gardiner, folding the letter.

"I am well pleased with the Cardinal's letter," he said. "I have a high opinion of his judgment, and he recommends you both to me."

Gardiner cleared his throat.

"We have come to you on a delicate matter, Your Holiness. The Cardinal has undoubtedly explained it, and I am commissioned to place the details before you. His Grace the King of England desires that you appoint a commission to try the validity of his marriage. He has been gravely troubled for some years because he married his brother's widow, and the deaths of all his male children have convinced him that he is under the judgment of God and living in conditions of scandal before his Maker and before men."

It was a good clear speech, and the Pope measured his man by the short way in which he delivered it.

Clement nodded. "I appreciate the King's wish for sons, and his scruples regarding the marriage. You say that you are petitioning me to authorize a hearing for the case; I presume you mean in England, with Cardinal Wolsey on the board?"

Foxe said coldly: "He is Your Holiness' Legate. We're asking nothing unusual in that."

"Two Cardinals must sit in judgment," the Pope said. "I must explain to you that the matter is a difficult one for me, as difficult as it is for your master the King. The imperial Ambassador has made strong representations to me about the question of Queen Catherine's divorce. I have to be impartial to both sides."

Gardiner spread both hands on his knees and said sharply: "Impartiality can be carried too far. The King's patience is at an end; he lays claim to Your Holiness' gratitude for his services to you in the past and his defense of your rights at a time when they were endangered by France."

"If you will help King Henry's cause and judge it fairly, you are assured of the protection of France as well as England when the war is concluded," Foxe interposed quickly.

Clement remembered their last offer of protection; a guard of French and English troops after his release from the Emperor's custody. That time he had thanked them graciously and rejected the proposal to exchange one set of jailers for another, preferring, as he said, to rely on the help of God and his own little body of loyal soldiers.

"I have no fears for my personal safety," he said gently. "But I have responsibilities greater than any debt I owe to any earthly King. Now, as to the divorce commission: an Italian must sit with Cardinal Wolsey, to make sure the judgment is impartial."

He returned to his thoughts. True, the war was going against Charles and the Empire. Clement had a mental image of the tall, cynical King of France parceling up his Italian possessions, on the excuse that he had failed to accommodate his ally, the English King. . . . Francis, Henry and Charles. They were all at his throat, all equally untrustworthy and unscrupulous; absolute monarchs who regarded him as little better than a petty Italian Prince with certain advantageous religious powers which could be turned to their purposes. Which one to choose; which one to trust with the security of the Church in Europe . . . God help me, Clement prayed, as he talked to the two English envoys, God guide me. Not just for myself, I'm mortal and all men die; but for my Church and all my people. I must have borrowed strength since I've none left of my own, but whose lance will shelter me without turning into my back?

He raised his head and looked from one man to the other.

He might have trusted England and, once he had her word, felt safe. . . . But he would never be safe with Francis. Francis was cynical and worldly beyond belief; his goal was power. Francis was worse than that strange, fanatical man Charles, King of Spain and head of the Empire. Charles wanted power too, but there was a vein of orthodoxy in him which might be united to his ambitions.

71

Foxe and Gardiner were both waiting, sitting a little forward on the edges of their chairs.

"We will meet again in a few days' time, gentlemen," Clement said, and I shall have two Cardinals with me to discuss the details in full."

When the envoys had gone, pages helped the Pope descend from the throne. Slowly, leaning on one of the boys' shoulders, Clement crossed to a side door set in the tapestry wall. The other page went ahead, holding a lighted taper, and the Pope walked to the still magnificence of the Sistine Chapel to kneel alone before the glorious high altar and pray that the Divine gift of infallibility might work once more through his feeble agency and direct his decision about the divorce of the King of England.

Sir Henry Norreys, Gentleman of the Bedchamber to the King, walked quickly down the gallery leading to Henry's private sitting-room. The gallery was filled with people as usual, sitting in the window seats, talking and laughing and leaning out. Some of them called to Norreys as he passed; he was a handsome, popular young man with an easy wit and a gallant reputation, and, like most of the men with whom Henry surrounded himself, he was a keen sportsman. His great friend Sir William Brereton looked up from a book of love poems he was reading to one of Queen Catherine's ladies who was perched on a window seat, giggling, and mocked Norreys for hurrying.

"You've grown fast feet, Hal; who's the fair quarry this time?"

Norreys laughed. "No woman, Will. I'm on duty today and I'm going to the King. He's sent for Master Wolsey."

Twelve months ago no one would have dared refer to the Cardinal by that nickname in public. But Norreys knew and so did everyone in the gallery that Wolsey's star was sinking; the day before, Dr. Foxe had returned from Rome, and judging by the King's smile and Anne's gaiety, he brought good news.

A few moments later Norreys had disappeared behind the velvet curtain that screened Henry's room from the public view.

"The Cardinal is on his way here, Your Grace," he announced.

Henry was standing by the open window, one hand on Anne's shoulder. Norreys saluted her, thinking how small she looked beside the King's great height. He was becoming heavier, and no amount of exercise undid the results of his enormous appetite. Looking at Anne, Norreys marveled. She was as slim as a reed, but he had often waited on them both at supper and seen her eat and drink with the capacity of a man. Nothing improved the King's appetite more than watching his mistress enjoying the food, and he often sat back, watching her and laughing.

She smiled at Norreys and twisted her fingers through Henry's. She liked Norreys; he admired her and she knew it; they often joked together in the King's presence.

"You're out of breath," she remarked. "I only hope the Cardinal bestirs himself as quickly about the King's business as you do."

"He's coming as fast as his short legs can carry him, Madame," Norreys answered, and a noise in the gallery outside confirmed the words.

When Wolsey entered, the King sent his gentleman away, and the curtain fell behind him, leaving the three of them alone.

"Your Grace," Wolsey said, and his voice was unsteady. As he knelt he saw the hem of a green velvet dress trailing beside the King's feet, and his eyes lifted to the oval face and the large dark eyes; the heavy lids closed over them for a second, and the hostility was gone.

"Madame," he said. Henry was smiling and gruff, a sign that he was pleased, and she was leaning idly against him. If he hadn't seen her expression as he knelt before the King, Wolsey might have trusted her smile and her greeting.

"We're pleased to see you, Thomas," Henry said. "Aren't we, sweetheart?" He pressed her shoulder gently, urging her to receive the Cardinal well. He was happy and full of hope, and he was generous at that moment to the man who had served him so well in the past, and was so pathetically eager to do so in the future. He wished Anne to be generous too.

"Nothing could please me more," she said graciously.

"Come, Thomas, let us sit down. I have good news to tell you."

73

Henry eased himself into a tall oak chair, and the Cardinal hesitated.

"Take the stool, my Lord," Anne suggested. "I sit by the King." And she balanced on the arm of Henry's chair, with her arm round his shoulder.

"I sit by the King." It might not have been a jibe at his expense; in any case Henry didn't see it. Wolsey ignored the remark and kept his eyes on Henry's face.

"Dr. Foxe came straight to me from Rome," the King began. "In our anxiety to hear his news, we sent for him in person, rather than wait while he made his report to you. There's no slight intended to you, Thomas."

Henry felt her stiffen against him as he made his attempt to salve what was left of Wolsey's pride. She'd be angry and upbraid him for it, but that was only a woman's pettiness. He patted her knee and continued.

"Foxe has accomplished the mission you set him. The Pope has granted all our requests and ordered a commission to try the divorce in London."

"Thanks be to God!" the Cardinal exclaimed. His heart was jumping with relief. The Pope had listened, then; his letter and his envoys had opened the way to Henry's marriage. He *must* regain his favor as a result; even she couldn't show enmity toward him now . . .

"He gave a written order, Sire?"

Henry laughed joyfully. "He did indeed. And the thanks are due to you, Thomas. I told Nan we could depend on you. Sweetheart, get the paper and show it to Thomas."

She moved to an oak cabinet which stood by the window and took a thick document out of a drawer. He recognized the heavy Papal seal hanging on a thread of purple ribbon. He rose and thanked her, and asked Henry's permission to read it by the window where the light helped his eyes.

Wolsey's back was half turned toward them as he unfolded the paper and began to read. Henry held out his hand to Anne, and squeezed her fingers affectionately. They waited, smiling at

74

each other until Wolsey turned round and came toward them.

"Well?" Henry asked triumphantly.

The Cardinal held the Pope's commission in his hands and hoped they wouldn't notice they were trembling.

"It is everything we could desire," he said. "Foxe and Gardiner are to be commended indeed."

"I knew you'd be pleased," the King remarked. "Even I could see that they'd succeeded. Now, Nan, my love, the time of waiting'll soon be over."

"Not soon enough to please me," she retorted. It was not the answer Henry expected, and he frowned. She was carping because he had thanked Wolsey, and God damn it, it *was* Wolsey who had planned the approach to Rome. Anne saw the frown, and immediately she looked at the Cardinal standing before them and smiled.

"Forgive my impatience, my Lord," she explained sweetly, "my love for His Grace is a cruel goad . . . I am deeply indebted to you for your help and I only pray that I can find a way to show my gratitude one day."

"Madame, your pleasure is my reward," the Cardinal answered. The King was in a good humor again; he was pleased that there was a sign of amity between them. It might yet be possible to trust his old Minister again if Anne trusted him and stopped sowing suspicions in his mind . . .

"May I take the paper and study it further, Sire?"

"Take it, take it, Thomas. We will see you in the great hall this evening."

Cromwell, the Cardinal's secretary, was waiting for him in the gallery. He had been standing at a proper distance from the curtained doorway, feeling ill at ease as usual among the groups of chattering courtiers. He hated the nobility with a slow, unwavering hatred. In their presence he was always made aware of his clumsy hands and feet and his unpolished manners. During the Cardinal's interview he had stood in the gallery and been ignored.

He walked back at his master's side, but neither spoke until

75

they left the gallery and passed into the empty anteroom leading to the great hall and the courtyard.

"What is the news? The rumors are flying that the Pope's granted a commission," he murmured.

"The rumors are right as usual and wrong as usual," Wolsey answered slowly.

"This is the commission, Tom, and in law it's worth less than the paper it's written on. The King didn't see through it and I dared not disillusion him."

For a moment Cromwell said nothing; Wolsey's pace had slowed to a dragging walk.

"Foxe and Gardiner!" he burst out. "Fools, thinking they could outwit Clement! Merciful God, I should have gone myself . . . But I was afraid, afraid to leave him to that night crow again after what met me when I returned from France."

"What will you do?" Cromwell asked at last.

Wolsey looked at him; his face was gray and the eyes were sunken.

"God help me, Tom, but at this moment I don't know. But if I'm going to keep my head, I'll have to think of something."

"I knew that wretch was not to be trusted!" Anne stopped pacing the floor of her room at Greenwich and swung round on her brother. George Boleyn leaned in his favorite position by the open fireplace, watching his sister who was pale and shivering with anger.

"Which wretch, the Pope or Wolsey?" he asked.

"Both of them! But especially Wolsey. Oh, God, I warned Henry he was false, and now it's been proved again. The commission is insufficient, he says, it still leaves the power of final decision to the Pope, whatever the Cardinals decide here! He lied and dodged for a few weeks while we deceived ourselves, and then he comes forward with this. Oh, he made little of it, of course, but it just means we're no more certain of the divorce than before."

"Perhaps he was afraid to tell you sooner," George suggested. "He's no fool and he must have known when he first examined

76

the documents, but at least he was honest enough to admit it in the end."

"Good Jesus," she said bitterly. "Don't tell me you're defending him as well. That's what the King said when I pointed it out to him. 'Have patience, sweet, he's going to send to Rome for a decretal defining the powers of the commission beyond any doubt.' Gardiner's starting off again . . . Patience! How easy for him to say patience to me . . ."

"Calm yourself, Nan," her brother begged. "You're over-wrought. It's no use raging, it won't hurry matters. And don't accuse me of defending anyone but you."

Immediately her face softened, and she came to him, and leaned gratefully within the circle of his arm.

"Forgive me, I didn't meant to spit at you. You just don't know how difficult it is, how wearing, always being with the King, amusing him, holding him off, waiting, waiting for the time when at least I'll be secure . . ."

"He loves you," George comforted. "No man could have given you greater proof, and everything depends on your keeping that love. For God's sake, don't snap at him, however you feel."

"I know," she said wearily. "But it's a hard fight, George, far harder than I imagined, and I'm only a woman after all, fighting the Pope, and the Emperor, and Wolsey, and all my enemies here. Not to mention the Queen."

"The Queen's no match for you," he answered. "And he hardly ever sees or speaks to her now."

"No, but he still sees his daughter!"

He was surprised at the bitterness in her voice.

"God, how I hate that brat. She's the image of him, too, which makes it worse. I've shown him how it upsets me, but he still visits her behind my back, and keeps her in royal state, just as he does her mother!"

"Mary is only a child of twelve, Nan," he pointed out. "Would you have him ill-treat her? She's his own child, and he's got a soft heart for children. Nan, surely you're not jealous of that?"

"I'm jealous of everything connected with that marriage," she admitted sullenly. "I'd never like the girl; she's too damned impudent; you should see the way she turns away when I approach anywhere near, and the way she speaks to me, at the times when she's forced to! I'd like to box her ears . . . But she's his daughter, George, the only child born in wedlock, and that miserable old woman never stops bleating about 'my rights and the rights of the Princess Mary, His Grace's heir'!"

"And that can only irritate him," George reasoned, "considering how much he wants a son."

"You don't know him as well as you think," Anne muttered. "The girl's a reminder. As long as he sees her he thinks of Catherine, and the little beast clings to his hand and makes him presents and cries over her mother. Jealous! Of course I'm jealous. I want him to forget he ever saw Catherine or ever had a child by her that didn't die at birth. I want him to love my child, when it comes."

It was beyond her to explain the fear behind her feelings; the emotional quicksand of depending on a marriage which might take months or even another year before it could take place, and knowing at the same time that so many factors were opposing it. Unless he married her, she was lost. She had enemies everywhere at court, people who had tried to patronize her and been viciously snubbed, people who resented her favor with the King and feared the power of her family and her political adherents. People who deplored the idea of replacing the regal Catherine with the granddaughter of a London merchant. And the men of her own party, Norfolk, Suffolk, Sir Francis Brian, the Earl of Surrey and many more, who saw her promise to destroy Wolsey unfulfilled, and the Cardinal apparently working in her interests.

She felt so tired suddenly that she leaned her head against her brother's chest and closed her eyes. Dear, faithful George, ready to advise or cheer her out of her fits of depression. And he wasn't happy himself. She thought of his wife, Jane, at that moment. That was their father's doing too; an arranged marriage with Jane Rochford to get back some of their Howard mother's estates, and George had never been happy with Jane and now hated her. She hated Jane too, for that reason principally, but also because there was something sly and malicious about the

78

woman which repelled her. The sharp exchanges which took place between the sister and the wife in the old days became intensified when Anne returned to court and seemed to have no higher prospects than the casual fate of Mary Boleyn. But things had changed, she thought grimly. Mistress Jane felt the whip of her tongue these days and had to bear it, because she knew that Anne was going to be Queen of England.

Neither of them heard the door open, and they stood there, George with his arm round her, looking down. Anne's eyes opened and she started.

Jane Rochford stood in the doorway with her hand still on the handle, staring at them without moving. Her pale blue eyes narrowed, and she held herself rigidly.

"Your pardon," she said quietly. "I had no wish to disturb such a scene of family affection."

Rochford's face flushed with anger. "Why the devil can't you come into a room like anyone else, instead of creeping about like a scavenging cat! What is it?"

He had moved away from Anne and they stood side by side. Jane's hand released the door handle and it clicked upward into place.

"I didn't expect you to be pleased to see me," she said. "From now on, my quietness won't offend you. When I come here again I shall remember to knock."

Anne moved one step forward, her right hand touched her throat in the gesture that was once coquettish and was becoming a nervous habit.

"If you tried to make George as good a wife as I am a sister," she remarked sharply, "you might find him more often in your rooms instead of mine!"

Jane Rochford looked at her for a moment and slowly looked away.

"I doubt if I'll ever accomplish that. George, your father wants you. That's all I came to tell you."

Anne turned her back and rested the toe of her red brocade shoe on the rim of the empty grate. They heard the door close again, and footsteps fading down the corridor.

"She's gone to cry and abuse me for not loving her, as usual," George remarked. He stretched. "Lord God, why did she have to hold the Rochford estates?"

"She's a vixen," Anne said. "And she knows you married her for the land."

"And she's tormented me for it ever since," he answered. "Tears and reproaches one minute and venom the next. I tried to be amicable in the beginning, Nan, you know that; but I'm weary to death of her. There's no peace with her, let alone happiness! Christ knows she doesn't love me and never did, but from the moment she married me she's grudged me anything that makes life bearable. If she's not jibing at you till I could strike her, and very nearly did on one occasion—she's jeering at Father and my friends. Now she's mad with jealousy because the King plays cards with me in the evenings. Sometimes I think she's out of her mind!"

"When I'm Queen we'll see what might be done to get the marriage annulled, if you like. You won't need Rochford estates or anyone else's by then. The King loves you; if he gives permission, Father can't object."

"Wait till the day comes," he told her gently. "And don't worry about me, Nan. She doesn't trouble me too much as long as we're at court. Take care of yourself. Rest and stop fretting or you'll catch this damned sweating sickness that's going about."

She shook her head at him and smiled.

"That's what the King said. The fever's drifting down from London, and he told me this morning that he's moving from Greenwich to Hunsdon. It's funny, George, that a man as brave as he is, should have such a horror of falling ill."

"Shall we be going to Hunsdon with him?"

"Not immediately," she said. "A little absence makes him miss me. And dear God, it gives me a rest! I wheedled him into letting me go to Hever for a few days before I join him."

"It'll be nice to go home," Rochford said. "And good for you to be away from court. Promise me you'll forget Wolsey and the decretal, or whatever it is he's after, and rest yourself properly."

"I promise." She reached up and kissed his cheek. "You'd better go to Father now."

By the autumn the court had returned to London, the outbreak of fever had subsided and the King and Anne were cheered by what seemed good news from Rome. The Pope had ordered the commission to try the divorce and the Italian Cardinal Campeggio was on his way to London, bearing the decretal Wolsey had asked for. It would soon be over, Henry rejoiced; the commission would pronounce his marriage invalid—obviously the Pope meant to accommodate him and he would be free to make his sweetheart Queen. In the first weeks of that fine autumn, Anne shared his hope, ignorant of the changing European situation.

The French had begun to lose the war. At the moment when their victory seemed inevitable, their Commander Lautrec died of the plague which suddenly swept through his armies and the Imperialists inflicted a crushing defeat. But the Emperor was shrewd enough to see that the support of the Papacy was wavering between France and England, his enemies, and himself and to recognize the value of that support. Heresy and revolt were spreading everywhere and Charles foresaw that his own system of monarchial autocracy and the authority of the recognized Church needed each other in order to survive. While the retreating French pillaged and ravished the unhappy Italian countryside, the advancing imperial troops maintained strict discipline and showed every respect for the Church, and Charles's agents arrived at the Vatican proposing an alliance with their master.

To Clement the position was clarifying at last. The Church had tasted the arrogance and greed of the French during their ascendancy and much as Clement hated him, Charles was proving the more trustworthy. And the Queen of England was his aunt. . . . Hurriedly, Clement sent a courier after Campeggio with fresh instructions. On no account must he let the decretal out of his possession—better destroy it first. No decision on the divorce was to be given till he heard from Rome.

5

It was early spring and the court had moved to Hampton. In the morning Henry and a company of gentlemen had gone out hunting, taking Anne with him. She loved the chase as much as he did, enjoying the fresh air and the excitement of the swift horses, struggling to keep up with him as he rode recklessly ahead. Norreys and another favorite of Henry's called Weston rode close beside Anne to see that no harm came to her, and when they stopped to change mounts, she spent a few minutes talking gaily to her two escorts. She enjoyed their company, and was beginning to like Weston, who was small and quick-witted, as much as the handsome Norreys. They loved the King and they admired her because he did, and there was no danger of his jealousy if she joked with them.

They ran the quarry down after more than three hours, and the King took the huntsman's knife and cut the stag's throat himself. He had beckoned Anne to come close, so that she could see his skill. She managed to shut her eyes at the worst moment, but she opened them and blew him a kiss of congratulation as soon as he straightened up and looked round at her. Not being squeamish, hunting exhilarated her, but the cold-blooded kill always shook her nerves. Afterward they sat down to a huge meal under the trees, served on gold plate by servants who accompanied the King and brought the food.

She sat beside him and took pieces of chicken and slices of game pasty from his plate, until he slapped her fingers, to the amusement of his friends. He loved the informal meals in the country, eaten sitting on cushions on the grass, with the dishes and cups and pitchers laid out on a white cloth. He squeezed her shoulder and gave her a sip of Rhenish wine out of his goblet.

"Never have I been so happy, sweetheart," he whispered. "A

fine morning's sport, a good kill, and my Nan here beside me."

And in a good temper. Much as he loved her, she tried his patience when she was quarrelsome and acid; it was the anxiety over Campeggio, and the coming trial, he consoled himself. She was becoming oversensitive, he thought, imagining slights from Suffolk and complaining because her aunt the Duchess of Norfolk and some of the great ladies tried to snub her when he wasn't there. Like all men, he thought her grievances partly imaginary and probably exaggerated, and he could do no more than tell her to be patient, as he had to be, and bear with it until he could present her to the court as his Queen.

After one angry quarrel he had walked out into the gallery at Greenwich and found her talking to Wyatt, fingering his sleeve, and smiling. The rumors of that old liaison returned on a flood of jealousy; he forgot his irritation with her in his rage that she should coquette with an admirer. He knew it was deliberate, but he was incapable of ignoring it; he interrupted them and peremptorily ordered Anne to come and walk in the gardens. Still fuming, he had challenged Wyatt to a game of bowls, determined to beat him in front of her. He had lost the game, but, to decide a shot, Wyatt measured a distance with a gold locket chain on which Henry clearly saw the initials A.B., and Wyatt nearly lost his head for that.

Anne herself had soothed Henry's rage; he knew she was satisfied by his jealousy, but he had no idea how terrified she was for Tom, that arrogant fool who had lost his temper under the King's taunts and risked his life by producing that damned chain. She explained away the chain to Henry's satisfaction. Wyatt was her cousin, she reminded him; he used to visit them a lot at Hever, and he stole the chain from her one day years ago and refused to give it back. He was jealous because the King's Grace was successful where he was not, she pointed out, knowing Henry's vanity. The King was too generous to punish him for a foolish display of pique.

She had saved Wyatt, but she took care never again to speak to him alone.

It was late afternoon when the hunting party returned to

Hampton Court. When the King left her, she took her embroidery frame along to the gallery, to sit and talk to Norreys and Wyatt's sister Margaret. Margaret was rather like Tom, dark and gentle and intelligent, and Anne liked her. They were sitting on cushions in the window seat looking out over the herb garden; she joined them, stitching by the fading sunlight.

Norreys was in the middle of an anecdote about the morning's hunt, when the hangings at one end of the gallery parted, and the voice of Catherine of Aragon's Chamberlain called out:

"Make way for Her Grace the Queen."

Everybody rose at once; only Anne hesitated a moment longer, so that when Catherine came through the doorway she saw her still perched on the window ledge with one foot swinging.

The Queen walked slowly with her head up and her eyes looking straight ahead. She was dressed in blue velvet, and a dozen huge sapphires shone in the heavy frame of her headdress. Her short neck was ringed by the ropes of enormous milky pearls that Anne had often taken out of their case and fastened for her in the days when she performed her duties as maid of honor. She had always envied Catherine those pearls.

Three of her ladies were with the Queen, and Anne stiffened when she saw the Duchess of Norfolk among them. The aunt openly hated her niece and loved the Queen; even the Duke's ambitions couldn't unite them, and with regard to Anne he shared his wife's personal antipathy.

The men and women in the gallery curtsied and bowed as Catherine passed among them. Twice she moved her head and smiled at a woman whom Anne recognized as Lady Kingston, wife of one of the King's officials and devoted to the Spanish cause, and again to someone else she recognized. She passed Anne as if she were invisible, but one hand drew in the skirts of her dress a few inches until she was beyond the window seat. Anne's face blazed red, and then turned suddenly white. The Queen had turned down the gallery toward Henry's rooms.

"Sit down, I beg you, Madame."

In spite of her splendid dress and her jewels, Henry saw

84

how tired and white she looked. And old, he thought uncomfortably. It would be so much easier if Catherine were young and less defenseless.

"Thank you, Sire."

He moved a chair for her himself, and avoided her eyes when she thanked him. He knew what he would see in them. Tears, and love for him, that genuine love which he resented so much because it made his treatment of her so much worse. If she had only hated him, or blamed him, or abused . . . like Anne, sometimes . . . he could have convinced himself that she deserved his unkindness and neglect.

"It was good of you to let me come," she said gently.

"Indeed, Kate, I've never wished to hurt you, whatever else you think," he answered slowly.

"I know that, and even if you did, even if you took my life, I'd still love you as truly as when we were first married. I've always loved you, Henry, both as a man and my King."

He looked flushed and quite handsome sitting there in the light of the spring sunset, plainly dressed in a white shirt and breeches of green velvet; his doublet hung over the back of his chair. In the old days she would have warned him he was creasing it by leaning back, and taken it away and hung it up herself, while he chided her for doing his body servant's work. But those days were past.

"I had to see you," she said. "I don't ask for your pity, but I beg of you, think what I've felt these last months, knowing Campeggio was here to annul my marriage, that everyone in Europe was talking about it! And never being able to see you alone and talk to you, even for a minute."

"I thought it was best," Henry murmured unhappily. "I thought we'd wrangle, and I didn't see how any good could come of it."

"Good always comes from husband and wife being truthful with each other," Catherine reminded him. He shook his head.

"We aren't husband and wife, Kate, and never have been. It's no fault of yours, nor of mine, God knows. We married in good faith, but the marriage wasn't valid. I'm convinced of that, that's why God's taken every son born to us. That's what's so hard about the business, but I've accepted it, and I only wish you'd do the same."

"I would if it were true," she answered, "but it isn't. Your conscience tells you we lived in incest, Henry, while mine tells me we lived together lawfully, joined by God. You mention the deaths of our children. . . . But what about our daughter Mary? God left her to us, even if he took the others. Oh, I know how you've longed for a son! Do you think I haven't wanted one too? I know you were grieved when our children died, but do you suppose I didn't suffer, I who carried them in my body and bore them, and saw them die before they left my breast . . ."

"I'm not denying that," he said. He had hardly thought of her feelings in his own disappointment, and he didn't want to hear about them now.

"But grief doesn't alter the fact, Kate, whether it's yours or mine. We've lived in mortal sin for all these years, and Campeggio's coming to see into it and conduct a fair trial."

"Fair?" Catherine questioned bitterly. "With Wolsey beside him and the revenue from his English cardinalate at stake? Henry, I've come to you for justice, not for myself, but for your daughter."

"Mary shan't come to any harm," he protested. He didn't want to think about Mary, either.

"Already you see less of her than you did," Catherine pointed out. "The child is devoted to you; and now she's grieving because she's not allowed to come to you."

Henry got up and poured some wine into a golden cup. He held out the pitcher to his wife but she shook her head. He came back to his chair, frowning and uncomfortable, and sat sullenly with his elbows on his knees, tipping the wine backward and forward in the cup, his eyes half closed. He was being spared nothing this time, he thought angrily. Catherine's grief over her children, her humiliation, her coming trial before prejudiced judges, and now the accusation of neglecting Mary.

He loved his daughter in his own selfish way, and above all he enjoyed her simple adulation. He was proud of her too, because she had his red coloring and green eyes, and was pretty and accomplished. She did him credit even if she wasn't a son.

86

He did love her, more than he dared admit lately, and whatever the outcome of his disagreements with her mother, the thought of injuring Mary never entered his head. She'd lose the succession of course, but that was no hardship; a woman had little chance of keeping the crown of England anyway. He meant to arrange a brilliant marriage for her, not quite as brilliant as if she were legitimate and Princess of Wales, but with a Prince of high birth and a rich dowry. He was prepared to go to endless trouble to make up to her for the loss of her birthright but he had reckoned without the jealousy of Anne.

Whenever he saw his daughter, Anne made a scene, sometimes sneering or else weeping and storming at him. Her weapons were cruel, and they won easily against the tears of his thirteen-year-old child. If it meant quarrels with Anne and disturbing the harmony of their life together, then Henry submitted and chose the easiest way for himself. He kept Mary at a distance; but sometimes he resented the necessity. He disliked being harsh to Catherine, but he hated being unkind to his daughter.

"I can't have the girl hanging round my neck with Campeggio here in England," he retorted. "She must be obedient and keep her complaints till the matter's settled."

"Mary will never disobey," Catherine said gently. "She fears you'll cast her out of your heart as you've cast me. Can't I take her one word of affection from you?"

He swallowed the wine and pushed the cup aside; he looked at his wife sitting quietly before him, her large eyes watching his face. Patient, gentle Catherine; God, she was serene even in distress. Suddenly, with one of his rare bursts of emotion, Henry's eyes filled with tears.

"Tell her I'll always cherish her," he said hoarsely. "As I do you. Oh, Kate, why in Christ's name couldn't a son have lived . . ."

She was on her knees before him, weeping helplessly as she clung to his hands. He squeezed them, and then put them aside. It was useless; if he listened any more he'd weaken and say something he would afterward regret. He couldn't soften toward her; she was the barrier to Anne, to the possession of that quick,

87

maddening body which would never be yielded outside marriage. And the son Anne was always promising him, the son with her black eyes and his red hair . . .

"Come back to me," Catherine implored. "Give me another chance; I can give you another child, I know I can, even now . . ."

If Anne had not existed, he would have raised her up and taken her back, and in his heart he would have been relieved. There need be no public trial with Wolsey and Campeggio, no need to disinherit Mary; no more struggles with the Pope, no more anxiety and frustration, not sure in his heart if he were married or free. . . . He would have taken her back and resumed his old life of calm domesticity, enlivened by a young mistress when he felt like it, with sport and hunting and his friends round him, and Wolsey back in his confidence.

"Forget this creature you're living with," Catherine urged. "That's sin, Henry, and a greater sin to cast off your true wife for the sake of your mistress. Send the woman away . . ."

At that moment the illusion of reconciliation fled. He looked down at her, his eyes still red, but he was frowning and his little mouth was drawn in a tight line.

"What mistress? Of what are you accusing me?"

Catherine rose stiffly to her feet; his tone had changed, and his heavy face was reddening slowly. Her fingers twisted in and out of the long rope of her pearls.

"Anne Boleyn," she answered.

"Anne is not my mistress," he said coldly. "Not now, nor ever has been. She is a woman of great virtue. The accusation dishonors her as well as me."

He felt righteous and ridiculous at the same time, as he saw the incredulity on his wife's face. Catherine knew him, and naturally she didn't believe that any little maid of honor could withhold what he wanted. He could hardly believe it himself. But she had charged him with something he hadn't committed; the fact that he wanted it so badly and had been denied it made him resent the imputation even more.

"You have an evil mind, Madame," he said shortly. "I've less

88

sin on my soul with regard to her than I have with you, God knows!" He was becoming really angry; his confidence was restored, he was firmly in the right and Catherine was wrong for once, and he revenged himself for his own qualms of conscience by turning on her bitterly.

"You come to me, pleading for Mary, and use the occasion to speak against one of the most worthy and virtuous women at court. You had her among your ladies long enough to know her character!"

Catherine swallowed; she was trembling with emotion.

"I know it well enough," she retorted. "And God pity me, I'd rather suffer the presence of her sister!"

The reference to Mary Boleyn brought Henry out of his chair.

"There's no comparison!" he roared. "What I did with one I've never enjoyed with the other! Withdraw, Madame, withdraw it, I say!"

Catherine faced him, blazing. She loved him as much then as when they had first married, and she answered with the bitter tongue of a desperately jealous woman, an old woman, with a young and beautiful rival.

"I was told she'd denied you," she said harshly. "And I couldn't believe that she'd dare. I couldn't believe that tradesman's daughter had snapped her fingers under her King's nose and refused him the favors she'd given others! By the living God, Henry, I thought more of you than to believe you'd descend to that!"

"Others? What others? What are you saying. . . . Name them, then. Name them!" he shouted.

"Wyatt," Catherine cried out, "and most likely Henry Percy as well!"

All her life she had disliked gossip, but she spat out the only two names ever mentioned in connection with Anne.

Wyatt . . . He panted with fury. It was a lie; it must be a lie. And Percy, that was a lie too. . . . He remembered his jealousy of that gawking Northumberland when he noticed that the new maid of honor preferred to walk in the gardens at Greenwich with him, instead of responding to the King. . . . And Wyatt's impudence with that gold chain, dangling the locket with her initials in front of his eyes. . . .

His enormous fists clenched, and a thick vein throbbed in his neck. For a moment there was silence; slowly his hands opened and he breathed hard. It was a lie. He knew it was a lie because she must be a virgin or she would never dare to marry him. . . .

"This does you no credit," he said at last. "I love her too well to be blackened against her. You'd have been wise to leave these things unsaid."

"Wise, perhaps," Catherine answered, "but not truthful. I retract nothing in respect to her, but I beg you to forgive me for accusing you. I see she *has* made marriage the price. Then you are determined to try to repudiate me?" Catherine's voice was low.

He spoke to her calmly now, as if she were a stranger.

"I cannot live in a state of mortal sin. Our marriage was illegal; I believe you were truly Arthur's wife."

She turned slowly, moving her chair aside.

"I was not, but now the matter doesn't depend on that. I had hoped to avoid this, Henry. I had hoped we might have resolved your doubts in private. The issue was foreseen by my father, King Ferdinand, when marriage between us was first discussed. He obtained a second bull of dispensation from Pope Julius, permitting the marriage if my first union had been consummated. The bull is in Spain, but my nephew Charles has sent me the copy of it."

Both were quiet now; Catherine stood listlessly in front of him, leaning on the back of the oak chair. She noticed that Henry's green and gold doublet had fallen on the floor. The sun had disappeared behind the trees lining the riverbank; the sky was a magnificent glowing pink streaked with red, and outside the oriel window, one of Wolsey's graceful gilt weathervanes turned lazily on top of an adjoining turret.

Already the room was quite dark; the linenfold paneling

seemed black, and the figures on the painted ceiling were indistinguishable. The King said nothing.

"You had better have the tapers lit," she muttered. Still he didn't answer, and she stood there helplessly, waiting to be dismissed. She wiped her swollen eyes with a handkerchief, and thanked God that the dusk would hide her face from the prying courtiers standing about in the long gallery, waiting to see the King go down to dinner. She wondered whether Anne would be among them, and made a great effort to compose herself. Henry's head was lowered; he was staring at his shoes, green velvet shoes with slashes cut across the toes. It was a new fashion which everyone had copied; it was rumored that he suffered from gout, and the new shape hid the swelling.

He looked up at last and said evenly, "The copy of the bull won't be enough. As your nephew's been so accommodating, let him send the original to England. I bid you good night, Madame."

She curtsied deeply, and he heard the door creak on its hinges as she opened it, and the murmur of her ladies' voices in the anteroom before the door closed again.

He waited some minutes, immobile in anger; rage with Catherine because she had upset him, and now threatened his plans with this new document, and a subconscious fury against Anne were mixed in a simmering emotional storm. He had an impulse to throw back his head and bellow, to strike out wildly with his big fists and bring someone crashing down, to relieve his feeling by sheer violence.

Women . . . women . . . His wife and his daughter and the woman he loved . . . At that moment he felt an extraordinary urge to kill them all, to be rid of them and the problems inherent in their existence; to be at peace . . .

He strode to the door and threw it open till it crashed against the paneled wall. He was aware of a group of startled faces in the anteroom, of mouths falling a little open and frightened eyes staring up at him. Courtiers and his new squire of the body, George Boleyn—he glared at Anne's brother and then looked away—and a man in dull black doublet and hose, with a heavy pale face and clumsy hands. Thomas Cromwell, Wolsey's secretary.

"Fetch me Hal Norreys," Henry roared.

For a second no one moved; his face was red and contorted with temper, and his huge body seemed bigger than ever as it stood in the doorway, both hands braced against the lintels as if he might tear the frame out of the wall. Then the Cardinal's secretary made a move; he bowed to the King, and backed out of the anteroom like an agile black beetle. Henry heard his voice calling down the long gallery, the plebeian accent emphasized by the distance, "Sir Henry Norreys to the King's Grace!"

A moment later Norreys came hurrying into the anteroom and followed the King into his private chamber.

That evening Anne waited in her own room dressed in a brilliant scarlet costume, cut low across the bosom, with trailing, fur-lined sleeves. It accentuated her coloring, and the King loved it. She swore while she dressed.

Catherine had gone to him and he'd received her—Anne's hand was shaking as she tried to fasten a pearl earring, and she suddenly flung the jewel across the room. She leaned against the oak chest, head down, and breathed hard to steady herself. Then she looked up, and studied herself in the steel mirror. Her hair was smooth and shining, drawn back in a middle parting from her oval face; she'd traced the outline of her brows with a stick dipped in black cosmetic, a trick she had learned from the French beauties, and she bit her lips to redden them. She looked beautiful, but decided that the graceful line of her throat was spoiled by the necklace of pearls and gold filagree. She took it off, thinking of Catherine's pearls, part of her magnificent dowry of jewels, and wondered for the hundredth time what she had said to Henry and how he had received her.

The smooth lovely face became pinched with fear. She was afraid of that dowdy old woman; afraid that if she reached the King she might weaken him, that the hold of years of happy marriage was basically stronger than his love for Anne. He had no right to listen to Catherine! Campeggio was in London, the trial for the divorce was soon to open at Black Friars Hall. That very morning he had come to her while she dressed to go hunting with him, and taken liberties and mumbled that he loved her better than life. . . .

She glanced down at the little gold watch on her girdle. They always dined together, so that whatever Catherine had achieved she would be able to undo. Turning to the mirror again, she rubbed a little jasmine-scented oil into her temples. Then she went to the fireplace and settled down in the Spanish leather chair to wait. Her lap dog dozed in front of the blazing logs, and Anne reached down to set it on her knee. It was a fat, silky spaniel, given to her by Henry.

The time went by and Anne grew rigid with nerves as she saw the hour hand on her watch reach the time appointed by the King, and travel halfway beyond it, and still no one came to call her. At last she pushed the spaniel down and went out into the gallery where there was no one but a page, squatting on the floor by the entrance to Henry's anteroom. She crossed to him so silently that the boy jumped when he found her standing over him.

"Get to your feet, boy!" Her voice was tremulous. The boy sprang upright, pulling off his cap.

"Where's the King? Has he gone to dine in the great hall?"

"His Grace is in his rooms, Mistress," he answered, nodding at the doorway behind him.

"Who's with him?" she demanded.

"Sir Henry Norreys."

"And who else?"

"No one, Mistress, only Sir Henry. The stewards took food and wine in to them awhile ago, and they said His Grace was throwing dice."

Throwing dice. She stepped back from the boy, her head turned toward the room leading off the little anteroom. Behind the closed door she could hear someone laughing. Henry's laugh. He was laughing and gambling with Norreys and had forgotten all about her, or he didn't want to see her. Catherine had said something; he was changed and hadn't sent for her . . .

93

She put out her hand for support, feeling suddenly faint.

"Nan? Nan, what are you doing here? I was coming to find you."

She opened her eyes and saw a flushed and smiling Norreys standing in the anteroom doorway. The dizziness receded.

"Who wants me?" she asked casually.

Norreys grinned. "Why, the King, who else?"

She smiled back at him, mocking and bitterly relieved.

"He wants you to come and play with us," Norreys added. "He's drunk half a gallon of wine and my head's reeling . . . He's in a high humor and calling for you."

"If your head's reeling, mine's aching!" she retorted. "Make my apologies to His Grace and say I've gone to bed!"

She went to her room and posted her serving-woman at the door the next morning to keep the King out, saying she was ill. She punished him for that two hours' wait by refusing to see him for twenty-four hours.

The legatine court opened the case of the king's marriage on June eighteenth and within a matter of days it was obvious that Cardinal Campeggio's only function was to obstruct. The case was conducted in public at the Hall of the Black Friars and both Henry and Catherine appeared to plead. Catherine defended herself with firmness and dignity, maintaining the validity of her marriage so persuasively that Wolsey thanked God when she refused to attend further or admit his right to try the case. The two Cardinals argued endlessly about the Second Bull of Dispensation, the original of which remained safely in Spain, but all Wolsey's desperate attempts to force a decision failed.

With increasing bitterness and frustration, Anne watched the farce played out at Black Friars and, turning to the disappointed King, furiously accused the Cardinal of being in league with the Pope and secretly working to prevent their marriage.

On the twenty-ninth the Pope and the Emperor signed a treaty of alliance; France was defeated and the Imperialists were everywhere victorious! In July it was announced in Rome that the divorce commission had been revoked. The case of the English

King's marriage, with the inevitable sentence, had been referred to Rome.

Wolsey was at York Place when he heard the news. For some time he sat with his head lowered, staring at the ground as if he had not heard. Clement had made his choice once and for all. The Church had allied itself with the Emperor. In spite of Wolsey's warnings Clement had sacrificed the Church in England. He had also sacrificed Wolsey.

6

THE ANTEROOM TO THE KING'S APARTMENTS AT GREENWICH WAS very quiet; the ladies and gentlemen of the court who sat or stood about were not talking and laughing as usual. Some had excused themselves and gone away. One had certainly gone to find Anne, and that was her friend Margaret Wyatt, who waited long enough to hear the angry threats of the Duke of Suffolk and then edged to the doorway and ran down the gallery. The door of the King's room was closed; his voice and Suffolk's could be heard but their words were indistinguishable. The Duke of Norfolk was leaning against the paneled walls, listening as openly as he dared, but he could hear nothing beyond angry shouting.

Suffolk should have waited, he thought; Suffolk's vile temper had got the better of him after the state banquet where Anne took the Queen of England's place and sat above Suffolk's wife and the Duchess of Norfolk. Wolsey had been dismissed in disgrace to York after the publication of Clement's decree revoking the divorce commission; the mighty Cardinal had fallen overnight, reduced to buying his life by bribes to Norfolk and Anne's relatives, and by abandoning everything he possessed to the King.

Anne had fulfilled her promise and destroyed him, but out

95

of the wreck of his fortunes, she had received his magnificent palace of York House, with its priceless gold plate, pictures and tapestries; her father had been made Earl of Wiltshire and Ormonde and her pup of a brother Ambassador to France. The Boleyns were climbing so rapidly into favor and office that the men who had no longer any cause to envy Wolsey, transferred their jealousy to them. Suffolk was the bitterest. He hated Anne and her family, and as soon as the Cardinal was stripped of his power and dismissed, he began intriguing to get rid of the woman who had ousted him.

There was no further need of her, he insisted. Wolsey was broken, and there were times when his yoke was more acceptable than the insolence and ambitions of Norfolk's vixenish niece. Norfolk listened, because he agreed in principle, but he was too wily to commit himself. Suffolk had some scheme in his head, he knew, and he had just found out what it was when the Duke strode into the anteroom, and loudly announced his intention of going to the King and denouncing Anne as the former mistress of Thomas Wyatt. The room stilled with terror as he said it, his thick beard quivering under his hard angry mouth; he was a big bull of a man, almost as heavy as the King, with a violent abrupt manner and furious courage. He was handsome in a ruthless way, and Henry's gentle sister Mary Tudor had loved him all her life, risking her brother's wrath to marry him.

Norfolk leaned against the wall, one finger rubbing his sallow cheek. Suffolk and the King were shouting at each other, and that meant that the fool had acted too soon. Norfolk knew the King; when Henry listened and was quiet, he was most dangerous. He could imagine Suffolk accusing her, his face blazing with the memory of his grievances against her, while Henry roared back at him in Anne's defense. He had tried to dissuade Suffolk in the anteroom, telling him the King was too besotted with her to listen to anything against her yet, telling him to wait for a moment when Henry was smarting after one of their frequent quarrels and might be swayed. But Suffolk only cursed him.

"She treats you and her aunt like the dirt she treads on,"

he snarled. "But the slut shan't insult my wife and seize everything for herself and her kin while I stand idle!"

Suffolk had failed, Norfolk knew even before the door crashed open and the Duke appeared, red-faced, with one hand on his sword hilt, and stopped in front of him.

"I'm banished," he choked. "Banished for telling the truth. The whore's bewitched him!"

Norfolk saw Anne standing in the archway from the gallery while Suffolk's voice still rang round the anteroom. She was dressed in white, but her gown was no paler than her face; he realized that she had heard every word. He raised his voice: "I'll not have my niece insulted, even by you."

When Suffolk turned away and saw her, he hesitated, and the hatred between him and the woman in the doorway passed through the atmosphere like a flash of lightning. Suffolk was walking toward her, but she stood rigid, blocking the way. The next moment he had shouldered her aside so violently that she stumbled against the door post and nearly fell. There was a gasp from the courtiers, and some of them started toward her. The Duke moved with them, but more slowly. He was glad Suffolk had pushed her; for months he had been longing to do something of the sort himself.

"I hope he didn't hurt you," he remarked. "His Grace has sent him from court, and I suppose his eyes were dimmed with grief."

She glared at him, holding one bruised arm against her side. "Don't concern yourself for me, Uncle. I trust you as well as I trust him!"

Then she disappeared into Henry's room. Norfolk left the anteroom and wandered down the long gallery; on the way he met Lord Guildford, newly appointed comptroller of the household after Wolsey's exile, and suggested a visit to the archery butts behind the palace. It was a fine spring day, and as they walked through the low-hedged gardens, Guildford asked him the results of the King's attempt to gain a favorable opinion from the universities of Europe.

"In England, the results have been as we expected. No one

dared to gainsay the King," Norfolk answered. "The royal commissioners saw to that. But there was more difficulty in France; the University of Paris refused to give an opinion on the divorce till King Francis intervened, and his intercession cost us dearly! Angers and Poitiers pronounced against it, Orléans and Bourges were in favor. We've poured out bribes to the faculties in Upper Italy to secure favorable opinions there, but our agents haven't been able to work in Spain or in Spanish-dominated Italy, so the universities there have pronounced against it. It's been a costly business, proving nothing."

"I hear the King is bitterly disappointed in the German universities," Guildford remarked. Norfolk laughed derisively.

"By God, that's the greatest joke of all. Master Luther and his disciples have declared the marriage to Catherine valid and binding beyond question! We've been dallying with them for months now, hoping to frighten the Pope by appearing to support them, and you know how much the King hates heresy, and we've gotten nothing out of it but a verdict worthy of Rome!"

They turned down a path into a little herb garden where the smell of mint and marjoram and violets was very strong. The gardens provided the palace kitchens with their seasoning, but they were prettily arranged with seats and statues among the ordered square beds. Guildford sniffed and then nudged his companions.

"There's Rochford in that place in the yew hedge, cuddling with someone."

It was Anne's brother, the new Viscount Rochford. As his uncle had prophesied, the King's favor couldn't replace experience and talent, and George had been recalled from France and the Embassy given to a more able man.

"It's Margaret Wyatt," Norfolk remarked, "telling the tale of Suffolk's doings, I've no doubt, and opening her petticoat at the same time. I can't say I blame him, insolent cub though he is. That wife of his reminds me of a grass snake."

"If the King hates heresy," Guildford interrupted, his mind returning to the main subject, "then why does he tolerate Lady

Anne reading a translation of the Bible, and surrounding himself with churchmen who lean to these ideas?"

"Because he has the same interest in the new teaching as she has," Norfolk retorted. "He thinks to use it for his own ends and that's why he meddled with the Lutherans in Germany. He sends their disciples in England to the stake fast enough! Madame Anne cares for the heretics because they're likely to support her against the Pope since the Pope doesn't intend to free Henry to marry her, and the new teaching is all for disregarding the Pope. Therefore my niece and her father and brother lean to the new teaching. That's simple enough, my dear Guildford, and it hasn't endeared her to our Lord Chancellor More, for example. There are many of us who want the abuses of the Church removed, but we're not out to make it Protestant, to suit my niece or anyone else. Nor is the King, be certain of that. She curbs her views before him, because she knows his religion's as orthodox as Clement's!"

"It's a twisted tangle," Guildford said, "and I think I'm right when I say that all of us wish it hadn't grown as snagged as it is. Do you really believe there's a chance of Clement's bending even yet?"

The Duke shrugged. "He's taken his stand with the Emperor, but he's temporizing still, hoping the King will see reason and cast off my niece. That's what we'll all be hoping for now, rather than see England torn asunder. My Lord Suffolk had the right method, but he used it at the wrong time. All we can do is obey the King, and wait."

Henry was very tender with her that summer; he was a man of many moods as she discovered while their relationship dragged on. Sometimes he was courteous and considerate with her, as he had been in the early days when he was trying to win her, at others ill-tempered and overbearing, or rough and unspeakably coarse. Intimacy was wearing away the façade of his manners; she saw him petty and vain as a woman at times, drunken and belching at table after an afternoon spent at his lute, composing.

He had great qualities; he was morally brave, he was kingly and politically astute. He was utterly ruthless in action, once he had persuaded himself that he was in the right, and he was finding it easier than ever to reach that conclusion about everything he did or said.

But whatever the circumstances, she could still win him back by a few words of affection, and by the tricks which she had perfected to arouse his eager sensuality. His tastes were as coarse as his needs, and of all his actions, they were the most honest, because he neither excused them or considered them unseemly. They were the King's wants, and that raised them above criticism. The attitude was typical and now that the tactful hand of Wolsey had ceased to guide him, it was pervading the court and the Council Chamber.

A new expression came into use; the King's will. The King's will is this or that, and it was quickly understood that whatever that will was, it was safest to obey it blindly and at high speed. Anne watched and encouraged him, reminding him constantly that he was the King and above all authority. Primed by her father and some of the Protestant-inclined clergy who attended her, she seriously suggested to him that the authority of the monarch was an extension of the authority of the Almighty. Whoever disobeyed the King was breaking a Divine law. Whoever refused to acknowledge the King's commands as binding above all others, denied the special position of a sovereign as the representative of God to his people.

It was a doctrine that appealed to him at once; his ego was large enough to agree with it, and his will and self-confidence shouldered the responsibility without a qualm. He was the King; God had made him so, and therefore he must be right. Nothing pointed out the enormity of Catherine's resistance more than this premise; and nothing placed the lives and properties of everyone surrounding him in greater danger. Even with Henry the process was gradual, for he was still sane, and his mind needed time to adjust itself to the height of this new pinnacle.

The adjustment was quickened by his new ease of conscience. The Queen, living in semi-retirement at court, neglected and humiliated and still clinging to her rights, was no longer a reproach to him; nor was his daughter Mary. Catherine refused to acknowledge that she owed him obedience in the matter of the marriage, and Mary supported her mother's claims and her own against his wishes. They were both in the wrong at last, and Anne and her adherents made sure that they had to be, by driving him to further unkindness against them.

The summer passed; the court moved from Greenwich to Anne's new house at York Palace, and the Queen was left behind because there were no apartments for her. There were balls and masques and hunting parties, and Anne and the King were the orbit around which everything moved, like satellites around the sun. In spite of the gaieties, there were disappointments. Anne's father had returned early that year from an interview with the Emperor Charles V, for the war was ended at the Peace of Cambrai, and Wiltshire had to face the furious King and confess that diplomacy and bribes of alliances and concessions had failed to move that cold young man from his championship of his aunt.

If the English could convince the Consistory of Cardinals that the divorce was just, would the Emperor cease to resist King Henry's wishes? The Emperor answered Wiltshire's proposal by asking whether the King of England would accept the verdict of the Consistory if it pronounced him truly Catherine's husband? Wiltshire dared not give the guarantee, and he returned to London, where Henry shouted that his feeble handling of the mission was responsible for its failure.

As a final debacle, the writ summoning the King to appear by proxy or in person before the Court of the Rota in Rome had been served on his Ambassador. Wiltshire quailed under the temper of the King, watched by Anne, who knew better than to interfere at that point. Later the breach was healed, but Wiltshire bought his forgiveness by an attitude of crawling subservience. The pattern of the future was already emerging.

The summer was over, and one day when the King was dining in the fine banqueting hall at York Palace, with Anne seated on his right hand, he heard the news that his old Minister Thomas Wolsey had been communicating with the Pope, and urging that a strong measure should be taken to bring the King to his senses, and necessitate his own recall.

The Lords of the Council and the woman whose hopes of advancement depended on the Cardinal never regaining his power forgot their differences. The King had been too merciful to his servant. The servant had rewarded him with treason. Henry signed the order for the Cardinal's arrest and committal to the Tower.

She was by his elbow as he wrote, and she noticed the angry glitter in his eyes, and the vein throbbing in the side of his neck. This time Wolsey would die. His was the power of life and death, and his was the divine right to punish disobedience as he thought fit. He had changed, since the day he sent Wolsey from court, ruined and despoiled of his possessions, but still free. They had tried to get him convicted of treason then, but Henry sent the Cardinal's former Secretary Thomas Cromwell to Parliament to plead the Minister's case, and he was acquitted. He had abandoned Wolsey for failing, but he had still relented a little when the man fell sick, thinking he was going to die, and sent him a token of friendship and made Anne do the same. There was still a softness in him that could be touched by servility, and might forgive. Now that had gone. She touched his arm and he grunted and turned round to her, his sandy eyebrows raised irritably at the interruption. She suggested that the Earl of Northumberland, Henry Percy, should go with the escort to arrest the Cardinal at York. He would make sure the wretch did not escape.

Northumberland went, and his muddled mind cleared long enough to avenge the ruin of his happiness with Anne by tying the dying Cardinal to his horse like a common felon, and forcing him through the cold, wet countryside toward London and his death, till he collapsed at Leicester Abbey and could go no further.

The King had Anne with him in his apartments at York Palace when he sent for the Earl and Sir Henry Kingston at the beginning of December.

The room was half-paneled, like the Cardinal's study at Hampton Court, and the upper part of the walls were frescoed.

The shield over the great stone fireplace had been scraped clean of Wolsey's cypher and replaced by the initials of Henry and Anne.

In spite of the cold and damp outside, where torrents of rain had raised the level of the Thames and turned the streets into a sea of mud, the room was warm, the polished floor spread with fine Persian rugs, and a magnificent Flemish tapestry hung over the door to keep out draughts. Candles were lighted, standing in candelabra of solid gold, and an oak sideboard stood the length of one wall, displaying plates and goblets and dishes, crested by the Cardinal's hat and arms of their late owner, part of his fabulous collection of gold and silver plate. The King stood by the roaring fire. He wore a doublet of dark green velvet, the slashed puffed sleeves showing inner sleeves of cloth of gold; the neck was open, revealing a narrow edging of miniver fur, and a great chain, encrusted with rubies and diamonds and emeralds, hung down over his chest. The little dagger at his belt was also set with the same stones. He looked gigantic in the flickering light of the fire and the soft candle glow.

Anne sat in a low chair by the chimney corner; her dress was dark blue brocade, with a paler velvet underskirt, and the long elegant sleeves hung over the arms of her chair and swept the floor. She sat very still and upright, her face outlined by a jeweled cap and a soft veil.

Percy came forward first, stooping as usual, and knelt to the King. He glanced quickly at Anne but his eyes were empty and they flickered away, back to Henry. Then Kingston presented himself; he was a gruff, thickset man, and Anne's lips tightened as she remembered that he and his wife were devoted friends of Catherine.

The King hooked his hands in his belt.

"I've sent for you to hear your account of the happenings at Leicester Abbey."

It was the Earl's privilege to answer.

"The Cardinal is dead, Sire."

He paused; he was nervous, and he found speech difficult without stammering.

"So your messenger told me," Henry answered shortly.

103

"His Grace wishes to know how he managed to escape his just punishment." It was Anne who spoke, and she addressed Kingston, who had taken Wolsey under his custody at the last stages of his journey.

"My Lord Northumberland can answer for that, Madame," Kingston returned. "The Cardinal was sick when he was delivered to me."

"Well?"

Again she spoke, anticipating the King, and the man who had loved her and completed her revenge on Thomas Wolsey, moved a step nearer and spoke directly to her for the first time in nearly a year.

"I forced him on as fast as I could," he mumbled. "I hoped to deliver him to the King's justice alive, but he was failing when I gave him into Kingston's care."

"We had to stop at Leicester," Kingston explained; he had turned deliberately so that he faced Henry, and avoided the figure, sitting, tapping her foot with impatience. She had destroyed the Cardinal, as she was trying to destroy the gentle Queen. He knew that Percy had been sent to make the arrest on her instigation, and, hardened to suffering as he was, he was shocked at the condition of the prisoner the Earl handed over to him. The proud, brilliant Prince of the Church was a trembling old man, soaked to the skin by hours of exposure in the fiercest weather, so stiff and cramped from his bonds that two troopers had to lift him from his horse. Wolsey was to die, but the unnecessary cruelty of his treatment was Anne's doing; she knew the temper of that stuttering lunatic Northumberland and what he would inflict on his fallen enemy.

"The Cardinal was dying when the monks at the abbey took us in," he continued. "If I'd proceeded, all I'd have been able to deliver to you was his corpse. He was tended, and everything was done to fit him to travel, but his strength failed completely; he confessed and received the Sacraments. He died a better Christian than he lived."

"Did he acknowledge his guilt or mention his treason in

communicating with the Pope?" the King asked roughly. Kingston shook his head.

"No, Sire. He only said as he died that if he'd served his God as faithfully as he had served his King, He wouldn't have abandoned him in his gray hairs. . . . They were his last words."

Northumberland said nothing; he was looking at Anne, watching the play of the firelight on her face, remembering the Queen's young maid of honor who had guided his clumsy movements through a dance at Greenwich, and enchanted him with her gaiety and her grace and her gentleness till he fell hopelessly in love for the only time in his life.

The features were still there, and the slender, voluptuous figure, but his body was dead to desire, and his heart was empty. He felt ill, and his hands were beginning to tremble. The hard expression in her eyes reminded him suddenly of his wife, that violent shrew whose tongue had driven him over the edge of sanity. They were separated now, but the harm was done. A harsh note in a woman's voice was enough to remind him, and a wild antagonism filled him for Anne because she had lost her sweetness. His pledged sweetheart sat in front of him, brazen and hard, and living in this great house as the King's mistress, powerful enough to destroy Wolsey and have the Duke of Suffolk sent to cool away from court for daring to speak against her. This was not the loving creature of his imagination, treasured like the Virgin, warped out of reality by the years; this was an ambitious harlot, who had crawled into the hay at Hever with her own Cousin Wyatt before she came to court and snared the King.

Everything he had ever heard against her and refuted, came to his mind and immediately found credence. He lowered his head and gripped his hands behind his back, fighting the images of her lying in other men's beds, when he had been fool enough to ask to marry her to get her into his. Wolsey had been good to him while he was attached to his household; he had had excellent prospects of remaining at court in the King's favor until he ruined himself for the sake of a clever adventuress who wasted no time in replacing him. His head ached violently.

Wolsey had been good to him once. He could remember instances of kindness which the memory of that one awful wrong had obliterated for so many years. And he had bound and harassed him when he was dying, and lashed on his horse through the mud-clogged roads to get him to London and the block for the sake of the woman sitting a few feet away from him.

Henry was still talking to Kingston; he could hear their voices. "You did your duty well, my Lord."

They were dismissed, and she was speaking to him, approving the cruelty he was already bitterly regretting. He didn't answer her; he dared not trust himself, in case he brought the fate of Suffolk on his head by shouting at the King to get rid of her before it was too late, before he blackened his conscience on her behalf and lived to see her for what she really was . . .

The tapestry parted, and the door closed behind them, leaving Anne and the King alone. She got up and went to him, linking her arm through his. Wolsey was dead. She shut her mind to Northumberland, now a stranger, sick and prematurely old, and the last whisper of nostalgia left her as he went out of the room.

Wolsey was dead; he was the one man who might have persuaded Henry to abandon the divorce; he was the last strong link with Henry's early years. She stood on tiptoe and caught him round the neck, drawing his head down till his mouth was level with her own. She kissed him slowly, till his powerful arms went round her, flattening her body against his, and his fierce urgency bruised her mouth. Deliberately she caressed him till he heaved and grunted with desire, and for the first time she responded genuinely, with a strange thread of love running through the fabric of her physical passion. He was hers, and he was the King. He was a man above all other men, as she had seen him that night, huge and splendid and virile, beside squat Kingston and wretched Henry Percy. He was going to get rid of Catherine and marry her and make her Queen of England; the struggle would soon be over and she could rest safely in the shade of his love.

"My love," she said suddenly. "My own dear love."

She was taken completely by surprise when he put her away

from him. His face was hot and flushed with passion, but he pulled her arms gently but firmly from round his neck and shook his head.

"Don't tempt me with sips, Nan, when you won't let me drain the cup. . . . It's late, and I've a meeting with Master Cromwell. I'll come and sup with you later, sweetheart."

She caught his sleeve quickly as he turned to go.

"Harry, Harry, don't leave me so; has something made you angry? You know I'd yield this moment if it were possible."

That was true for the first time in three years; if they'd continued, she might well have done so. She was too feminine to see the logic in his refusal to go on, suddenly jealous that talks with Cromwell or anyone else should matter more to him than making love to her. Then a doubt struck her, and she paled.

"You regret Wolsey's death!" she accused. "For all your high words you were still under his influence!"

The King looked down at her, and prized her fingers free of his sleeve. His expression was curiously blank, but his light eyes were steady and cruel and he stared at her for a moment without answering.

"For one who knows me well, you make many mistakes," he said quietly. "The Cardinal betrayed me; his resisted my will. If I have a regret it's that he didn't live to feel the ax. And disabuse your mind of one thing, Nan, I'm under no man's influence; and no woman's either, unless I choose to be."

He picked up his velvet cap from a chair and pulled it squarely on his head. Then he left her without kissing her or looking back.

She went to the fire and stood watching the flames playing about the sides of the logs. It was just as well he went, because her temper was rising to the point where it would have exploded in a furious quarrel, and in her heart she knew it wasn't safe to quarrel with him now, that he couldn't be treated to scenes like any ordinary man. She had taught him the value of his position, urging and insinuating that he was a being apart from humanity by reason of his kingship; too mighty to be thwarted by anyone, even the Vicar of Christ, much less a mere wife and a Cardinal Minister. Now her theories were rebounding on her own head. She laughed furiously, enraged with herself because in a moment of weakness she had expressed her love for him, and on an impulse she drew back her foot and kicked the logs. They toppled, and a shower of golden sparks flew up the chimney. Her embroidered velvet shoe was black and ruined. It didn't matter; there were over two hundred pairs in her shoe chest.

And blue didn't suit her, it was an anemic color, favored by the Queen.

She would give the dress away; and she would go and change it now, so that when Henry came back to her for supper, he shouldn't be reminded of their disagreement. She was being clever, and she knew it; this was how she had caught and kept the King and made him want to marry her; not by shrieking like a fishwife, but by policy. When she was Queen of England, there would be no need. He had always treated Catherine well until the last year or so, and he would be more attentive and indulgent to her than he had ever been to his first wife, because he loved her. She was sure of that love, and her temper cooled; patience, patience, she counseled herself, and smiled because she sounded like her crafty father. All would be well when she was married.

When Henry supped with her that night, her fractious mood had been discarded with the magnificent blue dress, which already lay folded in her tirewoman's chest, along with other gifts of clothes and gloves and little trinkets. Oppulence had never made Anne mean. She was so gay during the meal that his spirits bounded; he roared with laughter and pulled her chair next to his so that he could hug her while he ate, and they shared each other's glasses, till his eyes grew bloodshot with wine, and his hands began seeking for her under the table. It occurred to her then, as she parried him, laughing, and insisted on a game of dice, that she must see that the King was drunk on his wedding night. He was blind and violent in drink; he would never notice . . .

The sun of the great statesman Thomas Wolsey had sunk and been extinguished. His benefices were distributed, his wealth

108

went to his enemies, and all that remained of his glory was the palace at Hampton, and the reforms he had instituted during his brief stay at York, where he lavished on his neglected priesthood the energies that had been so long expended on politics and self-aggrandizement. The Cardinal's sun had vanished, but another star was rising. A less brilliant star, and as yet small, but it burned with a fierce concentration of cunning and ambition. The star was his old secretary Thomas Cromwell.

It was the measure of his skill that he managed to avoid the fate of his master by parceling out Wolsey's possessions to his enemies, and gaining the patronage of Norfolk himself, while he worked quietly to save the Cardinal from the sentence which finally overtook him. He was loyal, while there was any hope, but by the time Northumberland rode out to take the Cardinal prisoner, Cromwell had entered the King's service, ironically, on Norfolk's recommendation. He was obsequious and efficient, and the Duke thought he might be useful among the King's officials. He was firmly entrenched in his position before the Duke realized exactly what he had done.

He was unremarkable, where Wolsey's ostentation had offended everyone, and he anticipated the King's wishes with a humility that fitted perfectly into the pattern of monarchial tyranny which was just emerging. And he protected himself and revealed himself at the same time by attaching himself to the service of Anne.

Catherine was doomed. Wolsey had said that once, and Cromwell had never forgotten. And unlike Wolsey, the woman had no grudge against him, and the King no pride to salve at his expense. He was the perfect servant, ready to propose measures which might have degraded the dignity of the King, and to carry them out by methods which it suited Henry to ignore. Tireless and tactful, he asked for nothing but the chance to get Henry and Anne what they wanted; and he knew that the rewards would follow the success.

He was a dull, sexless man, and when he came to Anne and offered to work in her interests, she recognized the motive and knew it could be trusted. He wanted power and favor with the King; she held the key to both. He hated the court faction which she knew opposed her: the Duke of Suffolk, recalled from his banishment by Henry, in spite of her protests; the Comptroller Guildford; the Marquis of Exeter; and the Chancellor, that irritating, righteous man that Henry liked, Sir Thomas More.

The Council had turned against her after Wolsey's death; the truce of self-preservation was broken when he died at Leicester, and they were fighting her openly. She knew that it was only a matter of time before her Uncle Norfolk abandoned his pretense and sided with her opponents, and to make matters worse, the Pope was temporizing and holding out hopes of reconciliation to the King if he would only give her up. The opening of the divorce case at Rome was delayed on one pretext after another, while the Papal nuncio appealed to Henry, and the French King promised to do his best to influence Clement on his English ally's behalf.

Her father went to France, where the King redoubled his promises of friendship to England, and yet managed to avoid offending either Clement or the Emperor Charles. The nations were at peace, and peace was essential to Francis, who had been soundly defeated in the last conflict. The Imperial armies were on his threshold in the Low Countries, and they were the protectors of Rome in Italy. The infidel Turks were threatening an invasion of Christendom, and the Pope paused in his attempts to unite the Christian Princess, to issue an order forbidding the discussion of the English King's marriage among ecclesiastical or lay faculties until the case opened in Rome. It was an effort to stop Henry's agents from bribing the universities, and it partially succeeded, but the arbitrariness infuriated England and incensed the King. And Cromwell was at his elbow with a suggestion which he thought might avenge the insult and prevent the recurrence of foreign interference with the wishes of his master.

Working in his little closet, often until the middle hours of the night, the drab, ugly figure drew the threads of a tremendous social revolution through his fingers, testing the strength and fiber of each factor, weaving and twisting until the strands became a pattern of law.

When he went to the King with the finished design, he called it the Act of Supremacy.

It was very simple, this lever with which to overthrow the authority of the Pope in England. It was a law proclaiming the King Head of the Church in England and requiring the bishops to take an oath of obedience to him in that capacity. He explained it carefully in his quiet voice, while the huge figure of Henry towered over him, and the small eyes watched him, till Cromwell had to look away. They were alone in the King's room at Windsor, a cold, stone chamber in spite of the tapestries and the thick candles standing in tall metal sconces on the floor, which had to be lighted even in the day, because the narrow windows gave such a poor light. It was a medieval room, and the January sun filtered weakly through the talc casement. Unlike the elegant apartments at York Palace and Hampton, the floor was thickly spread with scented rushes. One of the King's hunting dogs had crept close to the crude fireplace and lay snoring, nose between its paws, one eye occasionally opening to watch the movements of its master.

"The device is simple," Cromwell explained. "The late Cardinal was under a charge of treason when he died; all those bishops appointed by him shall be summoned under a nominal charge and ordered to clear themselves by swearing obedience to you and acknowledging your supreme authority. Most of the bishops are Wolsey's nominess; the few who aren't are too old to offer any resistance."

Henry looked at him, frowning. "The Commons will support the measure, but what of the Lords?"

Cromwell's round face turned up to him.

"The Lords may be less willing, Sire, once they recognize how much your power will be increased. The Lords have always resented the authority of the King, and tried to limit it. My late master once said to me that the union of the Church and the Monarchy was the best safeguard against the ambitions and disloyalty of the nobles; he was right in his day, but no longer. The Church has dared to set itself above you, and the time has come to bring it into subjection before it has time to ally itself with the Lords. Wolsey believed that the King needed the Church in order to restrain his nobility. I believe the King can reduce both."

"The Cardinal was a wise man, before he became a traitor," Henry remarked. "But I am wiser; I know the temper of the Lords well enough, but the Lord's don't yet know mine. They think because Wolsey fell that his power shall be distributed among them. They're mistaken, Tom; that power is mine, was always mine, as *he* discovered when he went against me. My Church must learn Wolsey's lesson, and the first thing we must do is involve the Lords in teaching it, before they see too clearly that after the bishops the Act will be applied to them. I shall discuss the matter with Norfolk and my brother Suffolk; they shall come into my confidence, Tom, and be entrusted with my plans until they can never withdraw. The first thing they shall do is go to the Queen and advise her to submit and recall her appeal to the Pope."

Cromwell's mind was racing parallel with the King's as he listened; he was amazed at the cunning of the suggestion. Acting as Henry's official emissaries, a body of the great English nobles were to declare themselves partisans of the divorce by exerting pressure on the Queen; the opportunity was tempting, for it appeared that he was delegating his authority to them, by asking them to bully Catherine on his behalf.

"As regards their feeling toward the bishops and this new Act," Henry continued slowly, "I suggest that a question be put to Lord Dacre. Let him be asked whether he agrees that matrimonial disputes should be within the jurisdiction of the civil courts rather than the ecclesiastical."

"A very fair question," Cromwell smiled. "As Lord Dacre is no partisan of the Lady Anne's, his reply should let us know what attitude the Lords will take."

Immediately the King turned to him, his thin red brows drawn down and that tight mouth pursed till it was almost invisible; Cromwell knew that expression and his smile quickly disappeared.

"It's no longer a question of who champions the Lady Anne," Henry said flatly. "The Lady Anne has no significance beyond the fact that she pleases me and I wish to make her my wife. This is no trifling love affair in which men side with one woman or another. The matter has gone beyond that, Master Cromwell. I don't deny it began in earnest with my love for the lady; that love remains as steadfast as ever, but now my right as King is at stake. I'm no lovesick fool to set empires battling because of a woman; that's the malice of my enemies. I tell you this," and he leaned over Cromwell, one heavy hand flat on his shoulder, "my conscience tells me Catherine's not my lawful wife, and my conscience doesn't lie. My honor also tells me that Henry, King of England, shan't go to his grave without a son to follow him! I know my will now, by God, and I've seen men try to thwart it, as they thwarted other Kings."

His voice became a bellow suddenly, so that Cromwell jumped in spite of himself.

"No one shall thwart me, not the Pope or the Emperor, or anyone in Christendom! And my subjects shall learn that all the bulls ever written from Rome are nothing compared to my word!"

"Your subjects are learning, Sire," Cromwell murmured. "They'll learn that Rome is very distant and the King's justice very near." Henry had released him, and he resisted the impulse to rub his aching shoulder.

"The Pope will reconsider when he sees the bishops submit," the King went on; his voice was level again. "We'll continue appealing to Clement for a stay of the trial until this thing is done. Take your papers, Master Cromwell, and go, now. I'm well pleased with you."

It had never occurred to the bishops that Cromwell's summons was anything more than a means of forcing a grant of money out of them for the King. The enormous sum of one hundred thousand pounds was offered to propitiate him, and then Cromwell struck his blow. The offer was refused; they were ordered to go on their knees and admit their offenses and expurgate them by acknowledging Henry as supreme Head of the Church.

Suddenly the significance of the move burst on the Lords spiritual and temporal. There was a concerted move of violent opposition when even the most timorous clergy recoiled, and the Lords forgot their jealousy of Church lands and influence long enough to make it clear that they would resist the measure. A petition signed by many bishops, including the formidable Fisher of Rochester, and backed by Warham, Archbishop of Canterbury, was delivered to the Council, deploring the attempt made on the liberty of the Church and the Authority of the Pope. Cromwell's scheme failed to materialize in full; the Act was amended so that Henry's clergy swore to obey him "as far as God's laws allow," which, as Anne bitterly pointed out, took all practical value out of the Act, and the laws hostile to Papal authority were withdrawn from Parliament.

In his anger and disappointment, Henry's wrath turned toward the man who had made the suggestion, but Cromwell had his safeguard. He sheltered behind Anne's skirts, and the King's rage was diverted to his nobility and his bishops. The method was the right one, as Cromwell pointed out as soon as he dared approach the King; he chose an occasion when Anne was with him, because he was sure of an ally. He had miscalculated on the timing, and for that he begged His Grace's pardon; but he also begged His Grace not to abandon the idea. He had overlooked one stumbling block, the Archbishop of Canterbury. Warham was the rock on which the scheme had foundered. The complaisant compatriot of the dead Cardinal had been so long subservient to the royal wishes that his opposition and defense of his clergy had come as a violent shock to the King. How dared he, he roared, after conductting, with Wolsey, the secret inquiry into the marriage all those years ago, after lending himself to every plan in the question of obtaining the divorce?

It was Anne who answered Henry, when Cromwell dared not.

"He's old," she retorted, "old and sick. He's thinking of his soul instead of his skin now, that's why he's prepared to defy you."

The King laughed harshly.

"In that case, we'll find an Archbishop whose years won't fortify him. And we shan't have to wait long! Find me a candidate, Mas-

114

ter Cromwell, and I'll propose him to Rome, and by God, we'll turn it so that the Pope accepts him!"

"I have the candidate," Anne said, "the very man. My father's old chaplain, Dr. Cranmer."

"Cranmer?" Henry frowned, trying to place the man.

"He has lately been in Rome," Cromwell explained. It was fantastic, Anne thought, how much the man knew; every name and face, every date and every letter connected with State business were engraved on his memory. And his facts were always right; behind Henry's back they exchanged glances, and he nodded. Cranmer was an excellent choice. He was brilliant and ambitious, and he had made one mistake which Cromwell and his patrons the Boleyns had discovered. During a stay in Germany he had broken his vow of celibacy and married a free-thinking German lady. The marriage was quietly annulled and the King kept in ignorance of it. If he ever showed signs of resisting the divorce, like so many of the bishops who had gained their appointments and preferments by pretending to favor it, they had only to remind him of Henry's views on married clergy . .

"The Lady Anne shows excellent judgment in suggesting Dr. Cranmer," Cromwell said. "He is a man of high moral standards and an ardent champion of Your Grace's rights."

"In which case the Pope's unlikely to agree to his appointment," Henry objected. The secretary bowed.

"I believe he impressed Clement very favorably," he murmured. "He had little chance of advancing your cause if he antagonized the judges and so I believe he presented himself as most loyal to the Pope, and thoroughly gained his confidence."

The King turned to Anne and laughed.

"In other words the fellow's a deceitful cur, trust my Lord Wiltshire to employ him! So he went out to help argue my case and sniffed round Clement's skirts, did he? What makes you think I can trust him if the Pope can't?"

"He's ambitious," Anne answered. "His fortunes lie in serving you, and he knows it. I can vouch for him; he's more diplomat than priest. The See of Canterbury will buy him, body and soul."

Cromwell was watching the King while she spoke. He always

watched Henry, so that already he knew every shade of expression; the flicker of an eyelid, and that ominous compression of his little mouth when something jarred. She was too outspoken, he thought; that last remark about the See of Canterbury was a mistake. The King was a hypocrite at heart, hadn't she learned that . . . Henry was ready to employ Cranmer, but he didn't like the implications being brought into the light. If his marriage to Catherine was going to be dissolved, it must be done with the trappings of orthodoxy, so that in time the King could deceive himself as well as others. He coughed, and made good her mistake.

"Cranmer will follow his conscience, Sire. He's clever, as my Lady says, but he's a true man of God. If he obtains the Archbishopric he'll use his powers for justice and your Grace's rights, without fear or favor to anyone."

The King grunted; he was glad Cromwell had said that. Sometimes Anne's cynicism offended him.

"Warham is too near death to trouble us much longer, Tom. We've agreed on his successor, so let's proceed to other business." He paused. Norfolk and Suffolk had headed the deputation to the Queen and demanded that she submit to her husband and withdraw her appeal to Rome. She had refused. She answered them with dignity and restraint, and took the opportunity to state her case in such clear terms that several of her tormentors left her presence cursing the divorce and all who had instigated it.

"The Queen persists in her obstinacy," Henry said at last. "The efforts of my commissioners failed to move her."

"In fact," Anne interrupted bitterly, "her efforts moved some of them! Guildford's become her partisan, for one."

The King's eyes considered her.

"Guildford shall lose his office and be exiled to his estates," he said shortly. "And Exeter with him and any others who opened their mouths in agreement with her. That should convince the rest that consent to the divorce is their only means of remaining at court."

"A few were fools," Cromwell remarked, "but the rest are wise. What does Your Grace propose should be done?"

"Catherine must bend," he answered. "My daughter Mary

116

will follow her example. She must be shown that her attitude can only result in evil relations between us. I've spoken to her often enough myself, and sent others to her, but nothing has any effect."

"It seems to me there's only one method," Cromwell said after a moment. "If Your Grace will permit me to suggest it."

The King nodded; he knew what was coming; he had heard it over and over again from Anne and resisted it, because he knew that she was motivated by jealousy. Even now he had no wish to hurt Catherine physically unless he must. But Cromwell bore the Queen no grudge and if Cromwell suggested the same course, he would feel justified in taking it.

"Send the Queen from court," Cromwell said quietly. "Place her in a house in the country, with a household, of course, and all respect. But remove her from your presence."

Anne stood motionless, almost holding her breath. She had begged and argued and stormed for this, and never been able to move him. If Cromwell could only succeed . . . A house in the country, that was the first step, nominal exile, and then actual imprisonment. If he consented to the first, the second would be easy, when he could not see his orders put into practice, or hear Catherine weeping, or know how she was being treated . . . There was some regard left for her, Anne knew, and the thought drove her mad with hatred and anxiety. How could he care what happened to her, how could he go on tolerating her at court, knowing she was doing everything she could to keep him against his will, when he was such a tyrant to others? Any other man would have sent the creature to the Tower two years ago, executed her, if necessary . . . Her mouth was dry and her heart bounded.

She was jealous, she whispered to herself, she, beautiful Anne Boleyn, was so jealous of an old woman that she could have screamed at Henry to kill her then and there . . . her daughter too. Anne's hands were trembling, clenched into fists in the shelter of the long silk sleeves.

That pale, haughty brat was fifteen now, and marriageable. She had her mother's dignity and her father's vivid looks, and her face was long and her eyes were red because she was always weeping over the estrangement between her parents. That was the gossip, often loudly repeated so that Anne could hear.

The Princess Mary's Grace. She used to be gay and laughing, with the promise of rosy prettiness, like her lovely aunt the Duchess of Suffolk; now she was pallid and often ill. The doctors said she was grieving because someone had turned her father against her and was trying to take her mother's place. Pray God, replied the fiend of jealousy in Anne's heart, pray God that the Princess Mary's Grace should die like all her mother's other brats!

"I shrink from hurting her." It was Henry's voice at last. "But her presence at court is unseemly now. She must leave."

"When, Sire?" Cromwell asked quietly.

"When we go on our hunting trip, in a month's time."

Henry had put his arm round Anne, and she turned her head quickly and kissed his hand. She was not quite sure of him, Cromwell thought suddenly. And the hatred of Catherine which affronted so many people, that was a symptom of that uncertainty. She would never admit it, she was far too proud, but the longer the proceedings dragged on, the more men who had to be cut down in the process, the less sure of herself Anne became. The strain must be enormous, and it was telling, was making her harsh and tactless with the King, and she was making enemies as if she couldn't help herself.

Whom could she trust, Cromwell considered. Him, but only as long as it suited his interests; her father to exactly the same degree. Her brother—yes, he was true to her, and she adored him, but he was young and comparatively unimportant, and not nearly as clever as her Uncle Norfolk. There was a man to watch; a man not to offend.

She was really alone, and in her instinct she knew it, like an animal in a jungle clearing, surrounded by attackers, waiting for the lion who sheltered her to move away.

She had only the King. Whatever the beginning, Cromwell thought dispassionately, this was her punishment. Sooner or later, unless he married her, he would tire, and when he did, the pack would leap on her and drag her down. One thing was certain; the King must take her with him if his plan to meet the King of France at Calais materialized. The idea was only tentative, but Henry was set on a fresh alliance with Francis, believing that the coalition would frighten Clement and the Emperor Charles as much as his negotiations with the Protestants at Lubeck and Hamburg. The alliance with France would soon be concluded, and the King hoped to demonstrate his friendship with the French King by making a State visit. Cromwell glanced at her as she stood, flushed and smiling with triumph, in the crook of Henry's arm, she had yet to realize, as he did already, that banishment wouldn't rid her of Catherine.

In time she'd see that and that was why it wouldn't be safe to leave her in England if the King went abroad. If anything happened to Catherine in his absence, the English people would march on King and government, with the full approval of the Lords and Church. The Church was in disrepute; its wavering authority was held together by the defiance of the dying Warham, and the people and the Commons welcomed the measures taken to reduce its privileges. The Church could be destroyed with safety; but Catherine and her daughter Mary were sacred to the people in their misfortune. If Anne or her faction harmed either of them, Henry would lose his throne.

He wondered if Henry knew how much his subjects hated the woman he wanted to make his Queen. Cromwell knew it, as he knew everything; he had begun recruiting the army of spies which was to make him the most dreaded man in England in the next few years. They brought him copies of street pamphlets, describing Catherine's rival in the coarsest terms; she was accused of witchcraft, of wanting to poison the Queen and the Princess; ironically, some even blamed her for the miserable fate of Wolsey. She was hated for her riches, and her arrogance when she appeared in the streets, while Catherine's generosity and piety were remembered and prayers offered for her safety in the country churches.

With a weaker or less politic King and a determined Church, the project of divorce would have been overthrown long ago.

Circumstances favored it, and Henry was proving a genius in turning those circumstances to his own ends. The prestige of the Papacy was at a pitiful level, and the vacillations of Clement for the past five years had done nothing to raise it. Henry had presented the Pope to Parliament as the Emperor's tool, refusing justice to England at the behest of Spain. He had also encouraged criticism of the Church, advancing the popular theory that the tithes due to Rome should no longer be paid, and cunningly held over Clement's head the threat of revoking them, while the divorce proceedings were in abeyance. At the same time laws diminishing the ecclesiastical jurisdiction were pushed through Parliament.

On the surface the measures satisfied the clamor for reform which was a genuine expression of the people's wish; but the objective was a lay and spiritual dictatorship, the King's was the ultimate tribunal, and no appeal was allowed from his judgment.

Anne was only the pebble which began the landslide. But she was fierce and feminine enough to try to solve her problem by killing Catherine if she got the chance; her servants at York Place had reported violent threats, as they reported her quarrels with the King and the fluctuations in their relationship. One act of folly on her part could destroy the chance of Thomas Cromwell's becoming the first man in England, after the King. Whatever happened, he repeated, she must go to France with Henry. He bowed to the King, and backed out of the room.

7

THE SUMMER OF 1532 WAS VERY HOT; A MOLTEN SUN BURNED down over the English countryside, drying the crops and drinking up the streams, turning the rough roads into a desert of dust and dried potholes, and the fever broke out in London, born in the stinking refuse piled high in the gutters of the narrow streets, lurking in the dirty rushes and impure water. The King and his household prepared to leave for Hampton Court, and the long train of wagons containing beds and linen and plate and clothes started on its way out of London to prepare the red brick palace for the King's reception.

Henry traveled by barge, with Anne and a company of ladies and gentlemen, and it was a gay journey, enlivened by music from the musicians who traveled in a boat close behind. The procession was watched by curious crowds lining the riverbanks, eager for a sight of the hated Boleyn whore who had cast a love spell over the King. The people were silent; their caps came off for Henry, but their mouths were closed and their hands still. She was dark in coloring, like a foreigner, and they hated the way she stared up at them and then leaned toward the King and laughed. "God Save Queen Catherine," one or two muttered, and the goodwives of London leaned forward, cursing, to stare after that slim figure in the brilliant dress, and spat into the water.

Their Queen was shut up in some manor house in the country, and the Princess Mary had been sent from court. There were rumors of a war with Spain which would ruin their trade with the Netherlands and bring them all to starvation, and the new laws passed by the King and his Parliament had taken the right of sanctuary from the Church so that no one had a refuge from the punishments of their Lord or the King's justices. It was all being done so that witch could become Queen of England.

The people turned away as the line of barges drifted out of sight down the Thames, and a ragged harlot ran down the dirty cobbled path, her skirts lifted above her knees, tossing her head and mimicking the court lady's mincing air. She drew a shout of approval from the spectators, by giving a familiar high pitched laugh.

"The Bullen Whore!" yelled an apprentice, and immediately the cry was taken up. Someone fell on one knee before the strumpet, and then caught at her skirts. The woman kicked at him, laughing, and pushed the bedraggled hair off her face.

121

She saw a potential customer by the expression in his eyes. The fever had improved trade; with death so close, men drank and wenched and parted more freely with their money.

"If I'm Nan Bullen I don't lie for nothing," she taunted. "Come on, then, King Harry, let's see your coin!"

The royal barge swung into the broader path of the Thames and the King leaned forward, one hand on Anne's knee, to watch the lovely red buildings of Wolsey's Palace come into sight, warmly glowing in the hot sun. The sight always gave him pleasure; the proportions of the house were beautiful, and the setting perfect. The country was very green, in spite of the heat; two thousand acres of park had been enclosed and stocked with game to provide the King with hunting, and a fine tilt yard laid out at the back with five towers for the spectators to watch the jousting. The gardens at Hampton were Henry's pride. As the barge neared the landing stage, he could see them spread out; neat squares of ordered beds, crisscrossed with little flagged paths among the flowers and colorful rockeries; a white statue set in the niche of low green hedges; a delicate fountain spray cooling the paved garden, which was his favorite because it was sunken and barried by a little wrought-iron gate. He used to wander there in the long summer evenings, hand in hand with Anne, and vanished into the blossom-covered arbor with the stone love seat, overlooking the lovely stretch of the river.

Wolsey had been alive then, and Catherine still at court; the divorce was dragging on, but he could forget it and leave the anxiety to the Cardinal. In those days he had never dreamed of breaking with the Pope.

There were times when he hesitated still, when something in him paused at the enormity of the thing he and Cromwell were prepared to do; times when the thought of Catherine living in miserable exile twisted his conscience and had to be justified by the excuse that she deserved it. He was the King; his will was the expression of Divine Authority in the country God had given him to rule. His conscience was the voice of God, and it told him he was right to put his wife away; right to break the power of his bishops and subjugate his Church; right to withstand the doctrine which gave a Pope authority to excommunicate a Christian King, to refuse him the sacraments and absolve his subjects from their oath of allegiance.

A hundred years ago no monarch survived under that sentence, but the power to enforce it was gone; Henry was not afraid of revolt and assassination. He held his people and his nobles in a grip of iron, because they had lost their awe of the Church and the fear of the King's punishment was greater than the fear of hell. Whatever Clement did, he was not afraid, and in those moments of strange conflict, he braved the abyss of spiritual damnation and looked over the edge and said once and for all that he didn't believe the Pope had the power to topple him into it. He feared nothing else; and he gathered his will and his belief in his kingship, and refused to fear that. He thought of the place he and his small kingdom held in Europe, and his heart lifted with pride.

Beside the mighty Emperor and the powerful King of France, England had shrunk to insignificance since the days of the great Henry V; Wolsey had tried to compete with them; Wolsey had gone to war and meddled in alliances like a warrior King instead of a priest, but his ambitions had never come to fruition till the battle with the Pope reached its climax.

He, Henry, had split Christendom. He was forcing Francis to act in his interests because Francis needed him as an ally against a possible attack by the Emperor. And the Emperor held back from war because he depended on English trade with his Netherlands, and because he knew Francis would stab him in the back at the first opportunity. The Princes in Germany were looking to England to help them in their dual struggle for religious and national independence of the Emperor, and the Emperor hesitated for fear that the King of England might induce them to open revolt.

He stood in the middle, and he could do as he liked because now he knew that no one on either side would dare to move, even

Clement. Clement had opened the case against him at Rome, and sent a personal message asking him to take Catherine back and send Anne away, but he still hoped for a solution, and even now showed himself ready to forgive and forget, if the King would do what he was told. And stop despoiling the Church in England . . .

There was nothing they could do, because the temporal Princes were guided by temporalities, and Clement knew that if he gave the sentence no one would agree to execute it for him. Clement was powerless, if one discounted the doctrine of his spiritual power, and Henry had discounted that; he had refused and rejected it and his mind spat it out violently, all the more violently because he had once accepted it so fervently that he had sent troops to the aid of another Pope, when he pronounced anathema against a rebel King of France.

The barge bumped against the parapet, and a few drops of water splashed up from the wall and sprinkled Anne's skirts. She brushed them aside with an exclamation; it was velvet, she said crossly to Henry's inquiry, and velvet spotted. He scowled and suddenly his pleasure was spoiled; he felt intensely irritated, and a deep flush of anger spread over his neck when he saw that Will Brereton, sitting behind them, had heard. Damn her bad temper, he thought furiously, damn her dress—Christ's blood, she had over a hundred . . . damn her for answering him like that before others. She was still smoothing the material, unaware that she had done anything to annoy him, and he saw the thin line of her cheek turned away from him. She had changed; changed since the days he sat fondling her in the gardens at Hampton, reading aloud the love poems he'd written to her. Changed from a lively companion and affectionate lover into a bitter-tempered shrew who remembered her place less and less as he exalted her. Catherine would have shaken her skirts and said nothing, but Catherine was gone. Catherine had resisted him and tried to put him in the wrong, and for that he could never forgive her, but in all her life she had never humiliated him in public. He had done everything for Anne; respected her honor, loaded her family with wealth and office, and striven for six years to make her his wife.

When the barge was moored and his chief waterman stood on

the landing stage, cap in hand, waiting for the King to disembark, Henry rose abruptly and stepped ashore without speaking a word to her. He called Brereton and Francis Weston to accompany him and left Anne to enter the palace with the rest of the company.

"I've been searching half Hampton for you!" Lord Wiltshire exclaimed. He had found his daughter standing in the Base Court, with Margaret Wyatt, watching the men at work on the great hall. The King was having it enlarged, and making extensive additions to the palace; in Wolsey's day it accommodated five hundred persons, but the King and his court were cramped for space. Little work was done in that heat; the builders and craftsmen had been ordered to finish their task for the day and then wait till the King left before they resumed their work.

Anne turned to her father and shook her head.

"I can hardly hear with the hammering. What is it?"

"I want to talk to you," Wiltshire shouted. "Privately, and in peace."

Tom Wyatt's sister heard him and curtsied and walked away.

"Come to my rooms," Anne suggested as they moved to the center of the court, but he gestured urgently.

"No, not in the house. We might be overheard." She looked up at him quickly and saw his narrow face pinched with anxiety.

"Come to the pavilion. We'll be safe there." The pavilion was a small open building, erected on top of an artificial mound, covered with flowering shrubs and rockeries; it was an acknowledged rendezvous, which the King and she had often used when it was too cold to sit by the river.

It was shady and cool inside; a withered nosegay lay on the ground under the stone seat. There Anne faced her father.

"You don't wear that look for nothing. What's happened?"

"A fine thing you did when you defied me and tried to marry Northumberland," he snarled. "You're like to lose the King through it!" She almost caught at his doublet and shook him. "What are you babbling about . . . Northumberland, what about Northumberland?"

"He promised to marry you, didn't he?" Wiltshire sneered bitterly. "Well, he told his wife so one day, and now the Queen's friends have reminded her. She's going to demand an annulment, alleging a pre-contract with you!"

She felt as if he'd struck her. A pre-contract, that was as binding as the marriage vow. If word of this reached the King . . .

They had contracted to marry, and by that token, Northumberland's marriage was null and void, but what good would it do her now? It was years and years ago, she thought hysterically; there was nothing between her and Henry Percy now, but this old indiscretion had to be brought up to menace her marriage to the King . . .

"It's a lie!" she spat out.

"It's not, and you know it," Wiltshire retorted. "Do you know what it is to try to marry the King when you've been the contracted wife of another man? Treason, Madame, high treason, and I don't have to tell you the punishment for that."

Her mind was darting like a snared animal, trying to see a way out; suddenly she found one.

"Treason for Northumberland too, not to have told the King when marriage was first mentioned between us! If I lose my head, Northumberland loses his!"

"That muddled loon? He's idiot enough to put his own head on the block in order to get rid of Mary Talbot. Don't reckon on him."

"I do," she said doggedly. "He loved me once; he wouldn't harm me."

Wiltshire laughed bitterly. "Harm you? God's death, your vanity'll kill you yet. Harm you? He hates the sight of you! He's told everyone he talks to that you're a merciless whore who trapped him and then the King, and once he saw you as you were, he'd as soon have given the Cardinal a ship for France as punish him for stopping the marriage between you! If he loved you once, he hates you now, be sure of that!"

"Not enough to die for an old promise," she retorted.

In the midst of her fear she was hurt in a way that she had forgotten she could feel. Hurt and fool enough to be near tears, because Northumberland hated her too. . . . Let him hate her!

126

Let them all hate her, and work for Catherine of Aragon. They would lose and she would win. She calmed down then, and stopped trembling.

"When a man lifts his arms to strike you, deliver your blow first," she said. "I'll anticipate my Lady Northumberland by going to the King and denying the story before she has time to tell it! And he'll believe me."

"You're very sure of that," Wiltshire remarked. But in spite of himself he was impressed.

It was a good motto, strike first. He began to breathe more easily; he had not forgotten that the father of such a scheming traitoress would hardly remain on good terms with the King.

"Do you think you'll be able to convince him?" he asked again. "Sure of it."

She sat down on the seat, both hands braced on the edge.

"The King's as much in love with me as ever," she insisted. "He won't thank that Northumberland bitch for trying to separate us."

Wiltshire paused, biting his lower lip. There was something he wanted to say to Anne, something which nagged in his mind, but which he had never had the excuse to bring up until now.

"The King's as much in love with me as ever."

But Wiltshire did not think so. He had not thought so for some months, though he kept the opinion to himself. He saw his daughter living in royal state, taking the Queen's place at court, free to wander in and out of Henry's rooms whenever she liked, able to quarrel with him and then cajole him back; powerful enough to get great nobles and her own aunt, the Duchess of Norfolk, dismissed from court because they offended her, but he was still uneasy. The King's feeling had altered, and it was entirely her own fault. Six years was a long time for a man to love one woman and to wait for the fulfillment of that love. It needed a woman of skill and tact, as well as fascination to achieve it; and recently Anne's skill was failing and her tact had disappeared. He knew how she restored peace between the King and herself after their quarrels; he could imagine quite cold-bloodedly how she could lead Henry along a sinuous path of practiced sensuality, until the consummation became a mecca of physical desire. But her tongue and her arro-

127

gance were destroying the strongest link in the chain she had fettered on the King: sentimentality.

Wiltshire knew his master; he knew his crudity, his immense self-will, his cruelty and his unexpected kindnesses, and he knew that the instinct which enjoyed playing the chivalrous lover was being frustrated. That was the bond which had held him to Catherine for fifteen years. She was submissive and affectionate. Anne might have the sensual capacity of the Grand Turk's entire harem, but without those two qualities, she would never keep the King.

"Whatever our quarrels in the past," Wiltshire said at last, "you are my daughter, and I'm going to speak seriously to you now. If the King accepts your explanation, I know what I advise you to do."

She looked up at him, her eyebrows raised.

"What? Not press for revenge on Northumberland's wife, I suppose."

"No," the Earl shook his head. "You won't wish to hear this, but I shall say it nonetheless. Give up your plan to marry the King."

Her mouth opened, and her hand flew to her breast, and then stopped at the base of her slender throat. She didn't believe she had heard him at all.

"I have a feeling," Wiltshire went on. "Don't ask me to explain it, for I can't, but I feel you should draw back. I can give you the practical reasons: the enmity of such a large faction at court, the difficulties of obtaining the divorce—rather the impossibility, for Clement'll never grant it now, and the King knows it. The chance that one of these intrigues against you will succeed. Not long ago, Suffolk tried and failed; now Northumberland. There'll be others; we're bitterly hated, Nan; George and I, and above all, you. Someone will succeed, and you know where that will end. You've seen the King turn; he loved Wolsey once, and you know how he served him in the end."

"Because I made him," she broke in, but he silenced her.

"On the day he regrets Wolsey, and he may, he'll remember that you were behind him," he said quietly. "You say he loves you, Nan. Well, that may be; he leches, and he's unsatisfied, I know

128

that; but I don't think he loves you as he did. There lies your danger, in that and the delay over the marriage. The Pope's arms are still open; he can be reconciled with Rome and not repeal a single act against the Church, so he has everything to gain and nothing to lose but you, if it comes to the point. And it may come to the point, maybe after a quarrel, when you've been fool enough to rant at him like any common goodwife, or when there's an intrigue that isn't mistimed or discovered by us first."

She stared at him, wondering and quivering with anger.

"You say give up? After all I've striven for, and suffered and schemed? After holding the King for six years and setting the Pope himself at nothing? Give up, from you?"

She threw back her head and laughed in savage mockery.

"You, who crawled and plotted to advance yourself from the day you were born? Lord Wiltshire, by God, and Keeper of the Privy Seal . . . rich and important, with the world at your feet and your daughter as the future Queen of England! Give up!" She almost spat the words. "Have you lost your mind, my dear father? What would such a future hold for me!"

"Safety," he said harshly. "And not only for you but for all of us!"

She laughed harshly. "Ah, now I see it. Now I understand. You've no fear for *me*, that *I* may come to harm. You've lined your own coffer by my efforts, you've got enough for yourself now, and you don't like the risk any more! You want to keep your offices and your honors and persuade me to give up my chance of being Queen. You're afraid for your own hide, and the devil take me and the years I've wasted. . . . The King doesn't love me! He only leches . . . Is that what you say? He may abandon me at any moment because of the Pope or a pack of intriguers? Well, you lie! I know he needs me more than ever; he couldn't do without me!"

"Your vanity'll be your death," he snarled again. In all the years he had never hated her as much as at that moment when she accused him rightly to his face. He was clear-sighted, and he knew in his heart that for some reason he was more afraid of Henry than of any of the factions he had used in argument. Every instinct warned him that Anne's hold was more tenuous than she or anyone supposed; if it broke, her whole family would follow her into ruin. And the partisans of Catherine and the Princess Mary would have no mercy. If she withdrew now, she could have wealth and a good marriage arranged for her, and he could assume the role of peacemaker to the King and his estranged wife. Catherine would be grateful, and Catherine was not vindictive. She was the only one who pitied Wolsey, once her remorseless enemy, when she heard of his disgrace. And the King liked him, because he had made an art of subservience. He had hoped Anne would listen, and he struck at her furiously in a last attempt.

"You're not what you were," he told her. "Go, study your mirror. You're thin-faced and shrewish and you've a mouth like a bear trap. There's never a gentle word or a sweet smile from you, not for nearly a year past, and you're not young any more, Madame. You're past twenty-five, and by God, you look every day of the age! You lash the King with that sharp tongue of yours and think he doesn't mind it. I've seen him redden and look at you in a way that might have warned a wiser woman. Go your own way if you will, but I tell you, don't count on me to support you when you go too far. You've nothing to give the King now but your body, and I swear the time'll soon come when he sickens of waiting for that!"

She stood up and faced him, quivering. So she was old, and her beauty was gone . . . was that what he thought? She couldn't hope to keep the man who'd loved her for six years and sent his wife and daughter into exile for her sake! She was so angry that she choked for breath, and for one mad moment her hand half rose as if to strike him. At the same time she was bitterly afraid and shaken. He believed what he said. He believed she was losing Henry's love and he believed it so strongly he was prepared to abandon all their hopes at the last minute.

Suddenly she became deadly calm; she straightened her jeweled cap and shook out her skirts and looked up into his pale, furious face.

"I thank you for this, in spite of all your venom, Father, because you've shown me what I should do. The King has waited long enough. He'll marry the mother of his son, and I'll be Queen of England yet. But I'll remember your words to me today."

She brushed past him, and walked quickly out into the glare of the afternoon, her wooden-soled shoes tapping on the curved stone path leading downward from the mount toward the privy garden and the palace.

She sat by her dressing chest for an hour while two tirewomen brushed and scented her black hair. It hung loose down her back, drawn away from her face by two combs set with pearls. She had bathed and rubbed musk-scented oil into her skin, and she was naked under a dress of soft white satin, the sleeves and bodice sewn with seed pearls. She chose a necklace of large pearls with a pendant formed of the initial B. She had worn it for the portrait Holbein painted of her a year before. Her brows were blackened, and she rubbed a red salve into her lips until it colored them and disappeared. The skin was drawn tight across her cheekbones, leaving a faint hollow that enhanced the size and brilliance of her dark eyes and the delicate line of her temples. The candles burning beside the polished metal mirror picked out the dull gleam of the jewels round her narrow throat, and caught the light of diamonds in her ears as she moved. On her left hand she wore Henry's ring, and a fan of white ostrich feathers with a silver handle lay on the chest. Her bedroom was piled with dresses of every color and material, flung on the bed where they had been discarded one after the other; the shoe chest was open, and one of her women knelt, fitting a white satin slipper onto her foot.

Her father was lying because he hated her, and had lost courage. She didn't look old or bitter; she had never been more beautiful in her life.

"Clear these things away," she ordered. "Put everything in order, and be quick! His Grace will soon be here."

The serving-women left her and began gathering the clothes and folding them away in the great clothespress that stood on one side of the room.

She got up and pointed to the pots and bottles on the chest, and her gold brushes.

"These too; and there's a slipper in the corner there."

The bed stood in the center, high and cavernous and piled with silk cushions; she had ordered fresh bedding and sheets, and had the hangings drawn back, and the hand-worked coverlet turned down. Her lawn nightgown lay on a chair and the velvet robe, edged with sable from the neck to the hem, was folded over the chair back, and the tiny slippers set together. Anne turned, and the satin whispered after her as she walked.

"Make a fire that'll last into the night. Then go."

When the King came to dine with her he was tired, for Cromwell had followed him from London and he'd spent the fine afternoon shut up in what had once been Wolsey's closet, studying State papers. An hour before he had been tempted to send word to Anne not to expect him; he would eat with Norreys and Weston and play cards with them afterward, and perhaps hunt with her in the morning. But the mood passed, and he came to her rooms.

He found them full of lights; there were thick wax candles burning by the tapestry walls and lighting the table, shining on some of thè gold plate which she had brought with her from York Place. In spite of the heat of that day, the evening was cool, and a log fire burned in the open hearth; some herbs had been thrown on it, which gave a pleasant smell, and he stopped in the doorway, pleased by the elegance and the preparations. She came toward him and curtsied, and then raised her lips for the kiss they always exchanged on meeting.

He caught her shoulders, his fingers tightening as she pressed against him, and her breath was warm.

"By God," he said quickly, "you've no right to look so, Nan. You take my appetite away and give me other longings."

"I hoped to please you," she answered gently and stepped out of reach.

"And you've succeeded, sweetheart. I've spent a weary day."

"Then you must spend a merry evening," she returned. "Come, sit down and drink some wine with me before we eat and tell me about the day and its weariness."

He stretched and yawned, watching her, feeling the warmth of good humor spreading through him, and the itch of desire in his body.

"I've a mind for ale instead," he said. "I'm thirsty, Nan, I could drink a cask of it."

She smiled. Wine tonight, not ale; wine was stronger.

"Try this, beloved. It's a fine malmsey I had specially served for you."

He took the cup to please her and drank it down in one swallow. She refilled it at once, and he forgot about the ale as she knelt beside his chair, her cheek against his arm, and listened while he talked about Cromwell and grumbled that his wrist was stiff from signing papers. She took his right hand in her own and kissed it, and the cup was full again with the strong sweet malmsey. He stroked her hair and wound long strands of it round his thick fingers. He hadn't felt content and cosseted like this for months, and his old tenderness for her returned, as warm as the wine in his belly. She twisted around to look up at him and shook her head when he offered her a sip out of his cup.

"You always said if I had a trouble I could come to you," she said, "but it can wait till tomorrow if you've borne enough today."

His large hand stroked her head and he smiled.

"I've a broad back, sweet, tell me about it."

"You remember the time I thought I loved Henry Percy?"

"I do indeed; you wouldn't look at me, you minx, and you sulked in Hever for months on end," he chided.

She forbore to remind him that he had sent her there, and said lightly, "I was very young, and I didn't know the meaning of love, never thinking beyond a few smiles and a kiss. Poor Percy was only a half-grown boy, and I wasn't much wiser. It was childish folly, Harry, and forgotten by both of us in a matter of days. Now his wife's resurrecting it, because she wants to be free of him."

"Resurrecting what? There was nothing between you?"

It was a question, and his tone had altered. She thought how pale his eyes were as she looked into them; the pupils had diminished to pinheads. He had short, sandy eyelashes which were almost invisible at a distance; his brows were fine and arched like a woman's but so light his face had a curiously bald look as it grew fatter. She knew he was becoming angry because the freckles across his short nose and cheeks looked darker, as his color changed.

"She's alleging a pre-contract, as grounds for an annulment," Anne explained. "What she and Northumberland do are no con-

133

cern of mine, but she's involving me in something that's nothing less than treason, just to obtain her own ends. If I was pre-contracted to marry Percy or any other man, I'd have no right to come to you."

"When did you hear this?" he asked her.

"Yesterday," she lied, "but I hadn't the heart to spoil the hunt for you by telling you. However, I thought it best to tell you now, before she makes an open scandal. Also, I wanted to deny it to you, Harry. I know you'd never believe it of me, but I wanted to assure you just the same. I'm promised to no man except you. And I've loved no man in my whole life, except yourself."

Immediately he was ashamed of his suspicion that the prepara-tions and her unusual sweetness were the prelude to the disclosure. She had known and been fretting since the day before, and hadn't liked to worry him. . . . He was moved too, by that declaration of her love, and roused by the lovely shape of her face as she knelt before him, with the hair which was such a feature of her beauty streaming down over her shoulders.

He held her face in his hands, eager to hear the words again. "You've loved only me, Nan? Not Percy or Wyatt . . . Wyatt's a fine fellow and no one could blame you. It used to be rumored in the old days . . ."

"Not Percy, and not Wyatt," she assured him gently. "Wyatt's my cousin; we played together as children, and he had a love for me once, but I never returned it. I love you, Harry, with all my heart, and you've never had a rival for it."

He caught her in his arms and kissed her, murmuring endear-ments, but with a great effort she freed herself, one eye on the empty wine cup. She could surrender now, but he was sober and she dared not.

"Come to the table," she urged him.

She served him herself; a great helping of lampreys, and spiced river trout, then a carving of mutton with a slice of game pasty in a thick golden crust. She poured his wine and he swallowed it eagerly, and sat down to eat, herself, when his plate was full, talk-ing and laughing and reaching out to him across the table. He drank a great deal, pausing between courses to refresh himself with quinces and the hard cool apples which grew in the kitchen gardens at Hampton. The golden wine pitcher was empty, and he grimaced as he put it down.

"I have another on the serving table," she assured him and brought it to him; she poured till it slopped over the edge of his goblet and then left the jug at his elbow.

His face was flushed, and he loosened the collar of his doublet, and eased the jeweled dagger belt round his waist.

He ate another helping of fish, while she sucked grapes and watched him; he laughed at her with his mouth full.

"What witchcraft do you practice on the cooks, love? I've not eaten lampreys as good as these for months."

"No witchcraft, Harry. Just a box on the ear, if it's not to your liking. And a silver piece if it is."

"They'll have a gold piece from me tonight," he promised. "Ah, Nan, what a good wife you'll make me!"

"The best in the world," she answered. "Let's drink to it, Harry. The King's goodwife! May his platter be full and his linen well stitched!"

They drank the toast, and he leaned toward her, refilling his glass and hers.

"And may his bed be warm, Nan!"

This was the moment and she knew it. His voice was thick, and his hand wandered, trying to set down the wine jug. When he did so, a red stain spread over the polished surface of the table.

She left her chair and went to him and stood in front of him without saying a word.

"You look like a bride," he mumbled, half to himself. He put both hands round her waist and noticed that she wore no corselet, without understanding why.

"I've waited, and waited, Nan . . . God's love, will the time never come . . ."

"It's come," she whispered. "My love can't bear another hour of waiting."

He raised himself slowly, unable to believe what he heard. Night and day for six long years he had wanted her and pleaded with her to surrender, and at first his mind rejected the notion that she

135

actually meant to yield. He was confused and heavy with wine and the food; his heart pounded as he drew her close to him, and pulled her up in his arms till her mouth was in reach of his own.

She caught him tightly round the neck, and kissed him first slowly, and then with fierce intensity; desire leaped in him like a sheet of flame. He heard her whisper against his lips, "No more waiting, Harry . . . Carry me, beloved . . ."

His chair fell backward as he picked her up, and for a moment he stood with her in his arms, the hem of her white dress touching the floor, and they looked into each other's eyes. Then hers closed, and her face was hidden against his neck. She felt him move with her across the room. He walked unsteadily, and the hangings which covered the entrance to her bedroom brushed against her as he pushed through them. Then the movement stopped, and she knew that he had reached the bed.

It was nearly dawn when she awoke; streaks of gray light patterned the floor through the edges of the window curtain, and the birds were roused and beginning to twitter in the trees outside. She turned her head and saw him lying beside her, one heavy arm flung outside the sheet. She moved cautiously, afraid of waking him, and lay quietly listening to the sounds of the new day. They had forgotten to draw the bed curtains and she could see the shapes of the furniture in the room, and the white dress lying crumpled and torn on the floor. She raised her arms above her head and stretched; she might have been at Hever, waking warm with happiness and Tom Wyatt by her pillow. It was the same feeling, relaxed and safe and curiously tender, so that she leaned over the sleeping King and kissed his forehead. At one point in the night he had wept like a child, and she cradled him in her arms, comforting this strange manifestation of passion which she didn't understand, until he slept, his head as heavy as a boulder on her breast. And then he woke again and turned to her with joy.

It was the end and the beginning; the end of the long cruel game she had played with him and herself, and the beginning of a new life, as if in the night she had been reborn. He was a strange man, she thought gently, sensitive and emotional, and nervous, in spite of his great physique; she saw that side of him when the wine had worn off, and he came to her after the first quick, unthinking consummation.

His expectation in her was fulfilled; the man who babbled his adoration a few hours ago could never be turned away from her now.

She lay back on the pillows, smiling, and went to sleep.

8

THE TREATY OF ALLIANCE WITH FRANCE WAS DULY SIGNED AND plans went forward for Henry's visit to the French King. In Rome, where the divorce case dragged on, prevented from coming to any conclusion by endless squabbling over points of law, the news of the treaty was received with alarm. The Emperor, busy repelling an invasion by the Grand Turk Suleiman, made it clear to Clement that he was in no position to enforce a sentence of excommunication with troops, at that time, so the Pope continued to work for a compromise.

Warham, the Archbishop of Canterbury was dead, having fought to the last to preserve the Church's liberty, and Clement knew that the ability of the English clergy to continue their resistance depended on the man who took Warham's place. He was heartened by rumors that the King intended to submit Dr. Cranmer as the candidate. Cranmer had spent some time at the Vatican and thoroughly gained Clement's confidence; his charm and loyalty to the Holy See contrasted sharply with the bullying worldiness of England's other emissaries. The Pope trusted and liked him, and after Cranmer spent some time at the imperial court, even the Emperor held him in esteem.

Clement prayed that Cranmer might be the nominee, and then in September all Europe heard that Anne Boleyn had been created Marchioness of Pembroke, granted lands and a large fortune, with the right of her sons to succeed her, regardless of their legitimacy. And all Europe jumped to the same conclusion. She had yielded and the King had given up his plan to marry her. Money and the title were the compensation.

The new Marchioness of Pembroke sat in her apartments at Greenwich Palace, listening to Margaret Wyatt playing a gay melody on her lute; she sat in a high-backed chair, tapping her foot and humming. She was dressed in a gown of soft gray velvet, with a silver embroidered petticoat, and white ermine tails edged her wide outer sleeves; the inner sleeve came to a point over her wrist and matched the shining petticoat.

The pale colors didn't suit her as well as her favorite scarlet or green or the dazzling white which enhanced her dark coloring, but they suited the huge sapphires she wore around her neck, matched by the stones glowing in the frame of her headdress. They were Catherine's jewels; part of her dowry from Aragon. Henry had sent for them and given them to Anne. The casket stood in her room, and there were sets of emeralds, huge and cold, like drops of living green, and the bloody warmth of rubies, made into necklaces too heavy for Anne to wear without alteration; the rings were too big and had to be adjusted, and there was a caul of pearls and diamonds that the King made her put aside for her wedding day. She often opened the casket lid and took the fabulous pieces out and looked at them, but the pearls she had especially asked for had been kept back by the Queen. They had belonged to the great Isabella of Castile, and she refused to part with them, even for Henry.

He had asked her what she wanted the day after that supper, bursting into her room while she was dressing to go down and eat the midday meal in the great hall. He sent her women out of the room and caught her up in his arms, his eager mouth closing her own, until he set her down and laughed with pure exuberance, telling her that she had made him the happiest man in Christendom and he wanted to give her something as a token of his love. The offer took her by surprise; later, she told him, feeling his urgency rising again with the contact between them; later she

138

would think of something. She never went to the great hall that afternoon; she lay in the King's arms in the privacy of her bed.

When they dined together that evening, she asked him for a rank in her own right which would protect her from the snubs of women like her Aunt Norfolk. He agreed immediately; when she requested a grant of lands and the right of her children to succeed her irrespective of legitimacy, he leaned across and held her hand in both of his, asking her tenderly why she wanted such safeguards. . . . Didn't she know his resolve to marry her was greater than it had ever been? Just the same, she should have them, in fact, anything she wished. His adored and beloved, he called her.

When she asked for some of Catherine's jewels he paused for a second, and his expression clouded; then it cleared, so quickly that she could never be sure afterward that she hadn't imagined it, and he nodded. She should have them. They were the Queen of England's jewels, and she was going to be Queen.

Her father was told nothing; they scarcely spoke after that bitter quarrel, but Anne saw him watching the King dangling after her, peevish if she were absent from him even for an hour, and knew that he was puzzled.

The announcement of the title was her answer to him, and she appeared at court wearing Catherine's jewels on the same day.

Nearly a month had passed since that night, when she walked through the gallery at Hampton with her hand on Henry's arm, and heard the whispers rising to an excited buzz behind them. He looked down at her and smiled encouragement, and patted her fingers, because he felt them clenched on his sleeve.

"We've given them something to mull over, sweet," he murmured. "They'll have more yet. Tonight they greet My Lady Pembroke but they'll bow to her Grace of England before long."

Before the week was out they were saying he had decided not to marry her; in the chorus of envy and slander that followed her there was a note of satisfaction. She might be a Marchioness with unprecedented rights and wealth, but she was only the King's mistress, when she had expected to be Queen. Anne listened and said nothing, marking her enemies down for the future. She would be Queen of England. For the first time in her life she was certain of that, because she believed fervently that their liaison would result in pregnancy. Whatever the outcome, she was secure, if her father's prophecy and the hopes of all who hated her were realized and Henry tired of her—she smiled at the thought—and she bore no child in time, she wouldn't be dismissed into obscurity like her sister Mary, with nothing but old scandal and her memories to remind her of Henry's love . . .

That same month her hopes had risen; surely she was fuller, she thought, standing sideways before her mirror. And appetite was said to be a sign. . . . But that same day the hope was disappointed, and she sent the unsuspecting King to hunt without her, in spite of his pleading. Wyatt's sister kept her company, so did Meg Shelton, whom she liked, and an impulse of malice suggested her sister-in-law Jane Rochford. It eased the pain of foolish disappointment to see Jane sitting in the window seat, enduring the afternoon because she dared not refuse the invitation.

How that woman hated her. She laid down her sewing and began to talk of the coming visit to France with Henry, and said clearly that her brother George must be among the company; she couldn't bear to leave him languishing in England, with nothing to amuse him. . . .

Norfolk was making the arrangements, and she decided suddenly to see him and discuss them. A page was sent with her message. The Marchioness of Pembroke requested His Grace of Norfolk to attend on her immediately.

She began sewing again, smiling at some verses Shelton and Margaret were composing, while two other ladies came into the room, and joined the gathering. They sat and stood round her chair, exactly as she and others used to do in the days they attended on Catherine. She was in Catherine's place, wearing her jewels, taking her seat at table in public, going to France with Henry. At that point she asked Meg Shelton the time. It was nearly four o'clock.

Norfolk had kept her waiting half an hour.

When her page announced him he strode across the floor, clattering in riding boots and spurs, his eyes screwed up with anger, ready to do battle.

He was furious at the summons. Just returned from hawking, he was tired and hungry when Anne's messenger came. He roared at the boy to wait, while he was served with food and ale, fuming at the impertinence.

So he was requested to attend her immediately . . . he dawdled at the table, wondering if he dared ignore her and not go. Then he remembered savagely that his own wife had been sent from court not long before because that bitch complained of her to the King, and he had had to beg for her return.

"Madame!"

She raised her head and considered him coldly.

"My good uncle, you're late."

"I had other business to attend to," he answered shortly. "What is *your* business?"

He was gratified to see her needle shoot viciously into the linen square and stay there, embedded like a tiny dagger.

"My business," she said deliberately, "is the King's; you'll come to realize that in time. I want to discuss our journey to France. His Grace has gone hunting, and I want something settled for him on his return. Here is a list of the ladies I wish to accompany me on the journey; orders to prepare themselves should be sent out as soon as possible."

Norfolk said nothing, but he had begun to smile vindicatively.

One of the women moved forward and handed him a paper; he looked up and saw that it was another niece of his; she had been one of Catherine's maids of honor, and now that the Queen had left the court, the girl spent most of her time at home in Wiltshire. She had come to Greenwich at the request of her brother, Sir Edward Seymour, who was a great favorite of the King's. But her visits were always short.

"Thank you, Jane."

He put the list in his doublet without looking at it. Edward Seymour's sister retired into the background. She was small and she moved very quietly. Norfolk glanced round at the others; Margaret

141

Wyatt was there, so was Meg Shelton. And Jane Rochford. He saw her narrow face watching Anne, and the expression of tight loathing surprised him. Anne had been tormenting her, no doubt; they'd always hated each other, and Rochford made no secret of his indifference to his wife. She would be pleased to hear what he was going to say.

"While we're on the subject of your accompanying the King to France," he remarked, "I may as well tell you of some difficulties which have arisen. His Grace was anxious for King Francis to present you to his Queen."

He paused, and Anne looked up.

"Well? What of it?"

"The Council received an answer from the French Ambassador this morning," Norfolk continued smoothly. "The Queen of France is indisposed, and cannot make the journey."

Francis was immoral and unscrupulous enough to connive at anything for his own advantage, but he refused to insult his wife by forcing her to meet Henry's mistress. That was the reason behind the excuse, and Norfolk knew that Anne knew it. The color crept slowly up into her face. He stood in front of her, one hand jauntily on his dagger belt, and smiled.

"I'm sorry to hear it," she said stiffly.

"I suggested to M. De La Pommeraye that the King's sister, Queen Marguerite of Navarre, might meet you instead," he continued. "But it seems King Francis had already proposed it to the lady and she is too occupied to join him."

Anne flung the embroidery aside and stood up. She swung on the women standing listening. "Get out; this isn't for your ears!"

"Don't fret, sister," the voice of Jane Rochford said as she passed her. "Someone will be found to meet you . . ."

When they were alone Anne advanced a step toward him, her hands clenched into fists, blazing with anger so that she could hardly speak.

"How could you," she choked, "how could you say that and humiliate me in front of them! . . . Did you hear that whey-faced bitch? 'Someone will be found to meet you'! So the Queen of

France won't meet me, and neither will Marguerite of Navarre! Wait till the King hears this!"

"De La Pommeraye made an alternative suggestion," Norfolk interrupted and she quietened immediately.

"The Duchesse de Vendome is willing to come."

"Vendome! Vendome? Do you know what you're saying?" she cried out. "He forgets, and so do you, my Lord, that I *lived* in France for eight years. I know the Duchesse de Vendome; she's the worst whore in France! Are they trying to insult me? Or was this your idea?" she demanded suddenly.

He was no longer mocking her; he was squinting at her and his face was cruel with hatred.

"I don't have to insult you," he retorted. "The suggestion came from France. Send a whore to greet a whore! That's what they think of you and that's what you are! You're the King's whore, whether or not he makes you twenty Marchionesses and decks you out in his wife's jewels!"

"I'll tell him what you say," she panted.

"Wag your tongue till it falls out!" he snarled at her. "He's got what he wants now; see how much heed he'll pay to you in a month or two! Ah, by God, if I'd known how you'd set yourself up, you ill-born slut, I'd never have helped you on in the beginning!"

"You helped yourself," she shouted. "You thought to use me to get rid of Wolsey, and you did! And you thought you'd have a cringing woman ready to whisper your words into the King's ear, ready to put her hands under your feet and push you higher in the Council and the Kingdom! That's what you wanted from me, that's why you urged the King to marry me. Your niece as Queen of England! Wasn't that the truth, Uncle? You wanted the power and the honors for yourself; you've begrudged every favor Henry's shown to my family. Oh, you've made a potboy out of my father, crooking your finger to see him come running, but you'll never master me! I'm where I am through my own efforts, and by God's blood and death I'll keep what I've won without any of you!"

"You'll have to, from now on," he warned her. "I've done with you and your ambitions. I'll do the King's will, don't hope otherwise, but as for you, Madame . . . Look to yourself!"

"I will," she shouted after him as he strode to the door.

"And look to the King, too," he jeered over his shoulder. "He's gone hunting near his daughter Mary's house!"

"Your Grace! Your Grace, they're coming. You can hear the sound of the horns down the valley!"

The speaker had put her head round the door; she was flushed and breathless after running from the parapet walk on the top of the house all the way down the staircase to the landing and the Princess Mary's rooms.

"Come in, Agnes."

The voice was quite deep, contrasting with the small straight figure of the heiress to the throne of England, who stood in the middle of the room. She wore a dark green velvet dress and a three-cornered headdress bordered with small emeralds; her hair was drawn back from a middle parting, and it was exactly the same red as her father's; the pale pointed face was lightly freckled, but the fine gray eyes were her inheritance from Catherine. She had the King's small features and she had shown the promise of beauty long before she was sixteen. It was a promise that illness and anxiety were delaying, for now she was too thin and too pale, and there were circles under her eyes from sleeplessness and fits of bitter crying. But forlorn and threatened with disinheritance though she was, banished from her father and now separated from her mother, she had a firm dignity of her own.

"How far down the valley is the hunt?" she asked. Her woman Agnes curtsied quickly and then closed the door behind her.

"About a mile, Your Grace."

"Then they shouldn't be long," Mary Tudor said. "I know how hard my father rides."

She had been too young to hunt with him, and when she was old enough her mother's lady in waiting had claimed that honor. But she could remember watching the hunt set out from the steps of Hunsdon and Richmond, and seeing her father's horse bound away under his spur, far ahead of the others. As a child she wor-

144

shiped him. He was so tall and splendid, and he used to take her on his knee and feed her sweetmeats till she was sick, and laugh and kiss her, scratching her skin with the rough golden beard round his chin. Those were her early memories, and her mother was always in them, smiling in the background at her husband and her daughter, sometimes taking the child away from him herself, and chiding him for spoiling her.

Later she remembered the court ceremonies; Mass on Easter morning, when she walked in procession to the chapel, with a long train born by a lady in waiting, and her own retinue; banquets given in honor of some foreign dignitary, where she came forward with the King, and they bent to kiss her little hand; and the jousts held in the tiltyard at Greenwich, where she watched the contestants from a tower, and had nightmares afterward because she dreamed something had happened to her father.

There were music lessons, with Henry listening while she played the lute or sat at the virginals, painfully trying to please him, because he was so accomplished himself. But she had no real talent; she played woodenly, however hard she studied, and as she grew older, her voice developed its gruff deep tone, and that spoiled any prospect of singing. But he loved her; he was affectionate.

"Shall I go back and keep watch, Your Grace?"

"No, Agnes, it's too cold now to stand about on the parapet walk. Fetch me a cloak and I'll go up in a few moments."

It was more than a year since she had seen her father; it seemed like a lifetime. Chapuiys the Spanish Ambassador had sent word that the concubine—his only name for Anne—had become the King's mistress at last, and that therefore her influence was sure to wane in time. Let the Queen and the Princess send the King fair words and wait, and above all, let him see Mary as he passed her house that day, and see her smiling and submissive. He might be softened enough by the sight to stop and let her come to his stirrup and speak to him. That was Mary's hope. For that reason she had dressed in his favorite Tudor green and waited ready, more than two hours before he was expected. It was also the hope of her household, who loved

145

the rejected child. Maybe the King would see his daughter waving from her lonely place of exile and be moved to speak to her. But he might not. Mary was near tears again, and her head ached intolerably as it always did in times of stress.

Her temperament was Henry's, without his vein of odd, secretive deceit; her temper blazed and her tears flowed, and in the old days she clapped her hands and laughed as heartily as a boy. But her stubborn, uncompromising honesty was wholly Catherine's legacy.

She spent hours praying in the chapel, and Catherine's letters urged her to trust in God and the power of his Sacraments; she heard Mass every morning of her life, and as her material troubles increased she clung more and more to the consolation of her religion. And to the advice of the Spanish Ambassador Chapuiys, whom she trusted blindly because her mother did, and through him the distant figure of the Emperor. Charles had their interests at heart; he was fighting their cause at Rome, and so far he had prevailed, for the Pope had not granted the iniquitous divorce and never would. Let the Princess Mary follow Chapuiys' advice, and maintain her rights to the English throne.

The high winding note of a huntsman's horn came through the open window, and the pain pulsed in her head. They were only a few minutes away. Agnes was at the door again, holding a long velvet cloak; she drew it round her and fastened the clasp with shaking fingers. Then she ran up the stairs and out onto the parapet walk on the roof. There was a cold wind blowing and it whipped some color into her pale cheeks. The height made her suddenly sick as she bent over the low wall to look down; the road ran winding past the house, and there were riders straggled across it, raising clouds of yellow dust. The horn sounded again.

"Madame, Madame," one of her ladies cried, "if they sight the stag now, they'll gallop past without seeing us!"

"With God's Grace, they won't," Mary answered shakily. "See, the horses are slowing."

The house was low-built; if the King passed at an even pace he would be sure to see the group of women and look up.

146

She stared, shielding her eyes in the effort to distinguish him from the others, but her headache and short-sightedness made it impossible.

"Can you see my father?" she implored. "He should be in the forefront."

"He is; there, I see him!"

"Quick, take off your cap. There'll be no mistake if he sees that red head!"

Mary wrenched it off, bringing some of her hair down round her shoulder where the wind caught it, and blew it wildly round her head like a banner.

It was not the King who saw them first, but Henry Norreys. He urged his horse alongside Henry's and pointed.

"Your Grace . . . Look, up on the roof there. It's the Princess and her household."

The King's horse jumped under a violent tightening of the rein. He followed Norreys' finger and saw the women standing on the roof of the manor they were approaching.

"I'd no idea it was their park we were crossing," he said in a flat voice. "God's body, of course, it's Mary's house. And there is Mary," he added.

His expression and tone gave nothing away; only his gloved hands betrayed him, dragging at the·rein till his horse curvetted in protest, and Norreys did not notice them.

"Shall I give the order to gallop, Sire?" he offered.

The King looked at him.

"You'll pass the word to slow down to a walk. And every man doffs his cap." He touched his spurs to the horse and pushed ahead of them all.

Mary stood by herself now, trying to keep the red strands of hair from blowing across her face. Twelve months, he thought, his head turned upward; his horse had slowed to a walk. He had thought of her differently since then, angrily, because she had defied him and taken her mother's part. He had forgotten that she was so slight; she looked even younger in that plain green cloak, straining to see him; he knew how bad her sight was, and suddenly drew his horse nearer the house.

147

The cavalcade moved forward slowly, the harness jingling in the silence, and the King came directly below his daughter and stopped.

His face was a blur to her, and her heart beat so hard she felt faint; she didn't know if he were angry or if he even recognized her. Agnes, Agnes, she thought wildly . . . if only I dare call her . . . she could tell me how he looked. . . . The company had stopped with him but she could distinguish no details, only colors; the courtiers in brilliant doublets over their buff breeches and high boots, the huntsmen dressed in the same Tudor green she wore herself. And the King, her father.

He was broader, surely, than a year ago, heavier and redder in the face; he straddled his powerful horse like a giant. Her lips moved, and her hands clung to the parapet, so that the cloak blew open.

Merciful Mother of God, let him make a sign, one sign that he's seen me and isn't angry . . . Mother of God, let me have one word with him!

He raised himself in his stirrups, and the next moment he had lifted the feathered cap from his head in a gesture of greeting. All his gentlemen followed suit. She curtsied to him, and smiled, and knew that below her he smiled back.

Mary. Memories were flooding back in those few seconds as he saluted her. Memories of the little girl who lived when all the rest had died, the child who had caught him round the neck and kissed him, and followed him through the court with her hand in his; Mary, who had made him proud of her in spite of the fact that she wasn't the son he wanted. Her letters, still written in a blunt style in spite of all her tutors' efforts, begging him to see her and to take her mother back . . .

If he sent for her, as he wanted to do with all his heart at that moment, it would only come to that in the end. And he had Anne now; he couldn't have Anne and his daughter as well. He loved Anne, and if he was sinning with her, then he had sinned with Mary's mother, for she had never been his wife. . . . He couldn't send for Mary and turn time back six long years because of Anne, and the plan to proclaim Mary a bastard to make room for the son he knew that Anne would bear him. . .

He covered his head and waved to her. Then his spurs jabbed at his horse's flanks, and the whole cavalcade surged forward. Within moments they were shrouded in dust, and then visible as they turned off across the green parkland, thinned out as the King set his furious pace. On the parapet, Mary Tudor watched them ride away, hearing the horns sound their high excited note that meant the stag was sighted.

It was October and Dover Castle was bitterly cold; a strong wind blew in from the Straits, whipping the seas into a low swell that rocked the *Great Harry* at anchor in the harbor and tore spitefully at the bright pennants and the royal standard flying from her masts, and the same wind wailed round the castle, filling the stone rooms with draughts in spite of fires and hangings.

Anne's room was high, with a view out to sea, but the small windows were latched and the curtains drawn, shutting out the sight of the gray harbor where the big galleon rode surrounded by smaller craft.

She had gone aboard with the King when they arrived, to inspect the quarters, and found everything as luxurious as sea travel could allow. The preparations excited her in spite of herself, and took the edge off her disappointment over the whole trip; but the hostile stares and murmurs of the sailors and the common people when they saw her sharpened it again. She had walked beside Henry wrapped in a thick cloak lined with sables, looking politely at everything he pointed out, and waiting while he talked to his seamen and forgot about her for a few moments, wishing bitterly that she had never agreed to accompany him.

The plans had been altered; the English ladies selected to attend her had been told their services were not needed; apart from her servants and the wives of some of the attendant nobles, she was traveling alone. No member of King Francis' women-folk had consented to meet the Marchioness of Pembroke, so there would be no brilliant arrival in France as the future Queen of England. She was going with Henry because he insisted on her company, and she was to stay behind in Calais while he went to meet his ally on French soil.

It was the afternoon before they sailed, and she sat alone in her room, embroidering. The room was lit by torches grappled to the walls, and two iron holders stood at either side of the fireplace, the thick candles impaled on a spike.

She paused, listening to the sound of footsteps on the stone-paved passage outside, and laid down her sewing as they stopped by her door.

"George! Oh, George . . ."

They met halfway across the room, and he hugged her; it was the first time they had met alone for weeks. Both were smiling, and he looked at her and shook his head admiringly.

"Sister, how are you? . . . God, I'm happy to see you alone for once!"

"We won't have a chance over there," she agreed. "And today's the first time he's left me to myself for more than a few minutes . . . Come, sit down with me and talk."

He pulled up a stool and she sat in her chair, leaning toward him with her hands clasped round her knees.

"Where's His Grace?" her brother asked.

"Seeing to some State papers brought from London," she explained, "so I left him and came here and sent for you. Have some posset, George; there's some on the table there, steaming hot. And give me some; I'm cold to my bones in spite of the fire."

"It's a vile day," he agreed, passing her a cup with the hot mixture of ale and wine and spices in it; she sipped, warming her fingers on the silver goblet, and smiled at him. Dear George; he looked so well in his rich doublet . . . no wonder Margaret Wyatt was said to be in love with him. Anne hoped she was. She hoped sincerely that George found with her gentle Meg the happiness he had missed with his wife, Jane. He deserved to be happy, she thought suddenly. Of all the people she had ever met, he was the best, though he was her brother. He was the kindest in his way, and he had courage; he was generous and endearing even in his faults. He loved bright clothes, and squandered a fortune on them, enjoyed drink and gay talk and pretty women, and he was always Anne's most appreciative audience. And he loved her. He loved her more than the favors she could give him, and that was something rare indeed.

"I've been down to see the *Great Harry* today," he said. "She's a splendid ship, Nan, and your quarters are royal!"

"The quarters are the only thing about this trip that is!" She retorted. "I wish to God I wasn't going."

"Don't fret over it," he comforted. "Go, and enjoy it, Nan; and be sensible, think how much your enemies would like to see you leave the King to his own devices for a while!"

She stared at him then.

"Why is it," she said slowly, "that no one trusts him—not even you? Why would you worry if he went to France without me, George?"

"I wouldn't," he contradicted quickly. "I just said it was wiser to go with him . . . there's no harm in that."

"You don't trust him," she said. "Nobody trusts him to be true to me. Except me. Why, George? What do you see in him that's hidden from me?"

"I see nothing, Nan." He frowned. "Nothing I could explain. I see a man deeply in love with you, but you're my sister, and I keep more of a watch than I would otherwise. I can't help hearing what's being said—it's said loud enough by some of them, so that I *shall* hear—that now you're his mistress he'll tire of you, as he does of everyone, and he's already given up his plan to marry you. It isn't pleasant, Nan," he pleaded. "I hate saying things like this to you, but I know men, and there are men like that. Men who only want what they can't have. I don't believe the King's one of them, but—"

"But it'll go hard with me if he is," she finished for him. "I know George; you're afraid because I've got so many enemies. Well, now I'll tell you of another type of man. And that's the one who tires of something if he waits for it too long. Our dear father pointed that out to me, as I told you. And he was right, though I'll never forgive him. That was my danger, George, and I saw it before it was too late for I was near losing him, and now—" she waved one hand, "I'm hardly allowed to move without him."

That was true and he knew it; it was all true. Henry kissed her in public, praised her to anyone he spoke to, and insisted on having her with him every moment.

"I begged him not to take me to France," Anne continued. "When I heard not one of these damned Frenchwomen would stir to meet me, I refused to set foot there. But he said if I didn't, he would cancel the visit. You don't know what it was like, George; he raved like a madman, and said he couldn't pass a night without me . . ."

Her emphasis on the King's sexual passion repelled and worried him at the same time. He had seen and heard Henry gratifying himself in the old days, and he knew the superficiality as well as the grossness of his feelings, the complete indifference to the means of that gratification, once the end was achieved. He looked away from Anne, because the images forming in his mind made him angry and for some reason more afraid than ever.

He caught hold of her hands and held them, anxiously searching her face.

"Nan, does he care for you apart from that . . . apart from bed, does he love you? If you were sick, Nan, and couldn't be used, would he still want you with him in France?"

She drew her hands away and stood up.

"It's not only what you think," she said quickly. "He's ardent enough, God knows, but there's more to his love for me than that . . ." She knew what her brother was thinking; he saw the King as a great sensual brute, rather as she had seen him before that night at Hampton. He was older than when George first came to court, she thought, and a lot had happened . . . In those days he may have been what George was suggesting but he wasn't now. He was gross, yes; in amorous preliminaries his taste was unspeakably crude, she had learned that long ago. But only since they were lovers had she discovered that his appetite was preyed upon by nerves.

Sometimes he drank heavily and then tumbled into her bed

and fell fast asleep with his head on her breast, and never touched her till the morning. She had had one violent quarrel with him when she discovered that he had stopped the hunt and made his gentlemen acknowledge Mary—Norreys had told her that as soon as they returned—but that night when they were reconciled, he only lay in her bed and talked till dawn. . . .

She wondered what George would say if she told him that. She nearly mentioned it, standing there, seeing her brother frowning up at her and biting his lip in anxiety. She nearly told him that Henry was far less the rapacious lover than he supposed, but she didn't.

"Listen to me, brother. I'm not offended by the things you say. I know the gossip—voices get louder when I pass too—and I can promise you I've thought of everything. I know the King loves me. I know too that he's more intent on marriage than he's ever been. Why else would he bother to visit Francis? Francis is going to be persuaded to intercede with the Pope, to meet him and plead for us in person. That's why we're going.

"Oh, I'm not the fool everyone thinks me! I've heard tales of Henry's fickleness from the time I came to court, God knows how many years ago. I insured against that by asking for the marquisate and a good grant of money. I told you, George, I'm not a fool. And if they're all right, including you, and he loses all his fancy for me, gets tired of my company and bored in my bed . . . if he even thinks of keeping me as the Pembroke and not bothering about the marriage, he'll never risk a son being born to me a bastard! That's what I gambled on, and I know whatever happens I shall win. And I want you to know it too, and not go worrying for me when there's no need."

He sprang up at once. "Why, Nan, you're not . . ."

She shook her head. "No, devil take it, I'm not. Not yet. But I shall be, George, and I'll bear a King of England yet."

He came and put both hands on her shoulders and they stood quietly for a moment as they used to do when they were children and one or other had annoyed their father.

"I don't care what you bear, Nan, so long as you're safe."

"The child will make me safe, old faint-heart; and in any event the King won't swallow me alive one night! You attend to Mistress Wyatt, and stop fretting about me."

He laughed, but he colored.

"How have you found that out? Did Meg tell you?"

"Meg didn't have to tell me," she smiled. "You must think we're all blind not to notice the two of you mooning at each other like sick calves and slipping out of sight when you think no one sees you. I've seen Madame Meg come in after a good tumbling, as pink-faced as you are this moment!"

"Don't tease me, Nan," he protested. "And don't torment Meg; she's sweet-natured and I'm fond of her."

"I know the Wyatts," she reminded him gently. "Sister and brother are much alike, George. God in Heaven, it might be a hundred years ago!"

"It might," he agreed. "I used to see *you*, once upon a time, letting Thomas out of your room at Hever. But you weren't pink-faced, you were much too brazen! Do you ever think of him, Nan?"

"No," she admitted. "I used to, sometimes, while the months dragged on. I used to think of the happy times we had together."

She moved away from him, back to the fire, and stood looking down into the flames.

"Do you know George, there were nights when I was tempted, knowing he was in the palace and the King was safe in his own rooms . . . He would have come, too. But I didn't. I remember what you said at Hever all those years ago. 'You can't have Tom anyway, whether you go to court or not.' And you were right. That dog Suffolk tried to ruin me by bringing up Tom and the past before the King ever put his hand on me. Christ knows what would have happened if he'd been able to prove I'd done anything *afterward* . . ."

She shrugged and turned to him again.

"It was all long ago, dear brother, and it's sweet to remember it; I think Tom remembers sometimes too, though there's no love left for me now."

"He can't forgive you for going to the King," George said.

"How like a man . . . *he* couldn't marry me; if I'd stayed with him and defied Henry I'd have only brought him ruin. But I don't suppose he believes even that now. I tried to tell him once, when I'd been at court for a year and he came on me when there was no one near and started asking me to be his mistress again. And I refused. I had to. He sent me a copy of a verse he wrote me. It was beautiful, George, but I had to burn it."

"I think I know it," her brother said slowly. "I always thought it was meant for you:

> "Forget not then thine own approved,
> The which so long hath thee so loved,
> Whose steadfast faith yet never moved—
> Forget not this!"

"That was the last verse of it," she answered. "But he wrote another, George, after he played that foolhardy match at bowls with the King, and dandled my locket chain in front of his nose . . . S'death, the lies I had to tell to explain that! It was long, and I can't remember it all:

> "Who's list her hunt, I put him out of doubt,
> As well as I may spend his time in vain!
> And graven with diamonds in letters plain
> There is written her fair neck round about
> 'Noli me tangere; for Caesar's I am
> And wild for to hold, though I seem tame.' "

"Even he realized it was impossible then!"

"As long as you don't regret him, Nan."

She looked at her brother steadily.

"I regret nothing; in my heart's core I regretted Henry Percy for a good many years, and look what he's become. . . . No, George. Tom said it best, as usual. Caesar's I am. And that's the end."

"It's getting late," he said. "I'd better go and see to my servants, Nan, if I'm going to sail with you tomorrow."

"Go, and God bless you," she said gently. "And pray for

155

a good crossing. Besides, His Grace may abandon me if I puke," she mocked.

"If he does, just send for me, Nan. Whatever happens, you'll have me beside you."

He left her, and she stood looking after him; he had laughed as he made the promise, but she was not deceived. If anything threatened her, it would be kept.

Henry had spent three days as the guest of the King of France at Boulogne. It was an extremely friendly meeting, marked by affectionate embracing and offers of precedence on the part of both monarchs, and the French reception was so lavish that Henry forgot his resentment at having been parted from Anne. He had left her at Calais and ridden out with a large and splendid company to meet Francis. At the end of three days, it was arranged that two French Cardinals should go to Clement at Bologna, where he was preparing for another meeting with the Emperor, and persuade him to procrastinate till he met the King of France. The Pope was to be assured that reconciliation was still possible, and, to draw him away from Charles, negotiations were to be opened for a marriage with his niece Catherine de Médicis and the French King's son.

Henry listened to Francis with open delight. He went out of his way to be gracious to the French nobles, even outraging his careful instincts by playing cards and dice with the most influential for large sums of money, which he contrived to lose. The charm which had attracted so many to him in his youth had lost none of its potency, and he exerted it to the utmost. He was good-humored and splendidly gracious, till his own entourage almost forgot the tyrant he had shown himself at home.

At the end of the three days the French King and his nobles traveled to Calais, to be Henry's guests, and word was sent ahead to Anne to prepare accordingly.

Calais Castle was a huge, cold, forbidding place, the fortress foothold of England on French soil, all that was left of the great conquests of Henry V. Anne made a tour of the rooms, ransacked the stores for beds and tapestries and furnishings and fitted out a suite for the King of France in the nearby Staple Hall. She had elegant taste, and she fought her boredom and uncertainty of the last few days by organizing everything to please Henry.

The great hall of the castle was a high, stone medieval room, bitterly cold and bare. She had the richest tapestries hung from ceiling to floor and the King's personal plate was augmented by the plate of the port authorities, so that the sideboards and tables shone with gold and silver.

Huge fires were lit to warm it, and the musicians practiced in the gallery above, their score supervised by Anne herself.

When Francis came he should find that the English had prepared as fine a lodging and entertainment for him as he had given Henry. Also he should find the Marchioness of Pembroke waiting as mistress of Calais in her King's absence.

The cavalcade arrived on Friday, and she waited in her own apartments, having watched them come into the castle from her window, and recognized the tall thin figure in splendid costume as the King of France. She remembered him well, as he dismounted; he had hardly changed in the years since she had lived at his court in France as plain, unimportant Mistress Anne Boleyn, and brought attention to herself by her wit and her flair for dress.

Late that night Henry came to her, looking flushed and exuberant. He stood in the doorway for a moment and then crossed the floor in a few strides and caught her up in his arms.

"Sweetheart! Oh, God's blood, how I've missed you, sweet!" The door was kicked shut behind him, and he wrenched her bed curtains aside and fell with her onto the bed, his weight driving the breath out of her body. Afterward they talked, and she got up to pour him some sweet wine because he was thirsty.

"It's been more successful than we could have hoped," he told her, propped up on the pillows with the wine cup to his mouth.

"Francis has promised to influence the Pope in our favor by every means he can, and he's consumed with eagerness to meet you again, love. He told me he well remembered you, the most bewitching Englishwoman in my sister's train, he called you."

"I was a child when I accompanied your sister here," she reminded him. "He's thinking of me at a later date."

She wondered how well Francis remembered her; whether he remembered all the young men who had tried to seduce the *Belle Brunette*, as they called her, and of the occasion when his own eyes had lighted on her, and a casual, lascivious hand had been stretched out, and skillfully avoided. Even then he was a notorious libertine, but without malice, and had never held that refusal against her. He didn't have to; there were a hundred women waiting to take her place.

She climbed back onto the bed, drawing the fur coverlet around her for warmth.

Henry explained the plan to influence Clement before Francis met him, while she listened.

"Harry, don't think me stupid, but why is he taking all this trouble on our behalf? Surely he doesn't care that much for friendship that he's willing to negotiate a marriage for his son and travel all that way to talk the Pope into granting a divorce?"

"You're not stupid, Nan." He grinned, "Only unwise in the way of politics. Friend Francis wouldn't care if I were chewed alive by the Devil, nor you either! But he cares very much for the Emperor's power. He's fought Charles and isn't likely to forget that little lesson. He doesn't want Charles to be supreme in Europe and one way of stopping him is to diminish his influence with Clement. There's a saying which I don't believe, but Francis does. Who holds the key of Rome opens the door of the world. . . . If he can divide Clement from the Emperor, and unite the Medicis by intermarriage with France, then he'll take all the pains he can to do it. And achieve our object in the process."

"How wise you are," she said wearily. "I knew there must be a trick somewhere, but I couldn't see it. He sent me a jewel by the Provost of Paris, did you know that?"

"He showed it to me," Henry said. "A fine ruby, cut like a drop. It'll look well on you, sweetheart."

"Was he pleased with his apartments?"

"Delighted; and so was I. God knows how you've transformed

the place, it's a joy to the eye. You're a clever woman, my love, and I'm proud of you indeed."

She smiled and flushed suddenly at the praise; and in response she bent and kissed him on the cheek.

"Now that you'll let me draw breath, I'll tell you how I missed you, Harry."

He patted her arm. "Did you, Nan? I hoped so." He yawned and stretched his thick arms above his head.

"Jesu, I'm tired. And it's late. Sleep well, beloved."

She sat up, staring as he threw back the covers and began searching for his clothes on the floor.

"Sleep well . . . where are you going?"

"To my own apartments," he said over his shoulder. Seeing her expression, he explained quickly, pulling his breeches into place, "It's not fitting for me to stay here openly while my brother of France is my guest. And it does you no honor, sweetheart. I must wake in my own bed tomorrow morning and breakfast in public as he does. Good night, my Nan. I'll send you word tomorrow."

On Sunday night the two Kings supped in the great hall in the presence of a crowd of French and English notables. The King of France sat on the dais at the right hand of the King of England. Francis was as tall as Henry, but lithely built, and his dark handsome face was lean, with a short black beard. He had a shrewd, saturnine face, the face of a sensualist, with the sharp eyes of a diplomat and a narrow cynical mouth. He was in a gay, bantering humor, and kept asking when he was going to see the Lady Pembroke and refresh his pleasant memories of her.

All in good time, Henry responded, and clapped him on the back. The musicians played above the noise of conversation and the clatter of plates as the guests ate and drank their way through twenty courses, and the roof of the hall filled with a blue haze of smoke from the torches and the great banked fires.

Eventually the tables were cleared and both Kings rose to move down into the body of the great hall.

"An excellent feast, my brother," Francis complimented Henry as they left the dais. "I can't praise your hospitality enough."

"It lacks only one thing," the King answered gaily, "and that lack is already made good!"

The minstrels had begun to play the graceful openings of a saraband and from behind the immense carved screen at the far end, a company of ladies wearing masks approached the two sovereigns. All were magnificently dressed, and Francis searched them all, trying to penetrate behind the silk visors and headdresses and distinguish the Marchioness of Pembroke, for he knew she was among them. It was difficult, until he slyly followed Henry's gaze, and picked out a slim figure in blazing red satin, with a petticoat of cloth of gold and a gold mask and headdress. She moved with the elegance of a swan gliding over water; she had always had that gift, he remembered, and she held her left hand close to the folds of her vivid skirt, so that it was partly hidden.

"I claim the fairest lady for myself," he said quickly to Henry. "The guest's privilege, Sire!"

She curtsied low when he approached her and answered him in perfect French. Holding the tips of her fingers, he began the complicated figures of the dance. Henry and the other gentlemen had also chosen partners, and they turned and swayed to the rhythm in two lines, making a pattern of brilliant color and synchronized movement in the center of the floor.

She remembered the first time he had singled her out for that honor at a court ball at his magnificent new Château Chambord. She had been very young then, and as vain as the peacocks he kept on his lawns; glad that so many were jealous of her, and flattered by his attention in spite of her indifference to him as a man. He hadn't changed at all, she thought, watching his narrow eyes through the slits in her mask. He could never look at any woman without conveying the cold lust of a forest wolf. . . . And he knew her, by some means or other, she was convinced of that. But if he liked to play at ignorance, it might be wise to humor him.

"It's said, the King of England cannot hide his stature, and the King of France his skill, Sire," she remarked. "Both are true indeed; I'm shamed by your performance of the saraband; I've never been honored by a more brilliant partner."

"You surprise me, Madame," Francis answered. "The King of England is famous for his talent. Isn't it true that he excels?"

"His Grace excels in everything," she said coolly.

"Not least in his choice of women; I hear he's made happy by the most enchanting of all his subjects."

"It's the subject who is made happy, Sire. Don't you think she's to be envied?"

The King smiled; she was clever and he liked clever women; she deserved to have him repeat her little flatteries into King Henry's ear.

"I shall answer that, Madame, when I see you," he said gallantly. The music stopped; he bowed to her and she sank into a deep curtsy. She smiled at him, and removed her golden mask.

It was the same face that he remembered; the same fine features and magnificent black eyes, but it was thinner, showing the line of her jaw where it joined the frail neck, and she had lost the smooth, careless beauty of extreme youth and irresponsibility.

"My Lady Pembroke!"

Henry was moving toward them, watching Francis, anxious to see what impression she had made.

"Indeed, it's the King and not the subject who's truly to be envied!"

"Well spoken," Henry agreed. He raised her to her feet and kissed her on the mouth. "But I'll not lose you to my brother Francis, however well I love him!"

She smiled at Francis, and held on to Henry's hand. "With all honor to our guest, I hope you won't," she said.

It was Francis who offered her his arm, while Henry gracefully gave way, and led her to the dais. The other ladies had also unmasked, showing themselves with wives and daughters of the English suite and garrison at Calais, and soon the music began again and the King gave permission for dancing while he and Francis and Anne sat together and talked.

They talked of the marriage, and the meeting with the Pope, and Anne answered and listened, trying to keep the anxiety out of her face because she knew it made her haggard, and banished the sudden pang of rage when she suspected that the King of France was condescending when he paid her compliments. She knew Francis, better than Henry or his Ambassadors, thanks to the years spent at his court, and she knew exactly how ridiculous he thought the situation was. She was Henry's mistress, and the obstinate fool was still going to all this trouble to legalize something he could enjoy in any case. . . . Defying the Pope and driving some of his best men from his service, men like Thomas More, for instance; bullying his daughter and banishing his wife and rewriting the laws of his kingdom . . .

Francis' attitude infuriated her. All this was nobody's concern except Henry's and Henry's people's; he could have his way in England, Cromwell had showed him how, through the Act of Supremacy. The devil take the Pope, and all these foreigners who wanted to interefere to twist the situation for their own ends, at her expense and Henry's. The devil take the interminable talk, the wrangling over trifles; above all, let something put an end to the cruel suspense, and set her feet on solid ground, let her relax her ceaseless struggling and feel safe. She had a trembling impulse to burst into floods of tears and run to her own rooms.

"I think my Lady Pembroke is tired," Francis interrupted smoothly. "This talk of policy and matters of state must be wearying for her, when she's done so much for our comfort and entertainment."

"With Your Grace's permission I'll retire," she said and forced herself to smile and kiss Francis' hand. He bent down and touched her lips with his mouth, and laughing, turned to Henry.

"I've a mind to adopt that immoral English custom into my own court," he said. "But I don't think Madame my wife would permit it. Like all Spaniards, my dear brother, she's an excellent woman, but overstrict. . . . Good night Madame, and my compliments once more. As I said, it's the King who's to be envied."

9

The french visit was concluded without incident.

Back at court new rumors were circulating. It seemed the King was spending more time with his gentlemen; that he no longer spent every night in Anne's room. . . . Eyes watched them everywhere, and tongues wagged, hoping for disaster; but no one watched more closely than Thomas Cromwell. The relationship was stabilizing, that was all, and the King's orders were unchanged. To get Cranmer elected Archbishop he was ready to pay the cost of the Papal Bulls out of his own pocket. And when it was done and Clement had fallen into the trap, the Act of Supremacy was to be applied to the laity under penalty of death.

As Cromwell saw it, nothing was changed.

Anne was alone in her bedroom; she and Norreys and Meg Shelton had spent the afternoon playing cards, but the time had come for her women to dress her, and she had sent them away. She was dressed and ready for the evening meal with the King. She wore white, with a long robe of crimson velvet over her dress to keep out the January cold, and a little crimson headdress, studded with rubies. One of Catherine's immense ruby pendants was pinned to her breast. It was already dark, and the curtains were drawn, shutting out the cold moonlight and the bare trees and the black stretch of the river dappled with light.

She moved to the mirror and looked at herself; she looked tired and her cheeks were thin. Instinctively, Anne picked up the little golden pot of rouge, and then put it down. Rouge wouldn't help her now. Neither would scent, or the tight fit of her dress under the crimson robe. She knew it, and the rouge pot rolled across the edge of the chest to the floor. Nothing like that was any use. She sat down wearily and closed her eyes. There was a little time before she had to go to him, a little time to face it and think, to face everything that was happening to her all at once.

He was falling out of love with her, after only seven months.

One of the logs crackled fiercely in the grate as the fire ate into it, and she opened her eyes and met her own reflection, staring as if it were a stranger.

He was tired of her.

Now.

It was done; said aloud, admitted. They were all right; all her friends and enemies, right from the beginning when they said that he would tire of her once she gave way. And he had, though it was still difficult to believe; it made her heart heave and loaded a great weight of fear and helplessness into her breast, so that she wanted to run to him and throw herself into his arms and beg him to deny it . . .

When had it begun, she wondered, asking the woman in the mirror? When was the first night he rolled over and slept and something told her he was disappointed? . . . The night they quarreled, after he had seen his daughter Mary? . . . No, not that night. That night he never slept with her at all. . . . Was it then? Was it satiation that made him unenthusiastic some-times, becoming more casual as the time passed, until she knew the impetus was gone? . . . Was that the reason? Was that when he began to lose his love for her? Her eagerness . . . the gradual surrender of herself in mind as well as body . . . the moment when he knew for certain that she loved him, that every endearment, every caress, came from her heart. . . . Was that what killed his interest? The huntsman turning his back on the stag when the chase was over. . . .

It showed in little things; the way he looked up when she came into a room; kindly enough, and with a warm greeting, but the expectancy was gone, the eagerness which once brought him to his feet with his hands outstretched and his eyes alight; his attention, which wandered at times when they were together; his invitations to Weston and Brereton and the rest of his friends to come and spend the evening with them, when once all he had wanted was to have her to himself.

And the nights when he didn't come to her . . . twice or three times in the week since they returned from France. And the nights when he came and she realized in helpless agony that he didn't really care whether he made love to her or not.

When they came back from France, she said to herself. That's when it was; only a few short weeks ago, when all their hopes were high and she felt closer to him than ever before; that was when the light of his love for her dimmed, faintly, like a blown candle flame, while hers flared like a torch, burning away her independence and her judgment, leaving her possessive and clinging and jealous, at the mercy of herself and her enemies, as only a woman of her kind could be when she loved without security.

She was his Nan, his sweetheart, but his caress was casual and his thoughts were often absent.

Anne's hand touched her breast, and the great rubies swayed on the points of the pendant like drops of blood. Was this what Catherine felt the first time he was unfaithful? Did the same dull pain throb in her all those years ago? Had Catherine and her own sister Mary and all the other women who had slept with him seen the same signs that she saw now, and felt the same fierce anguish of despair?

They hadn't kept him; kind, dull, pious, damnable Catherine had never really had him, not as she had—that was one compensation—and she had believed in her pride that she would succeed where everyone else had failed, that the desire he placed such store on was really as compelling as he made it out. That was her mistake. She laughed wretchedly to herself and leaned forward, mocking the reflection. It was the lust of the mind, the lure of preliminaries, the itch of curiosity . . . a woman had more hope of keeping a libertine like Francis through sensuality than Henry Tudor! Then the mocking face contorted. Her own words to her brother George came back to her! "There's more to his love for me than that." There were tenderness and generosity, companionship and protectiveness; had they no value? They still remained to her; they hadn't faded like his passion.

Couldn't she control herself and be content with those? Where's your cool head, Mistress, where's the sharp sense that got you a fortune and a marquisate in time? Fool, she spat at herself, fool, fool, to fall in love with him at the end like this, and sit here making grief lines on your face. If you've lost his love you haven't lost the rest. . . . Gather your wits now, and thank the living God for the ace he's put into your hand. Get up and go to him now and play it. And even now, her hope insisted, you may get him back.

She rose quickly and looked at her body in the mirror, and pulled the loose red robe round her.

Supper was laid in the King's room where the fire was built up, filling the room with cheerfulness and heat. He sat drinking by himself, with a fur-lined doublet pulled over his open shirt, staring into the fireplace. He was tired and hungry and she was late. He was also low-spirited, and depression made him restless. He felt more like company than dining alone with Anne, and he shifted irritably because he didn't like to send her word and alter the arrangements at the last minute.

He was unused to quiet and solitude; usually there was a crowd round him and something to be done; his mind was always occupied these days with the things that used to be attended to by Wolsey, but he dismissed them and let his thoughts rove to himself and his own feelings.

He frowned; it was a mistake to sit there thinking when he should have sent for his gentlemen and avoided the introspection. He didn't want to be alone with his own restlessness and boredom and above all he didn't want to be alone with Anne that night.

There was no reason for not wanting her, he protested. She was gay enough these days and sweet-tempered . . . it would have been easier if she were difficult. He could have blamed his feelings on that, or his lack of feeling, he admitted suddenly. That was the truth. She didn't anger him as she used to in the days before they became lovers, and she didn't torture him,

166

either, so that in spite of himself he came back for more. In the old days he would have looked forward to her coming; he would have sat waiting with his eyes closed, indulging in those heated imaginings of what they would do when the meal was over, till he was quivering with impatience. Dalliance with her had been an extraordinary agony of pleasure; it promised the kind of fulfillment he had wanted all his life and always found a disappointment. Now the promise was a fact, and the part of lovemaking he liked best was robbed of its subtlety and its suspense. There was no need to stop short and protest that he wanted to go on. What began could be finished, had to be finished, and the finish had become as ephemeral with her as with all the other women he had known.

At first he had believed in the miracle; consummation was a magnificent relief in the first weeks and he had plunged into it like a man dying of thirst with his head in a well. Then it began to fail him, and the shock of that failure had driven him back to Anne for a denial of his fear. Again it failed, and he had no excuses left except the one he made to himself as he sat there in the middle days of that cold January.

He was tired of her body. He had waited and wanted her for too long, and found in the end that she was only a woman like any other. There was nothing wrong with his manhood. He was just out of love. . . . The ardor, the excitement—above all, the promise was gone; he had nothing left to look forward to; she had given it all, and after the first emotional and physical catharsis his desire was emptied. It had happened before. With Catherine his wife—but then she was old—and with Bess Blount, who gave him a bastard son, and Mary Boleyn. And all the others he had sampled over the years. All had palled on him quickly; disappointed him, even, but disappointment was the most acute of all with Anne. No woman, he thought suddenly, had ever held out such hopes and proved such a disillusion. . . .

Anne wasn't like the others, to be sent away without explanation when he wanted someone new. She wasn't just his mistress. He had turned his kingdom inside out to marry her, banished his wife, estranged his daughter, and embarked on a vast diplomatic and political campaign to secure his freedom. He couldn't abandon her, he said quickly to himself; she had done her best . . . besides, she loved him.

Admittedly, Catherine had loved him, and that had made it difficult to hurt *her*. Less difficult now because she was out of sight and still thwarting him, though it would gain her nothing. His mind was made up. He had taken his stand against the Pope, and if he sent Anne away, he would never demean himself by taking Catherine back.

He bore Mary no malice; God knew he would have loved her and had her with him, whatever Anne said, if she would only admit that she wasn't legitimate. But no girl could inherit the throne of England! The last Queen Regnant was the Norman Matilda, and the country ran with blood for twenty years. He must have a son; a strong son like himself, a son he could teach to sport and rule as well as he did. A King of England.

The woman who gave him that would never be asked for anything else. Neither beauty nor wit nor the pleasure he thought he'd found with Anne. Nothing like that mattered, he cried to himself, and covered his face. Only the son. Only the secure succession and the fine motives, and the great power he was arrogating through leveling the English Church. If lust came into it, if he abandoned Anne now for that, then he had to admit that he was base, as base as his enemies said he was, and small, with a vision restricted to his own loins. . . . No! His head came up. No! His flesh was unimportant. He hadn't been cruel to Catherine and his own child and struck down his old servant Wolsey for the sake of his flesh. God knew that, God *must* know it. . . .

"Harry."

He turned to see her standing in the doorway; he hadn't heard her come in. He forced himself to smile.

"Why, Nan; I was nearly asleep."

He got up and came to her, and kissed her automatically. He was irritated suddenly because she looked pale and he felt himself constrained to make an effort when he didn't want to.

"You look weary," she said.

"I am." He seized on the excuse and yawned. "I need sleep, sweetheart. Come and let's sup; you must be hungry."

"Supper can wait for a while," Anne said. She went to the sideboard and poured out a cup of wine for herself; then she hesitated. This was not the way to do it. This was the clumsy way of a woman who was about to lose her temper. He yawned when he saw her and said he needed sleep. . . . God in Heaven . . . the hand holding the wine jug shook, and tears of pain and anger filled her eyes. Slowly she poured out two cupfuls, and the temptation to break down and storm at him passed.

"Do you remember the night I first came to you?" she asked him.

"I do, love. What of it?" He watched her, puzzled.

"We drank a toast, then, Harry."

She came to him, holding out the cup of wine. "Take it. Do you remember the toast?"

He stood still with the cup in his hand looking at her, beginning to feel angry. He didn't want to be reminded.

"We drank to me, Harry. To the King's goodwife."

"So we did," he agreed. "I drink to you again, sweetheart, all the days of my life."

She shook her head and smiled strangely at him. This was the moment she had foreseen all those months ago when she quarreled with her father and writhed under the jibe that she was losing her hold on the King. This was the safeguard against the warnings of her friends and the hopes of her enemies. She would have given anything not to have had to use it, but in the pain of hurt pride and disillusion there was a mixture of hope. Hope that his face would soften and his arms open; that the man who was slipping further and further away from her every day, almost without noticing, would come back with his love alive again.

"Not to me this time," she said. "I give you another toast. To our son!"

169

His mouth opened and the raised cup stayed in midair. Then it struck the wall, and the contents streamed over the floor as he flung it aside and reached her in a single movement.

"Nan! Oh, Nan, my heart's life! Is it really so?"

She nodded, her face pressed against his shoulder, her hands clinging to him more tightly than she knew.

"I am with child; I suspected, but I waited to be sure. Now there's no doubt. . . ."

"God be praised," he exalted, squeezing her in his excitement. "God be praised, Nan." He kissed her vehemently and then stopped, shaking his head. "I must be careful of you now, love. No thoughtlessness." He bent and picked her up and walked to a chair with her. He sat, cradling her in his arm, and stroked her cheek.

"You're a sly minx, keeping your secrets from me, eh? My little pale Nan . . . I thought you looked pinched and not yourself lately."

"Are you pleased?" she asked him, looking into his flushed, delighted face. There was no indifference in it now; he was tender and solicitous like any husband. She moved closer into the circle of his arm and tears of relief came into her eyes.

"Pleased? I'm the happiest man in England! It'll be a boy, Nan; I know it will!"

"The son I promised you," she murmured, "with my black eyes and your red hair . . . do you remember, Harry, how we used to talk of it and long for it?"

"By God I do," he retorted happily. "Sitting like this more often than not, with you on my knee . . ."

He recalled the past with ease then, remembering only the sweetness of that long courtship and forgetting that in the final phase it was losing taste. . . . A son. God's answer to his prayers, God's answer to the unhappy self-examination he had indulged in before she came to tell him. Dear Nan. He kissed her affectionately. Boredom and disappointment faded from his mind in the overwhelming joy of Anne's news. She was pregnant; she was the proof of his vigor; her son would be the proof of his manhood. But she was pale, and he frowned, remembering that she was narrow. She must be careful. Nothing must happened to endanger the child. But nothing would happen. God had taken Catherine's children only because they were born out of deadly sin.

This child would live, he said to himself, holding Anne on his knees with both arms round her. It would live and it would be a boy.

On March thirtieth Thomas Cranmer was consecrated Archbishop of Canterbury. Clement had accepted him with alacrity when his nomination arrived at Rome, and he had the Englishman's private assurance that he intended following in Warham's footsteps, and doing all in his power to protect the Church's independence, and persuade King Henry to take back Catherine as his lawful wife. At the same time, the prospective Archbishop received clear warning from Cromwell that his first duty would be to take whatever action it pleased the King concerning the divorce, and to impress on his flock, both lay and clerical, that complete submission to the royal will was the only right course. His own example, the Secretary added dryly, would be the best way of convincing them. Cranmer gave his assurance. The King would find him an obedient servant in all things.

The new Archbishop was a man of brilliant intellect and great personal charm, but his years abroad had made him more career diplomat than priest, and the obstinate resistance to the inevitable, as in the case of Bishop Fisher, struck him as merely stupid. He was not a heroic man, nor a ruthless and determined one, like the ugly little Secretary who had no social graces. The separation of the Church from Rome was coming, and to refuse the See of Canterbury, which was the pinnacle of his ambition, or to quibble over a few diplomatic lies to the Pope, never entered his head. Henry held the real power, and as Archbishop he was ready to do whatever Henry wanted.

"My Lord Mountjoy is here, Madame, asking to see Your Grace."

Catherine of Aragon looked up from the book of devotions

she was reading and laid it down on her lap. The light was trying her eyes; she was becoming as poor-sighted as her daughter Mary. The King had given her into Mountjoy's keeping when she arrived at Ampthill, and he disguised his function of jailer as well as he could by treating her with every courtesy. When he came to her apartments it usually presaged more instructions from the King.

She nodded to her serving woman, and rubbed her aching eyes with a handkerchief.

"Thank you, Bess. Send him in."

When Mountjoy came into the room he bowed and stood awkwardly in front of her. Her patience disconcerted him; she was always sitting in her chair by the window, looking out over the park as if she were actually confined to the room as well as the environs of the house. She wore black, and it accentuated the tired, unhealthy pallor of her face; she wore few jewels, and her headdress was plain velvet. Mountjoy had seen the King's messenger ride off with the casket to give them to Anne Boleyn.

"Your pardon for disturbing you, Your Grace," he said.

Catherine smiled. "You're always a welcome visitor, my Lord. My life is lonely, in spite of your kind efforts. What can I do for you?"

Mountjoy steeled himself.

"A deputation has come from London," he answered, "headed by the Dukes of Norfolk and Suffolk and several other Lords, who wish to see you."

A deputation. Catherine said nothing for a moment, knowing what that meant. Another attempt to cajole or bully her into giving way. The gentle gray eyes hardened into stone. She placed the religious book on the low table beside her chair and folded her hands tightly, drawing herself upright.

"I will see the deputation. I don't expect I'm to be given any time to prepare. Let them come in, my Lord."

"Madame . . ."

Mountjoy hesitated; he had seen the attitude of Suffolk and

the rest when he met them in the hall below. Something was in the air; this was more than the periodic attempts to put pressure on the Queen. He could tell by Suffolk's aggressive bearing and the tough, impatient demand of Norfolk to see her at once.

"Madame, if it will help you, I can tell the Lords to wait awhile. This is my house, and I can protect my guest from molestation . . ."

"I am no guest, my Lord," Catherine reminded gently, "and you know it, though you've tried to make me feel one. Don't bring the King's anger on yourself for my poor sake. Go down to the deputation and bid them come to me here. And thank you."

She was standing when Norfolk and Suffolk came through the doorway; tired and ill though she was, it was a means of making them stand also.

"Gentlemen."

She greeted them calmly, watching Suffolk's fierce bearded face as he approached her, noting that Exeter and the Earl of Oxford had come this time.

They bowed to her, one after the other, and she inclined her head slightly and waited.

"Madame."

It was Suffolk who began, "As His Grace's brother-in-law I am commanded to convey a special message to you."

"If the King's message is written, then kindly give it to me and I will read it myself," Catherine interrupted; he had taken a parchment out of his doublet. The Duke ignored her outstretched hand.

"The message is also from the Council, of which my Lord Norfolk and myself are members," he continued. "We represent the Council. And my instructions are to read the message publicly."

"In that case you shall have a public answer!"

Catherine's voice had deepened with anger, and her Spanish accent was suddenly very pronounced. Norfolk watched her covertly and without pity. She was expecting another appeal to abandon her opposition to the divorce, a more forceful appeal than the others, but that was all. It would be interesting to see her reaction when Suffolk read that paper. Suffolk was enjoying the situation, unlike Exeter and the others, but then Suffolk had a natural talent for bullying women; it was supposed to be the secret of his attraction for them. Norfolk smiled crookedly. It certainly didn't attract his niece; it was difficult to judge whom Anne hated most, Suffolk or himself. . . .

"The King's Grace in concert with the opinions of his Council and the wishes of the nation, require that the Princess of Aragon shall relinquish all forms and titles pertaining to Queen, neither signing herself or permitting those around her to address her in such manner from this day heretofore, the said forms and titles being expressly prohibited under pain of the King's displeasure, being unlawful, illegal, and contrary to the truth, inasmuch as the said Princess of Aragon was never wife to the King's Grace. The King is most graciously pleased to bestow the title of Princess Dowager of Wales on the said Princess of Aragon, and out of the regard and respect he has for her, to allow her a pension of £8000 a year to maintain herself as befits the widow of His Grace's royal brother Prince Arthur. Given this eighth day of April in the year of Our Lord 1533 at our palace of Greenwich.
Henry R."

Suffolk rolled up the parchment. "Our names are also fixed to the document, though I've spared you the reading of them."

For a moment she said nothing, looking from one to the other, glancing in cold loathing at Suffolk, who stared back without wavering, though he reddened slightly; then at Norfolk, whose squint was an advantage at such times; to Exeter, who had once been banished for speaking in her favor but had been frightened into submission and sent on this undignified errand to teach him the lengths his King was prepared to go; he bit his lip and looked away and the Earl of Oxford was staring out of the window. She came to Mountjoy; he was the King's man, body and soul, but he was chivalrous and the attitude of the crowd of men standing there browbeating a lonely woman had distressed him.

"I see," she said at last. "In other words if I relinquish my rightful title as Queen of England and accept one which annuls my marriage and bastardizes my daughter, His Grace will make me a handsome allowance.

"He underestimates me. I refuse the order and the bribe. As you enjoy imparting bad news, my Lord Suffolk, return with that answer to the King! Tell him the Queen prefers the quiet of Ampthill and is happy to remain here."

Suffolk stepped near her, and his eyes were merciless.

"Don't count on staying here, Madame," he advised. "Ampthill's a pleasant place compared to some His Grace could choose for you!"

"If His Grace chooses the Tower," she retorted slowly, "I should go there as Queen, and as Queen I shall die."

She was terribly pale and in spite of her outward calm she was trembling. There was a movement and Mountjoy pushed past the Duke of Norfolk.

"Let me get Your Grace a chair."

Norfolk swung on him.

"Didn't you hear the King's order? What's this 'Your Grace'? . . . Address her like that again and you'll go to the Tower before she does! And now, Madame," he turned to Catherine.

He knew Henry's temper; whether he hated Anne or not, no man who valued his head had better show mercy to Catherine. Suffolk bullied her because she was helpless; he was going to give her the *coup de grâce* because it was expedient.

"You speak brave words," he said, "but they're as hollow as your rights. You're neither wife to the King nor Queen of England, and you haven't been for the last three months. The King married my niece Lady Pembroke in January!"

Her control broke then; not in tears as Norfolk expected but in a blaze of Spanish rage, as royal as her mother, the terrible Isabella of Castile, Catherine turned on him then, white-faced, with one shaking hand flung out in dismissal.

"Then your niece has just committed bigamy! She's not the

175

King's wife and never will be, as long as I'm alive. And any child born of her will be a bastard the same as Bess Blount's brat! Now go. You have my answer for the King, now go!"

They turned their backs on her without a word, and the door slammed behind them, leaving her alone, listening to the shouts and footsteps in the hall below, and the noise made by their departure as they left for London and the King. Now that she was alone the anger drained out of her; her shoulders sagged and she groped for the chair Mountjoy hadn't been allowed to bring her, and sank into it.

He had married her. In January, while she still hoped for a reconciliation, the hope bolstered by her knowledge of how quickly Henry tired of any woman, and while she still wrote encouraging letters to Mary . . .

The creature was pregnant, of course.

Catherine sat forward, hunched and old; remembering her own ill-fated pregnancies, terminated by miscarriage or the death of the newborn, her heart ached with jealousy for the young and healthy woman who had fulfilled herself in Henry's love. He hoped for a son. That was why he had married her illegally; the child born of Anne Boleyn was going to be declared England's legitimate heir. The great upheaval which for seven long years had rumbled under the country's social and religious structure like an unbelievable earthquake was about to erupt and bring it crashing down to make way for the child in embryo. The ruins would bury Catherine, and she knew it. She would be cast off now, by any means available; even death.

Slowly she rose, and for a moment stood helplessly in the empty room, hesitating; then she turned automatically toward the alcove were an oratory had been set up, guided by the dim red light from the Sanctuary lamp which burned in front of the altar. She knelt in front of it, and covering her face with her hands, began to pray. Not for herself, but for the seventeen-year-old girl confined to a house many miles away from her mother and her friends. Her own struggle was all but over; Mary's was just beginning.

10

THE MORNING OF WHITSUNDAY, JUNE THE FIRST, WAS CLEAR AND brilliant. The sun shone, sparkling over the red roofs of York Place, now named the Palace of Whitehall, casting a golden sheen on the river. It streamed into the room in the royal apartments where Anne Boleyn was dressing for her Coronation.

She sat down while her woman fastened her jewels; the heavy diamond headpieces which had belonged to Catherine of Aragon pressed hard on her small forehead, and already her head ached. She was numb with tiredness; the night before, after her royal progress from the Tower to Westminster, she had hardly slept at all.

"Your Grace's mantle is ready. Shall we fasten it now?"

She looked into Margaret Wyatt's excited face and shook her head.

"Give me a moment, Meg. We're in good time."

"It's a perfect day, Madame. Everything smiles on you!" That was her cousin, the young Duchess of Richmond, Norfolk's daughter.

"Everything but the citizens of London!" It was said before she could stop herself. The sun was shining and she was going to Westminster Abbey to be crowned Queen of England, but the people hated her, and yesterday they had had their chance to show it. She would never forget that progress from the Tower. It was Henry's idea; let the people see her in all her beauty and majesty, and she would capture them as she had captured him. It was a gallant speech, but she was not deceived. The marriage had been made public, and the outcry in churches and towns all over the country had upset him; it was only equaled by the furore in Europe, when the trick they had played became known. The marriage was reviled; the hurried ceremony performed in this

177

same palace by a common friar in the presence of her father and her uncle, a few days after she told Henry she was pregnant, had been kept secret until the time of Cranmer's consecration.

As a reward for the hole-and-corner wedding, as the King put it, she should be crowned and acknowledged with all the magnificence at his disposal. But the display was not for her, and she knew it. The progress was not done to please her; it was to impress Henry's subjects that she was truly Queen, that the child she was obviously carrying would be born legitimate. That was the reason; that was why he had absented himself from the ceremonies of the last two days, leaving the limelight he loved to beat on her head alone. He wanted his people to acknowledge her; to take her to their hearts as they had done with Catherine. To cry "God save Queen Anne," instead of cheering his divorced wife and bastardized daughter whenever they appeared outside their houses.

She knew the real motive for the money he spent on the pageantry which was to culminate today; that was why she had chosen Catherine's personal barge for her State journey up the river from Greenwich to the Tower. It was the sort of mad, futile gesture which she couldn't stop herself from making, and which always rebounded on her own head. He had been furious when he saw them burning the Aragonese arms off the barge and fitting it out for the new Queen; the mask of loving solicitude slipped for a moment, and she saw his rage glaring at her out of his little pale eyes. And the words which always struck straight at her heart when anger let them slip. "How dare you take my wife's barge!"

She rounded on him with such violence that he withdrew, reminded of the child, the precious son she carried, and for its sake he gave way, and she made her brilliant journey up the river, followed by the whole court and the Lord Mayor and aldermen of the great City of London, sitting under a golden canopy in Catherine's place. The river was a glorious sight, crowded with gaily decorated barges and over two hundred small craft which sailed out to see the spectacle. The City Companies' boats were more magnificent than many of those owned by the nobility. The City was the center of English wealth, and the dour Lord Mayor, Sir Stephen Peacock, was as important in his own trade citadel as many of the Lords who stood at Henry's elbow.

If the City acclaimed her, it would have important effects in the country and abroad. And the City had been informed quite clearly of the King's interest in her reception.

After the journey by river, she spent one night in the royal palace at the Tower, unable to rest before the next day's ordeal because she had to be present at a formal banquet, and then walk through the court on Henry's arm, exactly as she had seen her predecessor do on State occasions. And she had no chance to talk to him and tell him she was nervous about her progress through the City the next day, because he left immediately to sleep in his apartments, while she was conducted with great ceremony to hers. She was Queen, and the Queen had less access to her husband than a maid of honor.

"One of you adjust this headpiece, for the love of God; it's cutting into my scalp!"

She watched them moving the heavy ornament further back till it rested on her hair, the diamonds flashing in concert with the big stones fastened in her ears and blazing in the brooch at her breast. She felt faintly sick as usual, but thank God the nausea was not too bad.

"Are you all right, Madame?" The Marchioness of Exeter asked her; as senior lady in waiting she might be held responsible, if the Queen fainted on her way to the Abbey. And considering the size of her belly, the Marchioness thought viciously, there was a good chance that she might.

"Perfectly, thank you." She knew Exeter's wife hated her; Exeter had once been banished for opposing the divorce. They had long memories, she thought bitterly, and they resented waiting on her. Her grandfather was a merchant; the splendid coat-of-arms emblazoned on her liveries and belongings had only one genuine quartering, the arms of Norfolk. To women like Lady Exeter, she was still a parvenu raised out of her station by an infatuated King.

A wave of dizziness swept over her, and she bit her lips, fighting it back. In the name of God, why had she lain awake, tossing and crying last night when she knew the ordeal ahead of her . . . Now she was sallow and sunken-eyed, on what should have been the most triumphant morning of her life. But she couldn't forget that drive through the City, swaying in an open litter hung with cloth of silver, the palfreys caparisoned in white damask. They had dressed her in a gown of silver tissue, and a mantle furred with ermine, and her magnificent black hair flowed loose under a caul of pearls. The wardens of the Cinque Ports carried a canopy of cloth of gold over her head, and her enemy the Duke of Suffolk rode escort beside the litter, with her younger uncle, Lord William Howard. The highest-born ladies in England attended her, on horseback and in gilded chariots, dressed in scarlet and cloth of gold, with a brilliant crowd of courtiers, priests and foreign representatives riding behind them.

The procession started from the Tower and moved through the narrow city streets, hung with bright hangings and banners, with tableaux erected on the way. A press of people jammed either side of her path, craned out of the windows, and balanced on the sloping roofs, staring at the glittering figure in the litter, sometimes so near that she caught the smell of them, and raised her scented posy to her nose. There was hardly any sound at all, except the clatter made by the procession though there were shouts here and there, but they only emphasized the silence; a few waved their caps; the rest remained covered while she passed.

The quietness and the hostility pressed in on her till she felt like beating it back with her fists, and the eyes of the people followed her; inquisitive and full of hatred. They murmured and pushed, and at one or two points where agents of the King were placed, there were desultory cheers, but they died away, and the procession crept on through the narrow streets. They halted to receive a purse of gold at Cheapside, which was the City's gift to her, and again at St. Paul's where a group of children shrilled some poetry in her honor. She thanked them, but her voice shook. So did her hands. They trembled so violently that she hid them under her skirts. The tears which had gathered in her eyes seeped back unshed. They shouldn't have that satisfaction. They shouldn't see how their silence and their hostile stares had hurt her; they should never know that she had hoped that they might welcome her, give her a chance to make herself beloved like that other, who brought them running to kneel when she traveled from one prison to another.

She had never hurt them, she almost cried out loud. If Henry was hounding their churches it wasn't her doing. Let them hate Cromwell, who had thought of it, or the King himself. Why must their eyes burn into her like that, especially the women. God protect her from the women who looked as if they would have torn her to pieces. They peered at her face first, and then their eyes traveled down, raking over the rich dress and the jewels, to fasten on her weary, pregnant body, until she suddenly pulled the mantle round her and sat holding the edges tight together.

The merchants of the Staple had erected a pageant at Leadenhall, depicting St. Anne, the mother of the Virgin. A lisping child had made her an address. From St. Anne had sprung a fruitful tree, she said, and they prayed God the same would be true of this Anne also.

She nodded, tight-lipped, and the litter moved on. St. Anne had borne one child only, and that was a daughter. The insult hadn't escaped her. The progress dragged on and on through the winding City streets until it came out into the Strand, within sight of the river, with the green of the countryside stretching away past the village of Charing.

At Whitehall Henry met her. He had come forward eagerly, his hands outstretched, in his enthusiasm not noticing her white face and quivering mouth.

"How liked my sweetheart the look of the City?" he asked heartily. It must have gone well for he knew how his people loved a spectacle, and he'd given them a rare one that day.

"The City was well enough, Sire," her voice was razor sharp. "But I saw many caps on heads and heard too few tongues!" And she brushed past him and fled into her room in tears.

The pregnancy had made her weak, she thought wearily; she had never imagined that a child could drain the strength like this. She wanted to sit back and laugh at that moment, with all the ladies standing round her in their scarlet robes and coronets, waiting to escort her to the Abbey, and let the laughter turn to floods of tears.

"If Your Grace is ready now," Lady Exeter prompted. "It is nearly nine o'clock and we shall be late."

"I am ready. Fasten the mantle now."

She stood while they brought the long mantle of royal purple trimmed with ermine. One of her new ladies in waiting, Jane Seymour, reached up to fasten the jeweled clasp across her breast.

"It's fixed fast, Madame."

She looked into the girl's pale round face, with the light green eyes meeting her own, and thought suddenly that the little Seymour was inscrutable rather than dull.

"Thank you, Mistress."

This was the moment she had schemed and fought for, during seven anxious years; this was the thought she had held before her mind when her courage failed or her resolution wavered. Anne, Queen of England.

It had always been a dream, a mirage which she couldn't help pursuing because of an inadequacy in herself that aimed at the highest point of ambition in order to satisfy itself. It wasn't enough to be beautiful; it wasn't enough to have lovers—she had never really wanted lovers anyway, except for Thomas Wyatt—the urge might well have settled for Northumberland, had she been allowed to marry him while she was young, but the King stopped her and unwittingly showed her the other prize.

Well, she had it now. She was the King's wife, whatever anybody said; Cranmer had used his authority as Primate to annul Catherine's marriage and legalize her own; she was carrying a Prince of Wales, and within the next half hour she would enter Westminster Abbey to be crowned.

She was about to become Queen of England. Her portrait would go up on the wall at Windsor, among the Norman and Plantagenet wives of English Kings and the daughters of France and Spain who had come to an unknown bridegroom, like Catherine of Aragon more than thirty years ago.

She had asked for the universe, and Henry had got it for her;

in the Abbey they would put it into her hand, symbolized by the Orb.

Beside all this, what did it matter if he no longer loved her . . .

"I am ready, Ladies. Let us go."

"Your Grace."

Cromwell spoke quietly as the hangings fell to behind him and he moved forward into the room. Henry was standing with his back to the window, and his face was in shadow. Cromwell regretted this as he always liked to judge the King by his expression. He looked even taller and broader than usual, with the light behind him, the strong light of sunshine, for the month was July. He was buttoned to the end of his heavy jaw in a doublet of blue and gold, with a jeweled chain around his neck, and a short half cloak hung from one shoulder, in spite of the warmth of the day. He stood with his legs wide apart, balancing his massive trunk in the attitude which reminded Cromwell of old drawings of the legendary Colossus of Rhodes. The days when the King dressed informally in an open shirt and plain breeches were past; he had begun to set great store by etiquette, and to demand a rigid observance of protocol at court.

"Come here, Thomas."

Cromwell obeyed until he stood directly in front of the King, and then he could see his face.

"I've just had a word with Her Grace's brother, Lord Rochford," the King said. "He's arrived hot from France with some news. The Pope has excommunicated me."

Cromwell had no idea what reaction Henry wanted. It was impossible to judge because his face was a mask, lit by the little glittering eyes.

He drew in his breath and gambled.

"Much good may it do him," he said coolly. "Who will he send to enforce it—the Papal Guard?"

Henry's head went back and he gave a shout of laughter.

"By God, you're a man after my own heart! There'll be some lily-livers when they hear this, but you nor I won't be among them!"

"What was the nature of the sentence, Sire?"

"Excommunication unless I take Catherine back as my wife and repudiate the Queen within six weeks."

"He's angry over the Archbishop's annulment," Cromwell said. "No man likes to be duped, and Cranmer certainly made fools of him and the Emperor."

"And so did we," Henry reminded him. "Those friendly gestures to the nuncio a few months ago cost nothing and achieved a lot. . . . Ah, did he think I'd turn my back on the sign God has given me? Did he think I'd repudiate Nan when I found she was carrying my son? That was my proof, Thomas! God heard my prayers and gave the answer. I'll have a Prince of Wales before the winter; that's my reply to fifty Popes!"

"And to the partisans of the Princess Catherine and the Lady Mary," Cromwell pointed out. Cranmer's annulment had made a bastard of Mary; like her mother, she was deprived of her rights and titles.

"There are many who cling to them," Henry said, and his eyes glinted angrily. "The people demonstrate wherever either of them appears. And the clergy urge them on. I won't have it, Master Cromwell! I'll not have any pocky priest questioning my actions!"

"Then now is the time to stop them, Sire, once and for all," Cromwell answered. "Reports have been sent me from all over the country where the priests have refused to pray for Queen Anne and have preached against her and the marriage openly. The offenders have been examined and punished, but making an example of a few individuals isn't enough."

"I know that," Henry said. "We must break the power of the Church over the minds of the common people before this sentence from Rome can be spread through the country. Otherwise, friend, we might have a rising. . . ."

"It's possible," Cromwell admitted. "And to *prevent* the action, we might as well use the severity that would have to be employed to put it down."

Henry looked at him. "You have something in that crafty mind, Thomas. Speak up; what is it?"

"First, Sire, let us consider the construction of the Church. Not on its highest levels; we're well acquainted with Convocation and the powers of the bishops. And being within reach of your hand, the bishops can quickly be subdued. One example might have to be made . . . Fisher of Rochester, for instance."

"Nothing but death will subdue him!" the King said.

Cromwell smiled gently. "Even so. Convocation can be bent; in fact, with Cranmer at their head, telling them by words and example that the King's will is their only law, we need hardly trouble about them.

"After the hierarchy, there are the parish priests, mostly ignorant peasants, completely cut off from the affairs of the country outside their own villages; few of them will be aware of the breach with the Pope for the best part of a year or more! They can be disciplined when necessary, like the few fellows I mentioned a minute ago, who spoke against the Queen. They can be bewildered and frightened, Sire, and they have a limited influence with their flock, being of no better learning or status than the rest.

"Now the danger, as I see it, doesn't lie with the highest or lowest, but with the section in between. The monasteries. The monks are not ignorant; they hold the only means of schooling in most parts of England, and their word is respected. As great landlords, they hold the livelihood of many of your subjects, and those who lost their pasture when their Lord enclosed the land for his own use have fled to the monasteries, where they eat and work under the monks' protection. There are many different orders, and the members don't stay all their lives in one village like the parish priest; they travel, hear the news of the outer world and pass it on. It's been so for centuries, Sire; the monks have been the couriers of the people. The news of Your Grace's quarrel with the Pope will be spread through England by traveling friars, like the news of your marriage. Another thing, the monasteries are wealthy, while the King grows poor."

"What are you suggesting?"

Cromwell folded his hands in his sleeves and said simply, "Suppression."

Henry considered him and then stroked the end of his soft red beard with one finger.

"In other words, close them down and disband the monks.

Silence them; break their influence. Then take their lands and money."

"Not all, Sire," he protested. "Those responsible for the suppression should receive suitable rewards."

Henry laughed. "And they'll suppress all the harder, eh? By God, Thomas, why not? What good do they do . . . they house outlaws—I stopped that by forbidding Sanctuary—but they still take in hordes of beggars and employ them, tilling their own lands and enlarging their own crafts, stealing their loyalty from the King at the same time. They teach book learning and treason at the same time, too. I'll found schools and scholarships to take their place, Thomas. And in some places, they live lives of debauchery that cry out for punishment!"

He had found his excuse, and Cromwell knew it. The real reasons, political and economic, for the destruction of the monasterial system would soon be forgotten by Henry, and his own put forward as a complete justification.

The monks were immoral. The monasteries were a scandal to the King's conscience, for their luxury and evil living, and defiance of the laws of God. The King's Grace would not tolerate such an open sore on the body of England. Cromwell could almost hear the speech in Parliament and the Lords, and see the King's eyes filling with tears as he described the peril of his subjects' souls with such an influence among them. The promise of a distribution of the monasteries' wealth would not come from Henry; someone else would mention that, and a whole crowd of righteous nobles would discover their consciences and set out with drawn swords to purify in the King's name.

Henry remained thoughtful and went on to prod his Secretary, "But remember affairs abroad are as vital as at home. I've sent the Queen's brother, Lord Rochford, back to the King of France. My dear brother Francis appears to be angry because the marriage took place without his being informed. He's bent on meeting the Pope, and in his frame of mind I think Clement might influence him against us. That meeting must be prevented until the Queen's child is born."

"I think my Lord Norfolk's offices might strengthen our efforts,"

Cromwell remarked. Privately he disapproved of sending a man as young as Rochford on such a delicate mission. He lacked the experience and he was too partisan to his sister.

"It's possible that King Francis may dishonor his alliance with you if this sentence is confirmed," Cromwell said, fingering his lower lip. He had never trusted Francis, and he had an uncomfortable feeling that Clement's action might restore some of the prestige his previous vacillations had lost. Papal excommunication, backed by the might of the Empire, could have one of two effects on Francis. Fear of imperial supremacy might drive the King of France to side with Henry, or he might decide his ally was likely to be beaten anyway, in which case he would certainly range himself on the side of the Pope.

"I know what you're thinking," Henry broke in on him. "You think we wasted our time going to France and making treaties with Francis. Well, who kept Clement lulled while I married Her Grace and got Cranmer consecrated Archbishop? Clement was so full of plans over this French meeting that he almost forgot what might be happening in England. He thought Francis was a true gauge of the situation here and judged accordingly. One hint of what happened in January, or the real intentions of Master Cranmer, and he'd have delivered his sentence months ago, and forbidden the consecration to Canterbury! No! Francis is angry, but make no mistake, Thomas; if he betrays us now, he'd have done so anyway as soon as it suited him."

"As usual the King forsees everything." Cromwell bowed. "But may I suggest finding other allies to replace the French King, if he deserts us?"

"Who? The German Principalities?"

"The Elector of Saxony, the Landgrave of Hesse, the Duke of Brunswick . . . they're all opposed to the Pope's authority. And some of the Bavarian Dukes. Catholic or not, they're all bitter enemies of the Empire. Let me send my friend Stephen Vaughan as your emissary."

"Send him," Henry agreed. "And I'll adopt your suggestion and order Norfolk to wait on at the French court. Rochford's well enough but he lacks his uncle's craft."

Cromwell hadn't thought there was much likelihood of Rochford's prolonging negotiations over the marriage and Cranmer's annulment. He and Anne were as anxious for a complete break with the Pope as Cromwell was himself; but the Secretary was ready to play for time so that Henry could consolidate his gains in England and bring the last independent elements in Church and State to their knees. Anne and Rochford were not. As Queen she had sided with the Reformers; she read the English translation of the Bible and pensioned priests of Lutheran tendencies out of her own pocket. She had obtained benefices for some of them, ensuring, as her Uncle Norfolk jeered, that Anne the Queen should be prayed for in some of the churches in England! Some of King Henry's young men, like Francis Weston, with whom she was very friendly, openly expressed sympathy with the new religion. Only terror of the King's orthodoxy prevented them from joining in attacks on the sacrifice of the Mass and the doctrine of Transubstantiation itself.

That was the logical outcome of Henry's defiance of Papal authority and his delegation of spiritual power to temporal courts. It was impossible to reduce the power and prestige of Catholicism as low as he was doing without exposing its most sacred dogmas to attack. The King did not see that, and Cromwell knew him well enough to know that he would never see it, or allow it in his lifetime. He would suppress the monasteries, dismiss the sentence of excommunication as an empty threat, while he kept his bigamous wife at his side in defiance of the Christian world, and still send heretics to the stake at Smithfield for denying the principles he had violated himself.

If Anne hoped to interest him in the new religion, she was making a mistake; she and her brother and their friends were ahead of the times in their opinions. Only men like himself, with no belief one way or another, were safe with Henry now.

"What are you thinking, Thomas?"

The King was watching him, half smiling; he liked mocking Cromwell as he had once done with the great Wolsey. Like Wolsey, Cromwell never retaliated.

"I was thinking how much you had changed, Sire."

"Changed? In what way?"

That was another weakness of the great; Cromwell smiled to himself. They could never resist hearing about themselves.

"Majesty is a strange thing; some men assume it, others have it from birth. You always had it; from the first moment I ever saw you when I was in the late Cardinal's service, I knew that I was seeing a man born to be a King. But in those days I never thought the quality could increase; yet it has."

"You flatter me, Thomas," the King said quickly.

Cromwell shook his head. It was curious to be able to pay a King a compliment and speak the truth at the same time.

"I never flatter, Sire. I'd be a fool to try to compete with the experts at court."

"I see through them," Henry said. "Don't think I'm taken in."

"I don't. That's part of what I mean. You were always a King, Sire; now you've become a great King. It might be that everything that's happened to you was only a preparation, a means of making you what you've become."

"It might," Henry said. "God knows, Thomas. He shapes the destinies of men."

"Kings are his instruments," Cromwell agreed, leaving his own train of thought to follow Henry's favorite theory. It was astonishing to think that Anne had first propounded it; she was clever and quick and fierce; Cromwell allowed her all those qualities, but he had never thought her intellectual. But of course, the idea was emotional; it was the cry of an impatient woman, ready to say any insanity to urge the man on to do what she wanted. But it had taken hold of Henry's mind and it grew tenacles until Anne's cry "Get rid of your wife and marry me. . . . You're God's annointed; how can it be wrong if you know that it's right?" became quite simply, "You're God's annointed; therefore how can anything you do be wrong?"

God was man's best excuse for his own weaknesses and evil-doing, if He was properly used. It was God's will. Under that banner one could pillage and murder and persecute, without any feeling of guilt.

It was better to be as he, Cromwell, was. It was better to kill and steal and betray without making excuses to oneself, whatever had to be said to the world. He believed in nothing, and therefore he sheltered behind nothing. When the time came, and it was surely coming, for much blood to be shed, for peasants and priests and friars and noblemen to die because they opposed the King, Henry would slay in the name of God; yet he was a great King as Cromwell called him, because he was a great man; even his weakness was on a massive scale. Where others strutted in their purple and grew vain, his belief in himself was already a mania.

"God has guided me." Henry's voice broke in. "Whatever I've done is to his credit, not mine, Thomas. Believe me, that knowledge makes me very humble. And very strong. That's the change you see and can't identify. Strength. I do what must be done without doubts. I've found the invulnerability of an Achilles, without the flawed heel. I'm immune, Thomas," he said slowly. "Immune from fear or indecision or petty pride; and immune now from pity, which is the worst of all weakness. Pity kept me a slave to Catherine for seven years, until I hardened my heart. Pity denied me my son for that much longer. I have done with pity."

"Yes, Your Grace."

"You once said your idea of a true Prince was the Grand Turk," the King pointed at him. "And I abused you as un-Christian, but there was truth in it. The heathen is brought up without conscience. The heathen is damned; but the Prince of heathens doesn't stay his hand or alter his will for kin or kith. Christian or otherwise, that, Thomas, is what makes a Prince."

Cromwell looked into his eyes without flinching.

"When the time comes to punish traitors, will you remember that, Sire?"

"I will," Henry answered him. "And they shall pay for it, whoever they may be."

Hampton Court in summer, the red brick buildings glowing like jewels in the green countryside, with the riverbanks bordered by flowering trees, and the palace gardens brilliant with shrubs and rock plants; the court was in residence, and smoke from the palace kitchens rose like gray fingers into the cloudless sky. In the window seat of her privy chamber, Anne sat sewing a tiny shirt for her son. He must be big, as her ladies said, for in the last three months she could hardly walk across the room without getting tired, and out of breath. The slim and lovely lines of her figure had swollen out, making her face and neck seem grotesquely thin by contrast. She was sallow, and the hair piled under her jeweled cap was lank and lifeless; there were hollows under her eyes. She had been crying that day, and the hands holding her needle trembled.

She looked up at the girl sitting opposite her on a stool, also sewing for the baby Prince, and her eyes dilated with hatred. The girl was plump and round, with a fine skin and bright brown eyes; she avoided the Queen's look and bent over her sewing. It was Meg Shelton, once Anne's dearest friend and companion. There was no friendship between them now.

"Madame, I have finished," she murmured.

"Then go!" Meg stood up, still watched by those wild, accusing eyes.

"I can't bear to be like this with you," she burst out, and suddenly her eyes were full of tears. She came and knelt in front of the sick woman, catching hold of her hand.

"Don't hate me," she begged. "For the love of God, Madame! Remember how we loved each other always? Don't hold it against me! I swear I couldn't help it."

"Don't lie," Anne answered hoarsely. "I saw him standing over you with his hand under your chin, tilting it up. . . . What for, Mistress? Answer me! What was the King stooping over your mouth for? To hear a whisper? Or to have a taste!"

"I don't know what he was going to do," Meg protested. "He came round to me and stood talking, saying things, and then he put his hand out and bent down . . . and you came in! I couldn't push him off, Madame! You know I couldn't . . . I didn't dare!"

"He did it because you've been ogling him!" Anne accused. "Don't tell me the King would pay his court without some signs of encouragement." She flung her lady's hand aside.

"You're a cheap harlot, that's what you are! So you think to profit because I've got such a belly now he can't get near me? Ah, by Christ's wounds, I'll show you differently in a few weeks. You think he'd look at you . . . ! After me!"

"Madame, listen to me, listen to me," she cried desperately. "I've never looked near the King. I swear that by Our Saviour. I've never raised my eyes in his direction! You know it's the truth while you accuse me; you know no woman's safe from his maulings now and that none of us dare do anything!"

"Why didn't you come to me?" Anne demanded, gripping the girl's shoulders, almost shaking her. "Why didn't you tell me?"

Shelton shook her head.

"Tell you that, when you're so near the birth . . . No, Nan, you know that's not possible. No one who loved you would have let you know such a thing!"

Anne said nothing; she sat, still holding Meg's shoulders, staring at her. Shelton was telling the truth, and in her heart she knew it. It wasn't the girl's fault, but the fault of that lecherous dog, whose hands were always promising what his body fulfilled badly, if at all, . . . She knew it was his fault. She knew Meg had done nothing but be there when he felt the urge to take a woman on his knees and play with her, as he had played with Anne herself. He was out of love with her, tired of her body, bored with her, indifferent. . . . He had caught the stag and brought it down and now he wanted something new to hunt. The pursuit, never the kill, she thought hysterically, her lips moving. He didn't really care for the kill. That was the secret. That was why he tired, and the legend of his great virility grew as he discarded one woman after another. And it was a lie; he wasn't virile in the sense the world accepted. He was a bad lover; he was unskilled and nervous and he didn't really like it.

To Meg's alarm, she threw back her head and began to shriek with laughter.

"Madame, Madame, stop it, for God's sake. You'll do yourself some hurt . . ."

She stopped, because the door had opened, and the King stood on the threshold, staring at Anne, scowling.

"You've been warned not to excite yourself," his voice cut

through the hysterical laughter and it stopped abruptly. She turned and looked at him, and her haggard face blazed.

"Good Meg," she said shakily. "Go now, while you have the chance." He came into the room and she watched him, an odd, tight smile on her lips. She had recovered herself, and her rage was rising slowly, recklessly, as he came nearer.

"Dr. Butts has forbidden these outbursts," he said sternly. "They might injure the child."

She smiled, showing her lovely, even teeth, and clasped her hands over her body.

"And so they might," she mocked. "And that would be disaster, wouldn't it, Harry?"

He glared at her, his eyes narrowing.

"It would indeed. God help you, if you lost the Prince through some tantrum, Madame!"

"But I'd be flat again," she pointed out, "and you could come to my bed, couldn't you?" The smile vanished and she pulled herself up from the window seat by the long tapestry curtain and spat the next words at him. "Then you wouldn't have to try to tumble my maids of honor, would you?"

"What's this?" He roared back, but his face had colored.

"What's this?" she mimicked bitterly. "I'll tell you what it is! If I find you pawing Meg or any other woman in the palace I'll jump from the first window I can find, and you can scrape your cursed Prince of Wales off the paving stones! I shouldn't excite myself, eh? I should be calm, watching you philander where you can, watching you paying other women attention and neglecting me! You think I'll bear the humiliation? Just because I've got myself sick and ugly in your bed, you think I'll stand by meekly and say nothing, while the whole court laughs at me and my women give signals from room to room when I'm coming so that I shan't surprise you! You think that, do you? Well, by the living Christ, I won't, I warn you."

He forgot her condition then, forgot how patient he had been with her the last few months, the evenings he spent in her company when he might have been gaming or amusing himself with a pretty woman; he forgot the fears of Dr. Butts that she was delicate and might miscarry, so that he kept all news of the excommunication from her. He forgot everything but the fact that she dared to abuse him. He was sick of her, and because of the child he'd been forced to show her more consideration than he'd ever given any woman in his life. She was misshapen and ailing; useless in bed or out of it, and now she dared to upbraid him, threatening to injure the child.

"You'll do what you're told," he shouted. "And you'll learn to close your eyes like your betters did before you!"

Catherine had borne it and said nothing. What was more, Catherine was royal while this woman was just a commoner; everything she had she owed him . . .

"And if you don't close them, remember this!" His voice rose to a bellow of fury. "You hold yourself high at this moment, but it's in my power to bring you lower than I ever exalted you! Remember that, before you dare to question me again!"

He banged out of the room before she had time to answer. She sank back on the seat, gasping for breath, one hand pressed against her pounding heart. "I can bring you lower than I ever exalted you . . ." She was his wife. She was the Queen. People bowed to her and said, "Your Grace." She signed her letters, "Anne, the Queen." And she was within a week or so of bearing his child. How could he say that to her? How could he? The thing was done; he couldn't undo it. Oh, he didn't love her, and when they quarreled the rows only irritated him where once they had driven him to despair. Their relationship was changed, no denying that, she told herself, thinking she was being calm and rational, while her hands picked at her skirts and the prick of hysteria tickled her throat.

Everything was changed between them now. She had just as many enemies as before, probably more, and the bulwark which protected her was no longer the King's love. That was quite, quite dead, she said, nodding to herself. And oh, merciful God, how it hurt her to admit that! Her face twisted and she began to cry, both hands pressed against her mouth. She'd taken it all for granted in the old days, when he hung after her like a lovesick boy; she'd laughed at him with George, and run away from court because his persistence got on her nerves, and waited smugly for the letters and gifts and entreaties to return. She'd wait in vain if she left him now. All he cared for was the child. She sobbed, searching for a handkerchief.

And she was jealous of him. Oh, so bitterly, desperately jealous, because she had nothing to offer him. She couldn't hunt, she couldn't dance, or even walk with him, and all serious discussion was forbidden between them because that old fool Butts had warned him not to worry her.

The doctor should have warned him not to philander in front of her at the same time! He should have told him that forced courtesy was not enough. She needed love and coddling, she wept; she needed him to be a little tender with her, just a little, and to waive these damnable court rules which kept them in separate apartments and separate beds and made a simple meal into a public ceremony. Since April she hadn't been able to slip into his rooms informally, as she used to do when she was plain Anne Boleyn. The position of Queen had opened a wide gulf between them which left him free to choose his companions without including her, while her life was bound by etiquette.

The gloss of her position was as bright as she had imagined it, when the crown matrimonial seemed the thing she most wanted in the world, but it was superficial and unsatisfying, and she had never expected to find that. State and precedence and the power to snub whom she chose couldn't fill the emptiness in her life; only Henry could do that, Henry whom she had never loved for all those years, who was not as good a lover as Tom Wyatt or even handsome any more; Henry, putting on flesh, short-tempered and domineering, had won her without her knowledge and then abandoned her when she needed him most.

The indifference in his eyes was agony to her; he seemed always on his way out of her rooms on some pretext or another, and worst of all, the itch to try a new woman was on him, and that knowledge nearly drove her mad.

She had caught him with Meg Shelton and kept her head at the time, pretending to notice nothing, though she shook with rage and hurt. And she had seen him look at others; oh God, how well she knew that considering green eye, moving over the quarry, judging the height and figure and the face as he had once judged her while she danced in the great hall at Greenwich. Why, why had he to do it, she demanded, wiping her eyes. He didn't enjoy bedding as much as most men; it was this love of crude dalliance that drove him, damn him, and when he had his way and found he didn't relish it after all, the swine began again with someone else.

He could lower her as high as he'd raised her . . .

It was only a threat, she consoled herself; a cruel one, because it struck her pride, and that had suffered sorely all her life. Too low-born to marry Henry Percy; fit to be the King's mistress but never his wife; known far and wide by Henry's subjects as the Bullen Whore. . . . That had come to her ears at last; some of the viler lampoons circulating about her had been left where she was sure to find them, even a book of prophecies predicting that a Queen of England would be burned at the stake about this time was laid on a table, open at the appropriate page.

Henry had struck at her brutally. Her betters had closed their eyes, had they. . . . Catherine again. "My wife. . . . My wife's barge . . ."

Why didn't she die, why didn't someone murder her and then he'd have to forget her. It would be "my late wife" then, Anne thought.

"Madame?"

She looked up and saw a young man standing, hesitating in the doorway. It was one of her musicians, Mark Smeaton. She liked Mark; he was good-looking, with a pleasing manner and great talent.

"What do you want?"

"I beg Your Grace's pardon, I thought the room was empty. I left my lute behind yesterday."

She saw him looking at her, and quickly straightened her cap with the instinctive gesture of coquetry; unfortunately the long loose silk robe couldn't conceal her shape.

"Come in then, Mark, and since you're here, you can play to me; pull that bell cord, I want my ladies."

"Yes, Madame."

He smiled at her and did as she asked. Some said the Queen was sharp-tongued and bad-tempered; he'd never found her so. Several of her women came in from the next room, where, as Anne thought bitterly, they must have been listening to her quarrel with the King. Smeaton settled down at her feet, the lute on his knee, and bending his dark head, began to play a melody learned from the King's Welsh harpist, which he knew his Queen especially loved.

At the end of August the King and Queen left Hampton Court and sailed up the Thames to Greenwich; the quarrel had been made up by Henry after three days of not speaking to her. It was Dr. Butts who interceded for her; he came to the King on his own initiative after a routine visit to Anne, and told him that Her Grace's time was very near, and it might be well to cherish her a little. Butts was a skillful physician, but he knew more of human nature than he did of medicine. The Queen was his patient; he had nursed her through the early stages of her pregnancy and the arduous program of her Coronation. She was delicate and not really suited to childbearing, but her greatest weakness was her temperament. She was highly strung and inclined to hysteria, and the strain on her in the past few months had been tremendous; it was a miracle that she hadn't miscarried. Her bodily strength was low and her nerves in shreds, and Butts knew that the coming birth would be difficult enough without an emotional upset with the King. Unless Henry mended the quarrel, which she was too proud and irrational to do herself, there was a danger that the child might be born dead. He said so, watching the King's face cloud with anxiety, and heard him mutter something to himself, and then he added quietly that the Queen's danger was considerable, though she did not know it; it would be a pity if she were to die in His Grace's disfavor.

No one had suggested such a thing to Henry before; so far he had thought of nothing but the child, haunted by the long line of Catherine's unfortunate infants; any suggestion of Anne and death had never crossed his mind . . .

"I had no idea she was in danger," he muttered. "If I'd known, I wouldn't have spoken to her as I did. Oh, God's death, why couldn't she have been strong, Butts? Why must there be all this anxiety over the simplest thing in the world, a thing all women do and have done, and were created for? Is it so terrible for me to want a son?"

Butts shook his head and smiled reassuringly.

"All will be well, Sire. Only say some kind word to Her Grace; and take her to Greenwich, or your son may be born here at Hampton!"

The King sighed. "I'll send word, Butts; knowing her temper, I doubt if she'll accept it, but I'll try. God's death, she's become a snapping vixen these last few months! Always her fangs bared and a bark for me . . ."

"Pregnancy has that effect on some women," the doctor replied. "With others it's nothing but tears."

"I've had plenty of those too," Henry retorted. "She's tried me sorely, Butts, and St. Michael himself would've lost patience with her the other day! But I'll mend it, and we'll go to Greenwich."

Butts said nothing; he could remember many instances when the man who stood frowning and making excuses had been wild with anxiety in case fever or sickness should carry off the woman he loved. She had snapped then, and with less right than she had to do it now, when she was his wife and bearing his child. They had quarreled like demons, but in those days Henry loved her. That was the difference.

And that was what the foolish woman wouldn't accept without a fight and, like so many women, couldn't see that giving a man a bad conscience was no way to win him back.

For her sake, Butts hoped she gave the King his son.

"His Grace is in a very good humor this morning, Madame." She looked up at Margaret Wyatt and smiled. They were sitting in her apartments at Greenwich; the King had joined them to go

198

to Mass and, in spite of herself, Anne flushed with pleasure when he was announced. He had bent over her, waving her back into her chair when she attempted to rise and receive him, and kissed her warmly on the cheek. Her eyes had filled with foolish tears, so that she turned her head away quickly to hide them.

Several of his gentlemen followed him into the room and soon broke the women up into little chattering groups. Immediately the atmosphere became transformed, and the King's laugh rang out. He had left her for a moment and was talking to her aunt, Lady Boleyn; much as Anne disliked her, she didn't mind. At least it wasn't someone young and pretty like Meg, or just young, like Jane Seymour, who sat in her usual place in the corner, sewing.

"He's had news of more predictions," Anne answered. She felt strangely well, almost lightheaded. "All the soothsayers in England promise that the child will be a boy!"

"And so it shall, my Nan." He had come back and overheard her and laid his hand on her shoulder and smiled at her.

She smiled back, so grateful for his friendliness that she had no pride left. Whatever had happened in the past, he had been good to her since they left Hampton. The quarrel was made up, and to his surprise she responded eagerly to his overture. She knew she looked ugly and enormous, and spent hours painting her face and rearranging her dress to try to please him. And he gave up his evenings with his gambling friends and left the women alone, because Butts said it was only a matter of days.

"How are you feeling?" he inquired.

"Unusually well," she said. "I woke this morning with an appetite and an energy I haven't had for months. It's a fine day, too. I expect you'll hunt this afternoon, or hawk?"

"Hawk, most likely," Henry answered her. "When the boy's born you must take out your own birds again."

Everything was arranged. The rooms in Greenwich were prepared, and a magnificent tester bed hung with rich curtains of silk and velvet, which was part of a French Prince's ransom, had been found in the treasury and assembled for Anne's lying-in. The proclamation was drawn up, bonfires were heaped all over England, waiting for the torch to set them flaming with the news of an heir for the throne; the Tower guns were ready to fire the salute which would tell the waiting crowds of London that the King had a son at last. And all the astrologists and fortunetellers assured him that the child was a boy and would live to reign after him.

Henry was happy that September morning, and he felt kindly toward Anne because she had been no trouble since their last quarrel, when Butts had alarmed him by hinting that she was in danger. He would not want her to die. He might be tired of her, and out of love, but provided he had the son, she could sit safely at his side for the rest of her life.

Right now she was smiling at him, and he thought dispassionately that she had the most beautiful eyes he had ever seen, even though pregnancy had taken the sparkle out of them. As he watched they blinked, and her face screwed up into a sudden grimace; then the eyes were open again, staring at him.

"Your Grace."

It was Francis Weston at his elbow.

"The trumpeters are outside; when will you and the Queen be ready to proceed to Mass?"

The King lifted the gold watch at his belt and looked at it.

"Soon enough, Weston, soon enough."

He wasn't looking at her; for a few moments she sat very still, feeling strangely isolated in the crowded, noisy room, with the early autumn sunshine streaming through the windows. She pressed both feet hard against the floor and closed her eyes. The pain was coming again.

Some one was beside her; she opened her eyes and saw Jane Seymour standing with her cloak in her hands, waiting to fasten it round her shoulders for the procession to the Chapel. The girl was watching her out of those flat gray eyes which never seemed to hold any expression.

The King had turned back to her and he too was staring; she was unaware of her white, frightened face and the hands pressed against her body. The next spasm came so quickly and with such violence that she caught her breath in an audible gasp.

She held out a hand to him and he took it awkwardly.

"Nan . . . Nan, what's wrong . . ."

She shook her head at him, gripping his heavy fingers as if she would never let them go.

"This is one morning I fear I'll have to miss Mass, Sire. Someone fetch Dr. Butts!"

11

IT WAS LATE IN THE AFTERNOON WHEN THE KING WAS BROUGHT TO her. She looked like a child lying in the enormous gilded bed, flat and motionless under the covers, and they had cleared away the basins and towels, and smoothed back her hair and wiped her face clean of tears and sweat with a cloth dipped in rose water.

Her eyes were open and they watched him as he came through the press of people in the room, and she saw his glance move swiftly to the midwife who stood at the head of the bed, holding a bundle in her arms. The bundle was wailing. Anne was too tired, almost disembodied, to move; it was impossible that after all those hours and that last unbelievable convulsion of agony, that she had a body left. She wanted to sleep, to die, if she could, but she held herself poised on the edge of unconsciousness, waiting to see him, petrified by fear and a feeling which was much like guilt. She knew by his walk and the expectancy on his face that no one had dared to tell him.

Even in that moment he remembered what was expected of him, and he stopped by the foot of the bed and saluted her and turned to Dr. Butts.

"How is the Queen's Grace?"

"Well, thanks be to God."

And then it came.

The eagerness burst out of him, and he caught the doctor by the sleeve.

"Now let me see my son!"

No one moved. For some seconds it seemed as if every person in the room had stopped breathing. It was Butts who answered.

"You have a daughter, Sire."

He said nothing; he stood without moving, while the news sank in, aware that the heart felt as if it were slowly being torn out of his body; it was the only way to describe his disappointment. It was a physical sensation and for the moment it numbed his brain. A daughter, another girl! He could see the Duke of Norfolk standing a few feet away, with his wife beside him; Norfolk's face was a mask, but the Duchess was plainly gratified. There was another one there who was as near smiling as she dared. He narrowed his eyes, trying to recognize her, and saw Jane Rochford, Anne's sister-in-law. . . . Hadn't she spent a month or two in the Tower at Anne's request, for speaking publicly against the marriage? This was her revenge, then, for that punishment. The bitch. The Rochford bitch and the Norfolk bitch, and all the others who hated Anne and begrudged him his son and were rejoicing because he only had another daughter, no better than Mary, after all. The rage rose in him till he trembled. He heard a whisper from the bed.

"Harry." It was quite unlike her voice. "Harry, I'm sorry."

Butts murmured quickly to him. "Try to make light of it, Sire. The Queen nearly died. I would have kept it from her if I could."

He came to the head of the bed and his heavy hand patted her cold one where it lay slack on the covers. It wasn't her fault, he insisted. No one should see how he felt; not one of the partisans of Catherine and Mary should have their guess confirmed by anything he said or did.

"Have good cheer, sweetheart," he said loudly. "We'll have a fine son yet!"

Her lips moved and words came. "Forgive me, Harry . . . I tried . . ." They seemed like a trumpet call to her, but they were too faint for him or anyone to hear, and she closed her eyes, shutting out the sight of his strained face and empty eyes. In spite of everything he had been kind, while she had lain there, quivering inwardly because she expected him to show his disappointment publicly, and she shrank from the ordeal. Only a daughter after all. When they showed the creature to her she turned her head away and struck feebly with her hand. A girl. After the months of dragging illness and that nightmare birth . . . Oh, God, she wouldn't think of that . . . she wouldn't think what he had said about a son, about enduring it again . . . and then this blow to both their hopes.

If he had turned on her then, she would have died.

Instead he looked at the infant in the midwife's arms, parting the edges of the shawl that covered her, and stared for a few seconds at the tiny crimson face, with a fuzz of bright red hair covering its skull.

Then he left the room with his head high, and his arm round Norreys' neck, and said in the same loud, harsh voice, "Thank God for our daughter, Hal. England has a fair Princess!"

The following Wednesday the child was christened at the Church of the Friars Minor at Greenwich. It was a splendid ceremony; the church was hung with fine arras; the font was made of silver and sheltered by a crimson satin canopy fringed with gold. The Dowager Duchess of Norfolk carried the infant Princess, while the Earl of Essex bore the gilt basins, the Marquis of Exeter the taper of virgin wax, and the Marquis of Dorset the salt. The child's grandfather Wiltshire and his son Rochford and its Great-uncle Norfolk were among the nobles who walked in the procession, and the Archbishop of Canterbury was godfather.

The Bishop of London, attended by four abbots, christened the child Elizabeth. Anne was slowly recovering in the palace, and the King didn't think it necessary to be present.

"There's no use pretending, Thomas, it's the worst blow to my hopes!"

The King glared at Cromwell from his seat in the Council Chamber after the other members of the Council had been dismissed. A dish of sweetmeats was at his elbow, with the quills, ink and paper necessary to the business of the meeting. Whatever Henry did, he managed to eat or drink something at the same time. In the month since his daughter's birth he had put on still more weight.

"I know it was a personal disappointment, Sire," Cromwell agreed. "Everyone hoped for a Prince, but at least it proves the Queen can bear living children. Her infant Grace is thriving, I hear."

"Everyone did *not* hope for a Prince," Henry retorted, ignoring the last remark. "A good many were hoping for exactly what they got. A girl! Think what proof it would have been to the world that my marriage was justified, if, after all these years, the new Queen had given me a son! By God, Thomas, probably the Pope himself would've retracted in the face of that. Now I'm in a weaker position to withstand his damned excommunication. I thought I'd have a Prince to show my people as an answer. . . . I was sure of it!"

"It's still possible," Cromwell comforted. "If the child had died or miscarried, it might have looked bad indeed, but there's every hope of a Prince next time."

Henry stared at him and put down the gold toothpick he'd been picking his teeth with. It rolled a short distance across the polished table.

"She's not strong, Thomas," he said slowly. "She almost died; the child's brawny enough, with lungs like a blacksmith's bellows, but *she* is not! Each time she bears a child there's danger to both. I hadn't reckoned on that when I sought to marry her."

Neither had Cromwell, and he kept his muddy brown eyes fixed on the gleaming toothpick so that the King shouldn't see the disquiet in them. A woman too delicate for childbearing was no ally in the circumstance, and no fit Queen, either! But who could have foreseen that, he asked savagely; Catherine was big-boned and wide-hipped enough, God knew, and she spewed out dead children like grape pips. . . . This one was delicately made, but some of the smallest women bred the easiest . . .

Really, there was nothing he could say.

"We must try to gain another stay of execution from Rome," he said at last. "It's not wise to risk a complete breach until we've made it law. We've temporized before, and each time it gives us the chance to advance a little. I suggest, most humbly, that you do the same now."

"I've no intention of doing anything else," the King snapped. "We must await the outcome of this meeting between Francis and the Pope; in the meantime, ask for a further prorogation of the sentence. And prepare some new bills to be passed through Parliament."

"If Your Grace will let me know what you require," Cromwell murmured.

"I will," Henry said. "First, an Act confirming my marriage with the Queen; second, an Act that the Realm should acknowledge the General Council of Christendom to be above the authority of the Pope . . ."

"That's complete schism," Cromwell said quietly.

The King looked at him; he had the toothpick again and he tapped it gently on the table.

"I am excommunicated by a suspended sentence, Thomas . . . don't beg the question. Suppression of the monasteries was your idea for the future, so why bleat about schism now? Hold your tongue till I've finished!"

The Secretary bent his head.

"Thirdly," Henry continued, "an Act whereby any persons obeying the Pope's commands in connection with the marriage with Catherine shall be guilty of treason. Get these ready for their passage through Parliament. In the meantime, when Clement meets Francis at Marseilles on October 16th, we'll send a straight-spoken Englishman to present our final petition for annulment from the Spanish marriage and recognition of this one. If that is refused, Thomas, and I feel it will be, since I've no son, and a daughter of four weeks isn't much better than a daughter of seventeen, then the bill goes through Parliament, and we break from Rome."

Cromwell hesitated. Anne was delicate, and those last words betrayed a great deal. "Since I've no son . . ." He was much bitterer than he let anyone see. The disappointment rankled; at first he had been sorry for the woman because of that ghastly travail, but she was better and now he had begun to think of her health with irritation. It was just as well to make sure.

"May I ask Your Grace one question?" he said at last.

"Ask it."

205

"Would anything persuade you to put Queen Anne away and take Catherine back?"

Henry waited for a moment before answering.

"Nothing, either in Heaven or hell," he said evenly, "would persuade me to bend to the Pope against my conscience and take Catherine back."

The Secretary bowed and some moments later he left the King and drafted letters to the two men Henry had suggested should go to France to plead his cause with Clement. They were a strange choice if he wanted a settlement—Bonner and Gardiner. The Pope knew and hated both of them; in previous missions to Rome they had distinguished themselves for their aggressiveness and impudence. Neither was likely to conciliate Clement, to whom so many affronts had been offered. But then Henry didn't really wish him to be conciliated. He was playing for time, as Cromwell advised, but not for much time, only a few months at the most, and then he would be ready to break and declare himself independent. He would push his tyrannical laws through a picked Parliament and use them to bribe or browbeat any opposition. Then the right to rifle the monasteries would be his, to pass spiritual as well as material sentences, to live and rule entirely according to his own will.

Cromwell knew the pattern; he had largely woven it himself, but he frowned because there was something which had happened at that interview with the King which nagged at him and wouldn't be identified.

Something had been said or done. But what, in the name of God? Something important. Nothing to do with France or the Pope . . . yes, wait a moment, the Pope. Would the King bend to the Pope under any circumstances? . . . That was it. Cromwell sat forward. He remembered now.

It was his question, asked to make sure that he hadn't made a mistake when he threw in his lot with Anne and her faction; the King's remarks about the child being only a girl had worried him in case he might suddenly do to him what he had done to Cardinal Wolsey once, so many years ago.

Change his mind behind his back; make peace with the Pope

and reinstate Catherine and Mary, and send the woman who had failed him into retirement.

And the King had answered him. That was the matter of importance which had been gnawing at him since he left the Council Chamber. The King's answer. Nothing in Heaven or hell would make him take Catherine back. He had left the first and most vital part of Cromwell's question, about abandoning Queen Anne, without an answer.

Three months after her birth, Anne's daughter was taken out of her care and placed in Hatfield House, with a large establishment. The baby bore the title of Princess of Wales, and in December Mary Tudor, having been forbidden to use the title Princess and officially designated the Lady Mary, was ordered to join the household of her small half-sister.

Disappointment, and the knowledge of Catherine's and Mary's satisfaction, had made Henry strike at both of them without mercy. He closed Mary's household at Beaulieu, giving the fine house to Anne's brother George; Catherine had already been sent to Bugden, which was primitive and distinctly unhealthy. As an added punishment, he sent Suffolk, who could always be relied upon to be harsh to excess, with orders to disband Catherine's attendants, and if she resisted, to imprison her in worse quarters at Somersham, unless she ceased her complaints and acknowledged his second marriage.

Suffolk was prepared for resistance, but he was not prepared for the sullen crowds of country people who emerged from the fields and villages and drifted toward Bugden, when they heard rumors that hands might be laid on the Queen.

Catherine defied him; she lost her temper and her dignity, and roared at him with a spirit worthy of Henry himself, and dared him to move her by force. If he did it, she threatened, the common people would tear him and his miserable troop to pieces!

He was forced to leave her where she was, but he drove her household out into the snow when they refused to take the oath of the King's Supremacy, and rode back to London in a fury. Nothing would move the woman, he snarled at Norfolk; if Queen

Anne was agitating and getting him set on these useless missions to wrangle with a stubborn Spanish mule, he'd better tell her that! Norfolk told Henry, who looked at him and listened, saying nothing, and then he went to inform his niece. They were still on bad terms, though etiquette forced them to meet and acknowledge each other. He was as bitter and unforgiving as she, and he had never forgotten her insults during that quarrel before she went to France with the King.

He found her walking in the long gallery at Whitehall, with Margaret Wyatt and her brother, and Sir Francis Weston. She had ordered some magnificent dresses after Elizabeth's birth; she was as slim as ever and the dress of black satin, with a surcoat of French velvet, fitted her to the waist like a skin. The neckline was very low, he noted, showing the fullness of her bosom, and the King of France's huge ruby hung on a chain of diamonds, the stone itself resting in the hollow of her breasts. She looked like a fabulous whore, the Duke thought, hardly able to believe that the anguished creature whose lying-in he had witnessed was the cold, glittering woman who turned to meet him now.

The body was well enough, he thought maliciously; the gorgeous funereal dress, with sleeves lined with white ermine, and the few, breath-taking jewels; but the face was drawn and pale.

"Your Grace," he saluted her as abruptly as he dared, and her eyes lighted angrily.

"My good uncle. What do you want?"

"I have a message from the Duke of Suffolk," he answered. He hoped she would keep her companions with her so that they could hear of Catherine's defiance, and spread it through the court. He hoped for anything which would discomfort her, he hated her so much. But she knew him too well to fall into that trap.

"Meg, and Francis . . . you may leave us. No, George, stay and hear what our dear uncle has to say. I'll swear it's good news, or he wouldn't have sought us out so quickly!"

They stood side by side while he described the scene at Bugden, with the same look on both their faces. Rochford was a head taller;

at one point he laid his hand on Anne's shoulder as if to comfort her.

"Nothing will move her," Norfolk concluded. "Nor the Lady Mary; I'm informed that she agrees to call the Princess of Wales sister, since His Grace admits he's the father . . ."

"She calls Bess Blount's son 'brother'!" Anne burst out, and Norfolk's sharp eyes noticed Rochford's fingers press her shoulder gently, warning her not to be goaded.

"It's Mary who is the bastard," George Rochford interrupted, "in the sight of God and man!"

"I'll give her Lady Shelton as a governess while she's at Hatfield," Anne said slowly. "And she'll take her meals in the common hall with the rest of the household or she won't eat at all. I'll teach her to insult my daughter!"

"Do what you can, Madame," Norfolk sneered. "I'm all for breaking the girl's spirit . . . your methods may well do it, if the King allows them!"

"It's the King who's proceeded against her, not I," she answered, and it was true. He had become as harsh as her jealousy could have wished and had wished, in the days when she dared to quarrel with him and accuse him of soft-heartedness toward his daughter. There was no necessity to upbraid him now, but the fact that he was cruel to Mary was small satisfaction. It was not done for her sake; nor for the sake of the baby she had nursed and grown to love, in spite of its sex. Henry was defending his own pride; he had chosen her and she had disappointed him, but he could at least vent his feelings on those who dared to point it out. And he was persecuting and humiliating his daughter because he still hoped to give the things he had taken from her to a son.

"As for Catherine of Aragon," she said contemptuously, "her disloyalty is just what I'd expect. It certainly won't please His Grace. Have you any more news, Uncle? I don't want to detain you from your business."

Norfolk flushed at the dismissal.

"None," he snapped.

She smiled and turned casually toward her brother.

"Then you may retire," she said over her shoulder.

When he had gone they faced each other, and her pretense had vanished. "Oh, George, George," she pleaded, "will I never have any peace?"

He took her elbow and guided her to her rooms.

"We can't talk here, Nan, because we might be overheard. And we must talk, I've hardly seen you alone for months."

The fire in her room had gone down, and he threw fresh logs on it himself, and kicked them alight, while she paced up and down, her long skirts swishing after her.

"Now," he said, straightening from the fireplace. "Now, tell me the true position."

"Which position?" she asked him slowly. "The position in Europe . . . you know that better than I do! Or the position at court . . . Norfolk's a good example. Full of hatred and envy for me, but afraid to do anything because of the King. The legal position regarding the divorce and my marriage? Christ knows! And I swear I don't care; I'm sick to death of all this wrangling . . . if I hear the words Pope or divorce again, I'll shriek my head off!"

"Stop it, Nan," he said harshly. "Stop it, and talk sense. You know what I'm asking."

"Ah, yes," she said slowly. "Of course I know. The position between the King and myself, isn't that what you mean? That's what everybody's puzzling over. . . . Within a year of the marriage he's grown cold and behaved like a brute in public, and then cherished me so I wouldn't lose his precious heir at the end. And what now? Now I've got my strength back and can inveigle him between the sheets again? Does he love me again, or is he still hoping for a boy?"

He breathed hard and smacked one hand down on the open palm of the other.

"Answer, in God's name, and stop asking me!"

She sat down suddenly in the window seat and turned her head away to stare out at the frozen countryside. The first two months of the new year 1534 were as cold as the last months of the old.

"I can answer only one thing with certainty," she said at last. "He no longer loves me, George. That's finished. It was finished when he married me. . . . I never told even you at that time, because I couldn't believe it myself, and my pride wouldn't let me. . . . If there'd been no child, I wouldn't be Queen today. It was finished and done within six months of my surrender to him."

He came and sat beside her, and patted her hand awkwardly. It was not like her to sit there with her shoulders sagging . . . she had never loved the brute anyway, he thought savagely; why was she so hurt now? For she was hurt; he knew her and loved her like a second self, and he knew that she was more wretched than at any time since the end of her love match with Henry Percy.

She turned and tried to smile at him.

"You warned me," she said, "but I wouldn't listen. You said he'd tire but I didn't believe it. I didn't believe a man who'd waited all those years and done so much would be sick of me after a few months. But by God, I didn't know him as he really was! Do you know the reason, George?" she demanded. "Well, I'll tell you this; it's not any fault of mine. I didn't stale on him or falter. . . . I'd have kept the love of any normal man to the day of his death, I can promise you that!"

George stared at her, frowning.

"Nan, what do you mean? What's wrong with him?"

She laughed shortly. "Nothing. He's a miserable lover, and he has no stomach for it; less stomach than I have, and I'm only a woman! He sleeps better in bed than he makes love; he tired of me because I didn't give him what those hours of fumbling promised. But Great God, no woman could! No wonder he lived amicably with Catherine for all those years when she was old and as fetching as a dry cask. He could take a mistress here and there—like my damned fool sister Mary—and then discard them when he wasn't satisfied, and no one thought the worse of him.

"Listen to me, George, for it's worth hearing. I've thought and thought of it all, lying there like a disemboweled animal, after the child, and all the months before . . . This talk of a marriage against his conscience . . . this yelping for a son! It may be true enough now, by God; he can convince himself of anything and, once it's roused that will of his would move a mountain. But it wasn't true when he began with me. Why didn't he put Catherine away and marry Bess Blount, if he wanted a son so badly? Bess had a boy for him who's walking round the court today! Bess was the obvious choice if a son was all-important. Oh, I know Wolsey wanted a French Princess, but these mutterings about annulling the marriage had been going on for years, only no one took them seriously, least of all the King.

"Then he met me, George. And he wanted to play with me like all the others, and try me out and see whether he liked it better than he had before. But I wouldn't let him. Whatever he thought he'd feel with me it wasn't the joy of an ordinary man when he takes the woman he loves . . . I realize that now. But he thought he would, and he'd waited so long and gone so far that it took six months before he would admit I meant no more to him than the rest. And then I was pregnant. So he married me, because of his pride and his obsession for a son; and I gave him a girl."

He didn't say anything for some moments, having no idea what to say in answer; healthy and uncomplicated himself, he could hardly grasp the mentality of such a man as his sister described. He kept seeing the King's huge body, still showing signs of muscle and vigor in spite of his weight, and the thing seemed impossible. He was a big, lusty, athletic man, tied to an aging wife who couldn't give him children. That was the picture which the world knew, and which everyone, the King's closest associates included, had accepted without question. Only Anne had dared to say differently. The other women must know; Catherine must know, but she said nothing. She was probably too plain-thinking and unimaginative to appreciate the terrible subtlety like Anne. And the others wouldn't complain. They were too proud to spoil the notoriety of being Henry's mistress, however briefly, by damaging his reputation as a lover. And too wise, he thought, suddenly afraid.

"Never speak a word of this to a living soul," he said. "Promise me that on the Cross, Nan. If you value your life, never say one word . . ."

"Don't worry, brother. He'd kill me, I think, if he ever had to admit such a thing to himself, let alone know others knew it . . ."

"What will happen, Nan?" he asked her. "Surely even if he's out of love with you, you've nothing to fear."

She rose and walked round, aimlessly touching the ornaments on the table and the mantle shelf.

"That's what I tell myself," she answered. "Even if he's out of love, I've nothing to fear. I'm his wife and crowned as Queen. I can bear living children, I've proved that, and I can therefore bear a son as well as anybody else. I've reasoned it out so calmly, you'd be proud of me, George, if you knew. But it doesn't alter the fact that for the first time in my whole life, I'm mortally afraid."

She stood still and let fall the fold of her black dress which she had held up as she moved.

"I can't tell you why. Nothing's changed, if you consider it. I've got the same enemies, and a few fair-weather friends who lick after me for alms and office; that old harridan and her daughter are still alive and trying to get the Pope and the Emperor to force me out and bastardize Elizabeth. But Cromwell's on my side, and the King won't move an inch to give way to the Pope and lose all the power he's won. And Cranmer's under my patronage; he's the Archbishop and very important. I've entertained him and he's shown himself most grateful to me. I got him the See, after all. Some of the Protestant clergy are with me as they know the only hope for freedom for their views lies in our faction. . . . They know none of *us* can afford a reconciliation with Rome.

"You *have* reasoned it out, sister," he interrupted gently.

"I'm learning, George," she said wryly. "Learning there's more to being Queen than being a mere woman with a crown on her head. I'm applying my wits to affairs now. And I'll have to, if I want to keep my place."

She saw his startled face and nodded.

"Yes, keep my place. That's my fear, George. I've failed him twice, and I'm a nuisance. If I have a full belly he's got to humor me to stop its emptying before the time, and if I've got an empty one he doesn't care. . . . And the curse of it, the thrice damned curse of it is, that I do care, and I can't help myself!"

"I can't believe," he said slowly, "I can't believe that you love him."

"Nor can I," she retorted savagely, "but I do, God help me. Not like Tom, or that wretched Percy . . . Not like them, not like anything I can explain. But I only know that when I see him stare at me and through me, it's like a dagger going into my heart. . . . I'd give anything to hear him say a loving word to me, and really mean it. I'd lie in his bed like a sister and be happy, if I had him to lean on and could trust him as I used to. But I can't; I know that and it's a worse torture to me than the rack. And when he looks at women, George, I'm so jealous I could kill him!"

"You do love him, then," he said moodily. "Oh, Nan, Nan, why did you ever embark on this? It was my fault, too, God forgive me. I can see myself standing in your room at Hever, saying to you, go to court, when his letter came, just because I was frightened for Tom and ourselves if you didn't. I was probably wrong; he might have accepted it and turned to someone else. You'd have been married now, and safe, if I hadn't persuaded you."

"Don't be a fool," she said quickly. "What's done is done, and it was my doing, not yours. I could have yielded years ago like anyone else instead of holding out for marriage and the crown. But I wanted them, George, though I didn't want him in the beginning. I used to lie at night imagining myself Queen of England, with Wolsey kneeling at my feet, and all the people who snubbed us and made fun of us because our great-grandfather was in trade, bowing and saying, 'Your Grace . . .' Well, Wolsey's in his grave three years, and the rest of it's come true."

"Try to be content then," he begged her, "and don't fret after him. God's death, Nan, keep your pride! You're Queen of England now, nothing can change that."

"That must have been what Catherine thought," Anne said quietly. For some moments after that, there was silence between them. There were many things he wanted to say to her, but words wouldn't come. Suddenly he thought of his father, and wondered whether he might go to him and tell him the position, trust him for once, hoping that he might be able to think of something.

Immediately he dismissed the idea. Wiltshire had done his best since the coronation; he was on fair terms with the daughter who had done so well for herself and her family, but he had always managed to be the King's man, to do the King's business about the divorce, and to make as few enemies as possible, while Anne and George made dozens. Their father was not really with them, certainly not in trouble. Anne sensed his thoughts with the uncanny instinct which was part of their intimacy.

"If you're thinking of Father, don't! He'd only say, 'I warned her to give up before she became his mistress, and the vixen wouldn't listen to me.' Which is true. He was afraid for himself then, and he'd be afraid now, if he knew how frail my hold on Henry was. He'd counsel me to retire if I could, and we both know that's impossible. Before the marriage, yes, but not now. No, George, say nothing to Father. He's never looked further than his own skin's safety, and he wouldn't change now."

"You're quite right," he said. "He might even tell Norfolk, and that man hates you enough to do anything."

"I'd like to know how he dares!" she exclaimed. "Look where he's got! A place on the Council, more influence at court and abroad than he ever had! Oh, he may hate me, George, but I'm not afraid of that squint-eyed fox. He won't push his niece off the throne of England."

"True. I must be going, sister; I'm on duty in the King's antechamber in a few minutes."

He came over to her and stood, looking down at her, with both hands on her shoulders.

"Don't worry, Nan. Promise me."

She smiled and shook her head.

"I won't. It's been a relief to talk to you, my own dear brother, the one person in the world that I can trust!"

"Till death," he answered simply.

The meeting between the French King and the Pope delayed a decision, just as Henry and Cromwell intended; by the time the news of acts passed in Parliament limiting the Church's power reached Rome, the King had strengthened his hold on his people, and proved finally that whatever happened, he was ready to defy Papal authority.

Wolsey's warning, so many years earlier, had proved correct. Nothing could stop separation between Rome and England. In February the Consistory of Cardinals considered the marriage of Henry and Catherine of Aragon and by unanimous vote pronounced it valid. After eight weary years of wrangling, threats and negotiations, the issue was finally decided. In the eyes of the whole Catholic world, Anne's marriage was bigamous. Catherine remained Queen of England and her daughter Mary the rightful heir to the throne.

"Shall I take the Princess now, Madame?"

Anne shook her head.

"Not just yet, Kate."

She shifted the child in her arms till it rested more comfortably against her arm, and smiled down into the small face, framed in a little lace cap, with a few strands of red hair showing at the forehead.

"Who would have ever thought I'd have had such a time bearing *you?*" she whispered. The child blinked at her and sucked its mouth in and out.

"Her Grace is hungry, I think," Anne said, smiling at the wet nurse. "She's thrived with you, Kate; she looks bonnier than ever."

"She's a fine babe, Madame, and the spit of the King's Grace!"

"She is indeed," Anne murmured. She gave her daughter one finger to hold and immediately the tiny fist closed on it. She shook her head again, still smiling. The wet nurse watched her sympathetically.

The Queen missed the child, that was obvious, and it was more than most of the great ladies did who bundled their infants out of the way almost as soon as they were born. Unlike most of the household at Hatfield, who were always gossiping about her behind her back and favoring the Lady Mary, Kate liked the Queen.

"She'll bear no likeness to me with that coloring," Anne said. "Except the eyes, maybe. They're turning brown, I think."

"If she has your face, Madame, and His Grace's hair, she'll do well enough," the wet nurse prophesied. Whatever anyone said about her, Queen Anne was a beauty, even if a little drawn these days . . .

Anne stood still for a few more moments, rocking the child in her arms. The feel of Elizabeth gave her strength for what she was going to do. She was so helpless lying there, staring up with her bright eyes and holding her mother's finger in a vise, and Anne felt the strange feelings of maternal love stirring in her again. When they took the child away and gave it a household at Hatfield she had cried; but it was the King's wish, and there was no redress. Possibly it might have eased her mind had she been able to care for her own baby, but such pleasures were denied the Queen of England. So she came to Hatfield with two purposes; to see her daughter and to visit Mary Tudor, who was lodged in the same house.

Suddenly she bent and kissed the child's forehead; the unexpected movement made Elizabeth cry, and the wet nurse hurried forward with her arms out.

"Here, Kate, take Her Grace now."

Lady Shelton stood waiting in the background; she had been sent for when Anne arrived and informed that the Queen intended seeing the Lady Mary. Shelton curtsied and repressed her astonishment; when the Queen suggested that the King's eldest daughter should attend on her, the good woman mustered her courage and said it might be better if the Queen went to the Lady Mary. Anne nodded grimly. It might indeed. The girl shouldn't be given the opportunity to refuse, and they could hardly drag her struggling to Anne's room.

"Have you informed Lady Mary that I'm coming, Shelton?"

"Yes, Madame. She is prepared and waiting."

"Good. Take me to her."

Mary was standing when the door opened, and she held both hands tightly clenched in front of her to stop their trembling. She was too short-sighted to see properly when the figure in the vivid scarlet dress came through the opening, but she colored

217

when Lady Shelton cleared her throat and said, "The Queen's Grace to see you."

Then the door closed, and the woman in red came near enough for her to see in focus.

She was older—years older, surely, than Mary remembered—and her hateful beauty was pinched now, with a look of pain round the curve of the mouth.

The scent of her came close, strong and heavy, till it made Mary feel sick, and the sunlight streaming through the open window caught a massive brooch of pearls and diamonds which had gleamed once on Catherine's breast.

The dark eyes looked straight at her.

"If you don't remember me, then I am sure you heard who I am." Her voice was rather quiet and much more musical than Mary's; but she held herself very straight and stared back without flinching.

"I heard Lady Shelton announce the Queen, Madame, but I have yet to see my mother here."

There was no answer Anne could give to that but the box on the ear it deserved; and she had not come to quarrel if she could help it. The girl wasn't going to curtsy to her and it was no use trying to make her. Anne walked to a chair by the fireplace and sat down.

"It would be better if you sat too," she said evenly. "I admire your loyalty to your mother, and I assure you, I haven't come here to wrangle or exchange insults. Sit down."

"I prefer to stand, if you don't mind." Mary would willingly have sunk into a chair, because her legs were trembling, but she remembered who invited her, and wouldn't yield an inch.

"Stand then, if you insist. It's of no matter to me one way or the other. But be sensible and realize this; whether you admit it or not, I am the King's wife and crowned Queen; nothing you can do can hurt me, my Lady, whereas I can hurt you a great deal if I choose."

"I am not afraid of anything you do," Mary answered.

She had spirit; Anne had to give her that, and it was surprising because she was rather small and insignificant-looking. Henry's red hair and sandy brows didn't suit a woman; nor did his freckles, which accentuated the girl's bad color and black-ringed eyes. Apparently it was true that she was delicate.

"I was warned that you were obstinate," she remarked quietly, "so I came prepared. Now listen to me, I have no ill will toward you."

That was a lie above all lies; she had been jealous of Mary since she was a child, but if she'd give up her claims to the throne and stop endangering Elizabeth's future by appealing to the Emperor, Anne would renounce that jealousy. She'd even do the things she was prepared to promise, if she could move one vital enemy out of her daughter's path and her own.

And though Mary was only eighteen and a prisoner, her submission would quiet half the malcontents in England.

"You love the King, your father, don't you?" she asked suddenly.

"I do; I love both my parents as much as any daughter could."

Anne turned around in her chair to face the stiff short figure, laced into an old-fashioned dress of bright green brocade.

"And I can tell you this: the King loves you. He's said so to me often, but he's also said that your obstinacy is turning his love into dislike."

She paused a moment, hoping the words had sunk in, and then went on.

"The King's will can't be flouted, Mary. All his subjects have learned this except you, and I've come to see you today to try to reason with you for your own sake. The King married me and made me Queen. It's so, whether you like it or not, and refusing to admit it will only bring pain to you without changing anything. Be sensible and trust me. I would like to be your friend. I have a daughter of my own now, and I'll treat you as affectionately as a second mother, if you'll let me.

"Mary, why don't you please your father and resolve all this unhappiness and strife? Come to court and make your curtsy to me, and I promise you needn't give place to your sister Elizabeth in order of precedence.

"You shall have every respect due to you, and I'll lead you to the King myself, and reconcile you both."

It was a temptation straight from hell for it was two years since Mary had seen her father and nearly as long since she had last visited her mother; she had been isolated and stripped of her rank and birthright as brutally as if she had committed treason. Lastly, they had sent her to live in the household of the bastard who had supplanted her; whenever she heard from her father it was a threat delivered secondhand, and her mother had been finally taken to Kimbolton Castle, where she was reported to be ill and in fear of being poisoned.

If Mary did as this woman said, it could all be over. It sounded so easy. Come to court and curtsy to me. Come to court; live in the luxurious apartments she remembered, move freely among gay young companions instead of semi-jailers, attend a banquet and dance again. Ride out and hunt in the free air, without someone to turn back the horse's head at a certain point. And see the King, her father.

At the longing to see him again and hear him welcome her, the tears welled up into her eyes and ran down her face before she could stop them. And he would welcome her if she did what he wanted. He would love her as much as ever, and now this creature had promised her precedence and freedom from humiliation as well. . . . She found a handkerchief in her sleeve and wiped her eyes. She had only to break her promise to her mother and she could be riding to London within twenty-four hours.

"I know no Queen to whom I can make a curtsy, Madame, but my mother, Queen Catherine. However, if you would do me the favor of interceding with my father for me, I should be always grateful."

Then she slowly turned her back.

She heard the chair crash back as Anne sprang out of it, but she didn't move. She preferred to think of her sitting down, scented and painted, the King's concubine, as she'd heard Anne called, in her elegant clothes and jewels. Also, she was crying openly again because her choice was made, and her human weakness trembled at the consequences.

"You little fool! God's blood, you'll be sorry you threw away this chance. Haven't you learned what the King can do by now?

He'll put you in the Tower as he put your mother into Kimbolton! He may even have you killed! For the last time, think again, and give me your answer in an hour or so, if you want time."

"You have my answer, Lady Anne."

She shrank because Anne had reached her and she was forced to look up. The desperation in that white face and blazing eyes startled her; the creature was afraid. In spite of her rich clothes and her self-assurance, Mary had lived with fear long enough to sense it at close quarters. Anne was very much afraid of something.

"If you want me to beg you," Anne continued her voice shaking, "I will. And not just for yourself this time, but for others. Since Rome affirmed your mother's marriage, an Act of Succession has been passed by Parliament, to which everyone in England has got to swear; do you understand? It gives the succession to my daughter Elizabeth or the male heirs of my body, and those who refuse to acknowledge that and admit the King as Supreme Head of the Church in England will be charged with high treason! It's no longer you and your mother and your rights, it's the lives of hundreds of Englishmen, men like Sir Thomas More, and your champion, Bishop Fisher. They're in the Tower already, and others with them. And there'll be more joining them even while I speak! Think of it; think how much blood is going to flow, and how one act from you could save so many lives!"

"God forgive my father," Mary answered her slowly. "And you, Madame, because his love for you began all this. The lives aren't mine to spare, even if I could. If others have the courage to die for their Faith, I hope I have too. I shall prove that when they ask me to swear to the Act!"

"And they will," Anne promised her. "By God, I'll see to that. You'd cut off every head in England rather than give way one inch. . . . I would have been your friend," she shouted. "Now as God lives, I'll be your enemy. Shelton!"

The governess opened the door so quickly it was obvious she had been listening. Anne brushed past her without another word and pulled the door shut behind her with a bang that was heard all over the house.

"Your Grace, I hope . . ." the woman began stammering.

"You've been cossetting her!" Anne accused. She was so angry that Lady Shelton shrank back against the wall.

"Now listen to me, Shelton. I've given her every chance to win back the King's good will and she refused me. You heard well enough, you were skulking by the door and I know it! But these are my instructions to you now: If she dares to call herself the Princess Mary, or pretend to any rights in the house, you're to box her ears for the cursed bastard that she is!"

The same day the Queen's litter started back to London, and hidden inside it with the curtains drawn, Anne's anger and despair found a release in tears. They were as copious and as wretched as the ones shed by Mary, who was locked in her room at Hatfield.

12

CLEMENT VII LAY DYING IN HIS BED AT THE VATICAN. ROME IN THE month of September was cool; he knew that the city would be at its most beautiful, and already the ruins of burned churches and buildings were either cleared away or covered over with plants and flowers, as if Nature was as anxious to heal Rome's scars as he was. The memorial to the imperial sacking of the city was a strong wild flower which grew and flourished in the ruins, where so many had died and so much had been destroyed.

It was the way of God, the Pope thought hazily. The ways of God were strange indeed; he wondered whether He had forgiven Charles for the terrible crime of pillage and slaughter. Clement never had; for he hated the Emperor in his heart from that moment and he hated him still as he lay there, preparing for death.

Forgive if you want to be forgiven. It was a hard dictum, and he couldn't follow it. He had failed to follow many like it; he did not die a good man. He had been weak and unscrupulous and worldly. He hated his ally Charles and he would die with that personal hatred on his soul. But he had made his enemy his ally, and he knew now in the last hours of his life, that the choice had saved his Church. The Church would survive. He would die, and the Roman mob, who had never liked him, were howling and hooting outside his window, but the Church would live. Her domains had shrunk. Germany was the home of the Reformers, and the King of England, whose refutation of Luther's heresy had won him the title of Defender of the Faith, had begun the great schism of his country from Rome, and was enforcing it with the dungeon and the ax. The Kingdom of Christ was smaller, Clement muttered in his delirium . . . but the Church was safe.

Spain and the Empire would remain in the Faith now, and so would France and Italy. He had won where nothing seemed possible but defeat, and he opened his eyes suddenly, staring up at the purple velvet canopy over his head. The physicians at the bedside were bending over him.

His mind cleared quickly and for a moment death receded.

The gates of hell shall not prevail. . . . Out of the indecision and the fear, the bribes and the baseness, good had come. In spite of his weakness and the venality of some of his methods, in spite of the wickedness of Charles, who now protected what he had so nearly destroyed, in spite of the Kings of France and England, the folly and unworthiness of the human beings concerned, he had made the right decision. The promise had been kept.

A few moments later he died.

The French emissary Chabot arrived in London that November. Rumors of the rift between Anne and Henry were spreading everywhere, and the French King decided to make a bold proposal designed to avert complete rupture with Rome even now, and to conclude a brilliant alliance with England. Chabot came to London to suggest that the Dauphin of France marry Mary Tudor.

If Henry wanted an excuse to get rid of Anne and heal the quarrel with the new Pope Paul, this was his opportunity. The Dauphin could not marry a bastard, so the Act illegitimatizing Mary would have to be repealed; the moment that was done, Anne and her child Elizabeth were doomed, and reconciliation with the Pope would follow.

And, as Francis dryly pointed out, his grandson would one day inherit the throne of England and join it to France.

Chabot received instructions to treat Queen Anne as coldly as he dared, making the official French attitude toward her clear, for the right eyes to notice it.

The right eyes did notice it; they were a muddy brown and the lids drooped over them, hiding what expression there was. They noticed the French emissary's curt bow when he was presented to the Queen, and they noticed the Queen's color change. They noticed her sitting beside him at the court ball given in his honor at Greenwich and saw the King get up and leave them with an excuse. The eyes left Anne sitting on her chair under the canopy, her fingers tapping nervously to the music, with the Frenchman sitting stiff and hostile at her side, while the King's massive figure moved through the press of courtiers round the wall and passed out of sight behind the great carved wood screen at the end of the hall.

With a murmured apology, Thomas Cromwell pushed quietly after him and slipped behind the screen into the cool gloom of the corridor. Ahead of him he saw Henry walking quickly as if in pursuit, and then Cromwell's sharp ears heard the light tapping of a woman's heels further up. They stopped, and a murmur of voices came to him. He moved forward till he saw them, standing together in an angle of the wall, and then he drew back, flattening himself out of sight.

Whoever the woman was, she was very small; he could see the shadowy figure topped head and shoulders by the King, and the King was bending down toward her. Cromwell thought he had her hand in his, and they were whispering. He began to edge forward, trying to hear, and then froze; his dagger had clinked against the wall. He waited, but neither the man nor the woman had heard anything; they were too engrossed. Especially the King. In a minute, Cromwell thought, he'll take her on his knee as he does with the others and start fondling. That was the King's habit, and Cromwell's spies, already posted all over the palace, had reported it. He never indulged in more than maulings, and this puzzled the Secretary.

But the identity of this new favorite was what was puzzling him now. Whoever she was, she had caught the King's interest enough to bring him hurrying after her in the middle of a ball, leaving the French King's emissary and his own Queen sitting in awkward silence. Also she had his respect, Cromwell thought, frowning. He had not touched her; beware the woman who played the game as Anne had played it in the beginning.

Cromwell edged backward carefully and saw a doorway, covered by tapestry. Gently he eased into it, letting the arras fall into place, so that he was hidden. And he waited there while the minutes dragged on until nearly an hour passed while the King stood in the draughty passage, talking to the unknown woman.

At last Cromwell heard the sound of footsteps. They were heavy and soft. He drew back the edge of the tapestry a few inches and saw the King pass alone. Still he waited. Then the light footsteps came, and her shadow preceded her. She was close to the wall, and the edge of her dress swept the tapestry. In spite of the dim light, Cromwell saw her face clearly, outlined by the three-cornered headdress and soft veil. He bit back a deep intake of breath and stood hidden till the small steps had turned the corner of the corridor and faced away.

Of all the women at court. Of all the beautiful women, the gay women, the women likely to attract a man who had fallen in love with the Anne Boleyn that Cromwell remembered . . . God's blood and death! He swore with amazement. The plainest and dullest little girl in the Queen's retinue. Then he remembered she was not a girl, in spite of her smallness and paleness. She was twenty-five. So she was the one; she was the reason why that dark proud woman sitting on her shaking throne in the great hall often reminded Cromwell of a tortured animal when he looked into her eyes.

"Jane Seymour," he said the name aloud. He remembered the others since the birth of Elizabeth; the statuesque beauty who tried to influence the King in favor of Catherine and the Princess Mary and lost his favor through her efforts; and Mistress Shelton, Anne's friend; he had made a parade of the girl who didn't appear to relish her position . . . one or two others who caught his eye for a day or two and were forgotten. And now this one. All had been watched. Wolsey had lost his place with the King through underestimating a woman's power. Cromwell didn't intend to make the same mistake. His spies should be set on Mistress Seymour, in case she amounted to anything serious.

It was the loveliest spring England had known for many years. Early in the year the weather became unusually mild; the fierce winter winds died down, and the trees and shrubs burst into early flower. In the first week of May the small villages held their traditional celebrations, half pagan, half religious, which had always been associated with the month dedicated to the honor of the Virgin Mary. May queens were crowned and the May pole erected on the green; there were processions and torchlight, and flowers in the churches where the rigor of the new doctrines had not penetrated, and on a scaffold at Tyburn the first English monks were put to death by the order of the King.

At the foot lay the bloodstained hurdles on which they had been dragged through the filth of the London streets, all the way from the Tower, and the spectators on raised stands saw them die by mutilation, watched by a great silent crowd.

These monks came from the Priory at Charterhouse, and some were old and feeble enough to be semiconscious after the hurdles; these died very quickly after being disemboweled. When it was over, and the heads and members were distributed to be hung on the City gates, the nobles who had watched left their seats and rode away. They were all safe; Norfolk, the Earl of Wiltshire, the Queen's brother Rochford, Sir Henry Norreys and the rest. They had sworn to the Act of Supremacy.

The Carthusian monks had refused.

So had two of the most famous men in England, Sir Thomas More, once Lord Chancellor of England and personal friend of the King, and the intractable Bishop of Rochester, John Fisher. He had entered the Tower as a bishop, but he left it less than two months after the Carthusians died, and he went to his death on Tower Hill as a Cardinal Prince of the Roman Church. In an effort to save his life, Pope Paul had conferred the red hat on him. Henry's answer was an offer to send Fisher's head to Rome, where head and hat could more easily be united. When the ax fell on Fisher it severed the last threads of pretense that the King either desired a just sentence from Rome or was willing to be reconciled under any conditions.

The Act making Henry Supreme Head of the Church of England had been passed in January, and commissioners were sent throughout the country to summon clergy and influential members of the laity to take the oath. Cromwell's legal instrument had come into full use at last; there was no Warham to denounce it, only Cranmer urging capitulation on his priests and his flock. Again the legal brain of the Secretary framed the laws to make denial of the Royal Supremacy an act of treason to the State rather than the heresy Henry himself believed it. Religion was the issue, but it was robbed of its heroic appeal by being inextricably tied to the State.

And in the same month of January, before that mild and lovely Spring, Cromwell was appointed Vicar General with a commission to examine churches, monasteries and the clergy. The Carthusians were the first victims of both the act and the appointment, and paradoxically the King who ordered their atrocious deaths, sentenced a group of Anabaptists to the stake a few weeks later. In the opening phase of the Reformation, men died for upholding the Pope and others died for denying parts of the Papal doctrine in which the King himself believed. The result was a horrible parody, which left the Mass as the accepted form of worship in the country and applied to Henry Tudor the Gospel promise that the gates of hell would not prevail.

The true Reformers were as persecuted as the stanch Catholics; in one of his bursts of violent autocracy the King forbade the printing of books explaining the Zwinglian doctrine, and English translations of the Bible were publicly burned. Many of the Reformers sheltered behind the Queen; the gentle Latimer, whose original opposition to the divorce had been overcome and whose opinions now leaned toward the new teaching, became her almoner and then Bishop of Worcester, thus taking the first steps toward the stake which waited for him in the years to come. And many others received clerical office and pensions from her, who were surprised that their arrogant patroness should so earnestly beg them to pray for her.

Anne herself had begun to pray and to read the English Bible, which had to be kept hidden from the King; she was groping for the consolation Catherine had had to find in piety. Courage was not enough, though she had never lacked it; nor strength of will, because will was useless without power, and Anne the Queen was far less powerful than her Uncle Norfolk or half a dozen of the great nobles. The realization had come to her slowly; the Queen was a lay figure, lacking even the power to dismiss a maid of honor without the King's approval. She had tried to get rid of one persistent rival when Henry's attentions became too obvious, and her order was simply countermanded. The lady was to remain in her service. She understood at last the helplessness of Catherine in the same situation.

But she couldn't afford pity for anyone, and the attempt to marry Mary to the Dauphin had convinced her that the girl's death was essential to her own safety and the inheritance of Elizabeth. She loved Elizabeth, but the child was growing up away from her, traveling to different palaces with the desperately sick Mary in her train. There was a time when Mary might have died, and the imperial Ambassador himself begged Henry not to force the Oath on her. Anne was there and she heard him. The Princess would never take it; the pressure was only endangering her life.

Her own position was tenuous enough, Anne realized, as she lay alone in her bed, the next morning weeping because the hope of pregnancy had been disappointed that day, and she had not yet dared to tell the King.

The hope of a son still brought him to her bed; and because she was the Queen she had to wait until he chose to do so. The initiative had to come from him. A mistress might slip into his rooms during the day, or make a tryst with him in the gardens, but the Queen was attended wherever she went. There was no privacy except in her chapel, and even there a lady had to kneel at a proper distance while the Queen made her devotion.

If the King came to her at night, he came in state, preceded by his gentlemen of the bedchamber, bearing a torch, and she received formal warning some time before. However she felt, it was unthinkable that the Queen could leave her rooms and go to him unasked. Custom hedged her in and made her helpless while it left him free to do as he pleased. And it gave other women the opportunity to do what she had once done so skillfully herself. There was another woman, then; she sensed it, as she sensed every change in him and every mood, watching him now as if he were a dangerous animal, with no feeling left in her but a remorseless fear and a wild hatred for him because he had given her everything she asked and then taken away everything that mattered.

Prayer did not help her; it couldn't calm her spirit, and her fear lashed into her tempers, so that by complaints and abuse she widened the gap between them, until he looked at her with his cold, empty eyes and left, often staying away for days. Her terror fastened on the Princess and her mother; it told her that without these two spurring her enemies into action, and constantly reminding the King that in many people's eyes his marriage to her was illegal, she might have found security. Without rivals, she argued wildly, there could be no danger. And she urged him to put his wife and daughter to death.

The advice reached other ears and the few who hesitated in their loyalty to her, though some of them owed her a great deal, shrank away and drifted toward her enemies. Her words suggested to Henry that no life was too sacred to be taken; his shrewdness dismissed the idea, because he knew that his people and the Emperor Charles would take up arms against him if he killed either the woman or her daughter. But others had quietly moved within reach of the ax.

On a blazing July day Sir Thomas More climbed the Tower scaffold and jokingly moved his beard out of the way. That, as he reminded the executioner, had committed no treason . . .

When Fisher died, the King openly rejoiced. But on that day in July he was found by the messenger playing cards with Anne in her apartments. He was bored and restless, and Mistress Seymour had retired to her brother's estate in the country for a rest. So he went to his wife, and for once she welcomed him without mentioning any of the topics he least wished to hear. She looked well, that day, he thought critically; there was no doubt she was elegant, and the pale green and silver satin dress was set off by Catherine's emeralds. The sight of his first wife's jewels had no effect upon him now. Nothing connected with her affected him any more, except to make him angry.

He was tired of Anne and he still had no son—he banished the memory of the false hope at the end of last year because it made him angry all over again—but Catherine's obstinacy was arousing every brutal instinct in his nature. Nothing of his compunction for her in the past remained; he had not seen her for years, and the mental image had gone right out of focus. She had nothing to gain by opposing him, and she was losing more and more; her only function was that of an irritant. When he received the imperial ambassador, her name or Mary's was always mentioned; when his daughter was ill, Catherine reminded him of her existence once again, by begging to be allowed to nurse the girl. There was a core of anxiety for Mary somewhere in his heart, buried so deep by self-will that he could never have found it, but it found expression by savagely refusing Catherine's request, and allowed him with a clear conscience to send Dr. Butts to Hunsdon to attend his daughter. His cruelty to the one wiped out his weakness for the other.

One of the instances which had angered him most with Anne resulted from that action. She had faced him like a tigress when she heard Butts had gone to the Princess, and dragged into the light the parental feeling he was trying to hide, accusing him of loving the rebellious bastard child of Catherine more than her own daughter Elizabeth. And the French proposal to marry Mary to the Dauphin had produced a tirade of abuse against Francis and a volley of threats which ended in his shouting at her to be silent. He was used to fear in his courtiers now; he knew the signs of cringing, the flattery, the uneasy smile, but it never occurred to him that the white-faced, furious woman was blind with rage because she was mortally afraid. He would not have excused her even if he had known. He rejected the French proposal, because he saw through Francis' diplomacy and had no intention of being reconciled to Rome. They presumed too quickly on Anne's failure to produce a son; he would still have his Prince even if he had to beget it with her when desire had turned close to aversion . . .

They sat by the window, with Sir Henry Norreys and Margaret Wyatt, and there was a pile of gold coins beside his elbow. Henry was winning, and he rearranged his cards with satisfaction. In the old days he used to lose if he played with Anne; she must have lost her skill . . .

"I bet three nobles, Sire," she said.

She watched him and smiled quickly when he lifted his eyes. She might delude herself that the old days of their courtship had returned, that this was one of the many gay games they had played for very high stakes, often ending with herself and Henry at the table while the others withdrew and looked on. Only the fact that she dared not risk winning destroyed the illusion. However good her hand, she had to misplay it and lose, if the game was to continue.

He was staring at his cards, hesitating on what stake to put up, and for the moment he had completely forgotten that one of the men he liked best was due to be executed that day. The cards had driven Thomas More from his mind. Until the last moment he had never believed that his former Chancellor would be fool enough to follow that bigot Fisher and a parcel of mangy monks to the scaffold, rather than take the Oath for his friend the King. More was cultured and brilliant; he was also one of the driest wits at Henry's court, and the King had spent many pleasant evenings with More and his family. More was loyal to him, and incorruptible, but he was worldly enough not to throw his life away for nothing; not to die for the sake of a Pope in Rome he had never seen, when favor and safety were promised by Henry himself if only he would take the Oath. As Cromwell said, if someone as universally respected as Thomas More acknowledged the Act of Supremacy, many who wavered would follow his example. This was the day set aside for his execution, but the King believed that the messenger he was expecting would bring news of More's capitulation. He would be genuinely glad to order his release and welcome him back.

"Six nobles," Henry said. His hand was very good.

"Sire," Norreys interrupted. "There's a courier just come to the anteroom door."

The man was waiting, cap in hand.

The King looked up and laid down his cards, "Call him in, Hal."

The messenger's riding boots echoed through the room, which was suddenly very quiet until Anne snapped her cards together and half of them slipped out of her hand and scattered on the floor.

There was a movement to pick them up.

"Leave them!" Henry's voice froze Norreys to his chair.

He turned to the messenger. "What news do you bring me?"

"Word from the Governor of the Tower Sir Henry Kingston, may it please Your Grace. The prisoner Thomas More was executed an hour ago."

Nobody said anything; Norreys opened his mouth to say something and then closed it at the sight of Henry's face. The King was not looking at him; his eyes were almost closed, but a deep red flush was spreading over his neck. He was staring at Anne, sitting opposite to him, and the rush of pain and guilt in his heart found a scapegoat, and suddenly his indifference and his boredom turned to hatred. More had not taken the Oath. More had died as other men were dying and languishing in prison because he had once loved this woman enough to make her Queen.

Henry threw his hand of cards down on the table, and his chair fell back, clattering to the floor behind him; his arm shot out, one shaking finger pointed at her in accusation.

"A good man died this day because of you!" The words were bellowed at her; he stood like a giant, hunched with rage and loathing, his hands itching to seize the table and overturn the cards and the money into her lap. He heard Margaret Wyatt gasp. Then he turned away and a moment later the door crashed behind him.

Margaret was at Anne's side with a cup of water, begging her to take it, and when she sent Margaret for wine instead, she found that Norreys' hand was on her arm, and his arm was round her shoulders. She was trembling and she let him hold her; she hardly knew what she was doing, or clearly heard his voice, urging her to be calm. And then she listened, and his face came into focus, a few inches away from her own. She saw him closely for the first time, and there was something in his blue eyes that startled her.

"Take no notice of him, Nan . . . sweet Nan, to hell with him and what he said to you. . . . He killed More as he killed the others . . ."

"As he'd kill you if he saw that expression on your face," she quavered. "Take your arm away from me, Hal . . . are you mad? Someone might come in . . . Margaret with the wine . . . I thought it was Margaret you wanted."

"It is." He recovered himself and stood up. She shook her head slowly; this was something new, something to stop her thinking about what had happened for a few more moments. If she thought about Hal Norreys' being in love with her she might yet stave off the hysteria rising in her throat.

"You looked to have me . . ." she insisted. At that moment she heard the sound of Margaret's soft velvet shoes crossing the floor with the wine she had asked for. How lucky Norreys was on his feet, and standing away from her. Probably Margaret had not noticed anything.

She took the cup and swallowed the contents.

"I'll go to my room, I think," she said, and the lady in waiting caught her arm and helped her up.

"I'll go to my room."

13

THE PLAGUE BROKE OUT IN LONDON THAT SUMMER, AND MANY hundreds died; the crops failed, and rumors swept the country that war with the Empire would soon destroy what remained of the Netherlands trade. The Emperor would invade England to protect the lives of his aunt and his cousin, whom the hated Queen Anne was planning to poison. The people suffered from sickness and hunger, and the heads of those who had been executed rotted on bridges and city gates as a reminder of the evils the King's marriage had brought to the country. Hatred for the woman concerned manifested itself in fresh demonstrations in favor of Mary, and sullen silence when Anne appeared. The silence was also accorded the King, who escaped the plague by making long progresses through the countryside, and amusing himself with jousts and entertainments wherever he stayed. The court traveled with him, and Anne, worn out with anxiety and strain, followed from one house to the next.

And when he came to her bed as he sometimes did, empty of love or true desire, and possessed her as nearly in cold blood as was possible to nature, a new terror emerged. He wanted a son by her; she saw it in his face when he bent over her, and felt it in every nerve of her taut body. The union was forced and joyless, but the outcome was her only hope. And it was the King himself who frustrated what he most wanted, in spite of her frantic efforts to fan his dying fire into a blaze. He was becoming impotent. She fought the realization for some time; it was too much to admit. He didn't love her or want her, he was drawing further and further out of reach with every day that passed, and on the progress she discovered that her maid Jane Seymour was the present object of his poisoned fancy; all these things she acknowledged, and submitted to the tortures of jealousy and loneliness which ensued. But the horror of this new development threatened her sanity. Impotent, not just tired of her and reaching out for someone else, but actually useless in her bed.

There would be no son if this continued, and whatever the real reason, she would be blamed. That was the way of men and Kings. It was never the man who failed; only the woman who was barren.

She said it aloud to herself one day when they had stopped at Winchester on their way back to London. The plague had abated, and affairs of State were mounting up; Cromwell had pressed for the King's return, and Henry had abandoned his traveling and hunting through the kingdom and turned back toward his capital.

Only the woman is barren, she repeated, till the words seemed to echo round the bedroom like a scream, and suddenly she threw herself down on her bed, laughing and weeping and tearing at the silken sheets. The irony of it, she choked, oh, God, the cruelty of this fresh danger . . . The sniggers behind her back, because it was over two years since the birth of Elizabeth, and there was no sign of another child; no one believed the story of a luckless second pregnancy. They said it was invented to gain time, and who knows, Anne wept hysterically, in her fear and insecurity perhaps she had deceived herself . . .

She was derided, while he came seldom to her bed in any case, and now, now when he did come, the desire ran out of him like wine out of a burst skin, and he sprang up and left her, saying nothing. But she knew how he had begun to hate her in his heart because she knew . . .

The fit of laughing came again, shaking her whole body; she pressed her hands against her mouth to try to muffle it. And like that, her sister-in-law Jane Rochford found her. She always moved quietly; the door opened and closed behind her and Anne heard nothing till the cool voice full of hatred asked her what was wrong.

"I heard the noise of weeping, sister. Is anything the matter? Are you ill?"

She raised herself from the pillows; the hysteria had passed, and she suddenly realized how she must look to this woman who was her deadly enemy. Disheveled and beaten, with her hair half down her back and her face hideous with tears. Jane Rochford moved slowly nearer to her, still making no sound as she crossed the floor; only the train of her blue brocade dress rustled after her.

"Forgive me for disturbing you," she said softly. "Is there anything you want? A glass of water, perhaps . . ."

"Nothing." Anne cleared her throat and pushed her hair back off her forehead. She sat upright on the bed and her feet touched the floor. Jane Rochford's pale lips opened in a smile.

"Who knows," she said slowly. "Your Grace may be with child . . ."

There was a Book of Hours beside the bed; it was heavy, with metal-tipped corners. Anne flung it straight at her head.

She sprang back, one hand flung up to shield herself, and the book thudded against the wall some feet away from her. Jane Rochford regarded the desperate, trembling woman with a faint smile, then bent and picked up the book from the floor.

"Your Grace may need this," she said.

Anne was standing, both fists clenched by her sides, fighting the impulse to launch herself like a tigress at that cool, mocking figure and quiet that jeering voice with a rain of blows.

"Your Grace may be with child . . ."

"Put down that book," she panted. "I wish to God that it had killed you!"

Jane Rochford rested both hands on her hips.

"Rages like these won't help you to conceive," she said. "I've consulted almost as many doctors as the King, trying to find a way to help you. It isn't easy to put a child in the womb, though, is it sister? . . . It's easy to mock me, and deride me to my husband, and have me sent to the Tower for saying the same thing as everyone in England: that Queen Catherine was a better woman than you, and made a better Queen. . . . It's easy to throw something at my head as if I were a scullery maid. But it isn't easy to give the King his son, and if you don't, dear sister, why, even I'll feel sorry for you!"

"Stop it!" Anne shrieked at her. "Stop it, or I'll tell the King you rejoiced over his disappointment. Stop it, for pity's sake!"

"I don't rejoice," she answered. "Truly I don't; I pitied Queen Catherine when she gave England nothing better than a spindly girl, just as I pity you. And I pity the King sweating his passion out with you for nothing. It's not right that such a man should waste himself . . ."

"Waste himself! Ha, by the living God, you don't know what you're saying. You taunt me because I have no heir for England. You stand there, torturing me with your malice, jeering at me as if it were my fault! Well, it's his, do you hear! His!" Anne's voice rose to a shout; her self-control gone, she stood shaking from head to foot, all the anxiety and humiliation bursting out of her in a flood of reckless words.

"It's his fault, not mine! Sweating out his passion, you say . . . I'm the one that sweats; sweats to hold it before it runs away before it's any use. He's useless in bed, do you hear me? Useless . . ."

She stopped and swallowed, and then slowly one hand crept up to her throat in the old nervous gesture, as she realized what she had done.

"You always hated me, Jane," she said at last. "But you shan't despise me. Now you know the truth, though I've no doubt you preferred the lie."

"I know nothing, and I heard nothing," Jane Rochford answered quietly. "If you've taken leave of your senses I've still got mine. I hate you, sister, as I never believed it possible to hate another human being, but what you've just said is beneath my contempt. I know the truth, do I? Well, I don't believe a word!"

"I said you'd prefer the lie," Anne said. "I don't care now what you believe. Hate me and be damned to you. And for God's sake get out of my sight!"

She turned away wearily, feeling sick with fear and despair, and yet too tired to struggle any longer, to threaten or cajole the woman in whose hands she had placed herself. There was nothing she could do; it was all said. Jane would betray her; she knew it, but the outburst had left her numb. She didn't care, she thought dully; God knew, she really didn't care. Let her go and leave her alone and do what she liked . . .

"You won't dismiss me so easily," the other woman said at last. " 'Go, get out of my sight. . . . You may leave, Jane . . .' Ah, no, Madame, not this time. This time you'll hear me. I hate you; just as I said, I never knew I *could* hate you as I do. And do you know why?"

Anne looked at her and shrugged. Her head was throbbing violently.

"I don't care. Spew out your venom if you want to; it means nothing to me."

"That I believe," Jane Rochford said and smiled again. "Nothing except yourself has ever mattered to you. Only your own vanity. Vanity, Madame. Vanity made you set out after the King, when you didn't care a fig for him; you wanted to be Queen of England, so let Catherine lie shut up in Kimbolton, where it's said you're having her poisoned . . . are you, sweet sister, or have you balked at that? Let Mary Tudor live under the threat of death, and she may die, judging by the King's way of dealing these days . . . Nothing has ever mattered to you except yourself. You've hurt and trampled without mercy!"

Anne swung on her, suddenly blazing. The accusation about poisoning Catherine stung her. It was on the edge of her tongue to say that the King had hinted at it, as a means of solving the problem of the Queen's existence without bringing her nephew the Emperor to open war. Henry would poison, Anne thought bitterly. But God was witness that she had never sunk to that. The ax, yes; a quick, fierce death to her enemies, but not that slow horror.

"You lie about Catherine," she said harshly. "Everything the King does is put down to me. But I've lost my influence; you said as much in your spite a few minutes ago. You can't have it all ways; either I hold the King's heart and have his ear and can be blamed for his doings, or I'm about to be cast off by him unless I have a child. One or the other, my dear sister-in-law, but not both!"

Jane glared at her, twisting a handkerchief between her hands. Her pale blue eyes had narrowed to slits. She looked strangely mad as her composure cracked, showing the turmoil of hatred and emotion seething in her.

"Anything evil in this court is your responsibility," she said fiercely. "If you'd come between George and me, you'd be guilty of anything!"

"George and you!"

Anne took a step toward her.

"So that's what it is, is it . . . all this shouting about Catherine and Mary and my cruelty to them. . . . You lying wretch, you don't care if they both died this moment! You don't care about anything except the fact that George doesn't love you, and you want to blame me for it!"

"I do blame you," the other woman quivered. "I blame you and only you. He would have loved me if you hadn't stopped him."

"You flatter yourself!" Anne laughed aloud. "By God, you do. I stopped George loving you? Ah, sister, you don't know much of life. *You* stopped him! You nagged and carped and jeered at him from the moment he married you, and when he turned away from you, you had to find someone to blame except yourself. You never made him happy. You never even tried. When were you loving to him, when did I ever hear you say a gentle word, or see you put your arms around his neck . . . Or did you think that sneering at him for a tradesman's grandson was the way to make him love you!"

"He never loved me," Jane Rochford cried out. "Never! He only married me for my inheritance. He wanted the Rochford estates, not me! And I knew it. If I said things to hurt him, he deserved them!"

Her face contorted and she began to cry, weeping noiselessly, with her eyes half shut and her thin mouth drawn down.

"George liked you well enough," Anne said. "He's not bad-natured, and if the marriage was arranged between you, I'd like to know whose isn't in these days? George would have tried to make you happy; he *did* try, for I saw him, but you wouldn't have it. Oh, no, Madame Jane, you married my brother and thought you'd be able to insult and humble him and make him miserable, and still have him dangling after you! And only when you saw you'd lost him did you find out this great love for him that I'm supposed to have spoiled! You were a spiteful bitch to him from the beginning, and if he doesn't love you it's your own doing. Try mending your ways, if you want him so badly."

"I do," she sobbed. "I do, I do. I want him to come back to

me. I want him to look at me the way he looks at *you!*" Her voice rose to a shriek and her eyes opened, glaring at Anne, vapid and mad with jealousy.

"You're the one! If it weren't for you, he'd have to come back to me!"

"You're mad," Anne accused her slowly. "By God, I really think you are . . ."

She saw the smile creeping back over Jane Rochford's white, wet face, and was suddenly afraid. The quarrel had restored her senses. She remembered her crazed outburst and the things she had said, the secret she had given away to that livid, quivering woman who had begun to sway back and forth like a cobra about to strike.

"If you think to destroy me," Anne said quickly, "remember this. If I fall, George falls with me. If I go to the Tower because of anything you tell the King, don't think he'll spare my brother. And you won't have the stomach to sail down the Thames at midnight and pick *his* head off a spike on Tower Bridge, as Thomas More's daughter did. . . . Remember that, Jane, before your jealousy tries to injure me. Remember that George will suffer with me. George, whom you say you love so dearly."

The woman's hands were at her mouth, and she was staring; Anne thought she was about to faint. She came and caught her arm, but Jane Rochford wrenched away from her.

"Don't! Don't touch me!"

"Collect yourself, then," Anne said. "Oh, for God's sake, woman, what's the use of quarreling like this? Go to my dressing mirror, if you like, and put some rouge on your face."

"I don't need it," came the answer. She looked at the handkerchief in her hands and pushed it into her sleeve. The color was slowly coming back into her face and she was calmer. She raised her eyes and looked at Anne for a long moment.

"You're safe enough," she said slowly. "Because I can't bring myself to harm him, even though he deserves it almost as much as you do."

She walked to the door and pulled it open, still making as

little noise as possible, and when she had gone Anne ran to the ewer and basin of water that stood in a corner and bathed her aching head. The water cooled it, and she leaned against the little chest, exhausted. The light was failing; it was October and already the nights came early. And the King was having a masque that evening to amuse himself before he set out for London the next day.

It was probably the last time they would be together for the next few weeks for when he returned to Greenwich or Hampton or Windsor, they were separated immediately by court custom. To-night was the last chance of drawing near to him again, the last time probably that he might be induced to come to her bed and try again, for God knew how long . . . The last opportunity to whip those flagging senses into potency.

She ran to her clothespress and flung the doors open, pulling out one dress after another and thrusting them back. There was a ballet to be performed in the middle of the masque, and she had the principal part. It was the stiff, stylized performance customary at such functions, danced to a solemn beat. Dull and dignified, unsuited to her purpose. She swore. That could be changed; she could send orders now to the musicians. But what could she wear . . . Her hand touched a bedgown of pale yellow satin, and she pulled it free of the rest and took it out. The color was one that suited her best, but the material was so thin as to be nearly transparent, and it was too long to dance in; she needed her sewing mistress. And her ladies in waiting, and her body servants. She swung quickly to the mirror, holding the yellow gown against her body, and moved so that the reflection in the polished steel swayed in the fading light.

Then she flung the robe on the bed and pulled the bell cord for her women.

Henry waited for her to begin the masque that night, as he had waited in the great hall at Greenwich nearly ten years before. It had been Christmas then, instead of autumn. No holly and ivy decorated the banqueting hall at the manor in Winchester, only tapestries, part of the furniture which traveled by wagon train

241

in the King's wake wherever he journeyed. And the hall was much smaller and less lofty; most of the light was given by sconces flaming in the walls, sending a thin haze of blue smoke into the center of the room. In the gallery musicians played the opening bars of a pavane, and a company of ladies, masked and costumed, began the measure. The King leaned back in his chair and asked Hal Norreys a question.

"The program has been changed. Her Grace was to begin the pavane."

Norreys bent down to him.

"I know, Sire; the Queen sent word altering it late this evening."

"The Queen takes too much upon herself," Henry said shortly. "The program for the masque was well enough as it was."

Norreys hesitated. God help her, whatever she did these days was wrong . . . but he'd try to put the King in a good temper and protect her if he could.

"She has a surprise planned for your entertainment," he explained. "I heard that Her Grace was anxious to make your last night in Winchester the gayest of the tour."

Henry turned back to watch the dancers and said nothing. In the corner of the hall, he saw Jane Seymour, demurely sitting with some other ladies, her eyes fixed ahead as usual, not looking at him or trying to attract his attention. Pale, gentle Jane, who was suddenly showing the spirit to refuse his advances. He had no idea how grateful he was that her obstinacy spared him yet another disillusion . . . And at times she relented enough to allow him a few liberties, as inert and submissive as a doll in his arms, with her strange green eyes half closed. She said so little always, having a curious quality of stillness which soothed him after the high-powered atmosphere in which Anne moved. Jane was noiseless; there was no wild laughter or spirited talk . . . and no fury. He wished that she hadn't taken up her place so far away from him.

In spite of himself he began to think about Anne again. Memories of that other evening crowded back, reminding him of his own dead impatience while he waited with Catherine by his side, fidgeting to see her. How he had changed, how flat and empty was the marriage he had once desired more than anything in the world; and how different was the woman who had enchanted him with her grace and loveliness that night so many years ago. So much had altered. Different faces surrounded him now; the chair as his side was empty; Catherine lay ill at Bugden. Very ill, from the last reports. He closed his mind to her quickly. A new Princess played in the royal nursery, while his daughter Mary pined in a suite of gloomy rooms, harried and restricted because she wouldn't take the Oath.

In the old days More would have been with him, and Wolsey, surrounded by a brilliant entourage of priests and gentlemen. But they were dead, and others whom he didn't like so well were in their places. And then the music changed, and the lines of women parted.

It was a trick of his imagination that the torches dimmed, so that he saw her through a haze of smoke, moving as if she floated; but the whole room became suddenly quiet, while the slow, sensuous notes of a single lute quivered on the air.

She was in yellow, and her arms and neck were bare; ropes of pearls were twisted through her flowing hair, and knotted round her narrow waist; the soft material clung to her as she moved.

He had seen her dance before, and been exhilarated by her skill, but never had he seen her dance like this. He knew she held his eyes, knew that unconsciously he had reached the edge of his chair and was leaning forward, watching that one figure drifting and swaying like a pale daffodil in the wind, guided by the notes of the lute. She bent, and spread her arms, till it seemed that the supple body was without bones, and stayed there, a few feet away from him, looking up through the slits of a tiny gold mask. Behind him, Norreys caught his breath, but the King heard nothing. Nobody moved. The ladies lining her path stood like statues in their stiff gowns, until the only living creature seemed to be the woman, moving with the grace of a serpent to the music.

The past fled from him while he watched her; everything

243

receded, the room, the courtiers, everything became unreal, while the desire which had been dead for nearly three years stirred in his blood, and mounted, singing in his brain.

Then it was over, and she turned and vanished, leaving the spell unbroken, and an incredulous murmur rising after her.

Within five minutes he had found her in her room.

"My Lord Suffolk," the Duke of Norfolk said, "you'll have to keep a record of my debt. I'm going to see my niece."

He stood up from the table where he and Suffolk had been throwing dice. In the first week of January, 1536, the court was at Greenwich; the weather was wet and dismal and there was nothing to do but gamble or play tennis if music did not appeal to them; neither man was interested in that gentle pastime.

Suffolk looked up and grinned unpleasantly.

"You're like the rest these days, hurrying to pay your court to good Queen Nan! Tell me, friend, is it true the vixen's got religious? I heard she spends nearly as much time on her knees as Catherine used to when she had the strength to kneel. And that she's given the fortune of £14,000 away to the poor in the last months."

"Fear of men has taught her fear of God," Norfolk sneered. "She's busy buying her soul with alms and paying her priests to send up howls for her intentions."

"It looks as if they've succeeded," Suffolk retorted. He was not grinning any longer. "There's no doubt about her belly this time. If it's a boy, we'll have to knuckle down to her for the rest of our lives."

"If it's a boy," the Duke remarked, "certainly. But let's wait till it's born before we despair. And let's wait to see if it lives . . . The poor lady suffered torture to give our King his little daughter . . ."

"Almost a rhyme, my Lord," Suffolk mocked. "Almost, but not quite. Go then, and don't keep Madame waiting. I'll total up what's owing."

Norfolk straightened his cap and smiled crookedly.

"I have other nieces beside the Queen," he said. "I'm going to Mistress Seymour!"

She was waiting for him in the chapel. The summons she had been expecting for the last few months had come at last. He was her mother's brother, and the head of her family, but unlike Anne she didn't approach him for support; she let him seek her out.

She was kneeling at the back of the church when she heard him come in, and turned around to make sure who it was. He was clever enough, she thought; no one could accuse them of conspiring if they happened to go to the same place to pray . . .

She stood up and brushed her skirts after their contact with the stone floor. She stood quietly in front of him, her eyes watching his face, and said nothing.

"You know why I want to speak to you," he began loudly and then stopped because she had put one finger to her mouth.

"Gently, Uncle. This is the chapel. We might be overheard outside. Yes, I think I know."

"I've heard a deal of talk about you and the King," he said slowly. "And strange talk it is. It says you refuse him. Is that so?"

"It is, Uncle. I have refused His Grace for months, and I shall go on as I've begun."

He considered her, frowning. She was so small her head was tilted right back to look up at him, and the dim lighting of the chapel made it difficult to see her face. She spoke in a flat whisper.

"Why?"

The answer came unhesitatingly; he never knew then or later whether there was a note of icy laughter in it.

"Because I'm virtuous, and the King respects virtue."

"I see." He turned half away from her, his mind racing. Who was behind it, who had told her to do this, to copy Anne and hold him off . . . And what chance had she anyway, supposing anything happened to that cursed pregnancy, or it was a girl or Anne died, as she easily might, judging by that one ghastly confinement . . .

245

"Who's been advising you?" he demanded. "No lies, Mistress, answer me."

"My brother Edward, and Sir Nicholas Carew, and My Lord Exeter and My Lady Exeter," she said simply. "But I had already thought of it for myself."

"And what did you hope to gain?" he wanted to know, anxious to shake the serenity out of her and see that pale enigmatic face dissolve in some expression he could read. It was almost easier to deal with that fiery virago Anne than fathom this quiet little snake . . .

"I hoped he might marry me, when he grew tired of Her Grace the Queen. Your other niece," she added. "If it weren't for her condition, I think he might have done it. He talked of it enough."

"Talked of it!" He did catch hold of her then, pushed off his guard by the revelation of how far things had gone without his knowledge. "Who knows of this? Have you told your brother or Carew?"

She nodded. "They know, and so does Master Cromwell, I imagine. He should, for he's been having me watched for some time now."

"God's death!" The Duke swore roundly in amazement. "How in the devil's name do you know that?"

"I noticed things," she told him gently. "Shadows around corners when I met the King in secret, and my letters look as if they're opened. I think you'll find that Cromwell knows."

"And he's done nothing," the Duke said, half to himself. Cromwell, the friend and partisan of Anne the Queen, knew there was an intrigue to replace her, and had done absolutely nothing. And as he thought about it, Norfolk understood his inaction. He was waiting, like the rest of them, waiting for the child . . .

Jane stood in front of him, her hands tucked into her sleeves.

"Will you support me, Uncle, if the opportunity occurs? I've thought very carefully, and I shan't act unless you do."

"I helped one niece to elevate herself," the Duke said slowly, "and small thanks I got for it. Why should I make the same mistake again?"

"Because I am not Anne," she answered softly. "I have no enemies as plain Jane Seymour, and I'd want none were I Queen. I only want to be Queen, Uncle, that's all. I don't long for power, as she does, or hope to interfere in the affairs of men and kingdoms; I only want to be Queen."

"If she gives the King his Prince, you've little chance of that," Norfolk said gruffly. "And a very good chance of going to the Tower, when Madame regains her health and strength. She's not a gentle rival."

"I know," Jane Seymour nodded. "I'm ready to retire to the country immediately if a Prince is born; but there is no prize without some risk."

"What is it in our blood," he fumed, "that sends us stretching our necks for the crown or the ax . . . I've seen it in her, much as I hate her, and now you too . . ."

"I don't know, Uncle," she murmured, "any more than I know why you seek me out now, when the Queen's with child and in high favor. It seems my prospects are fading fast! Supposing she knew you'd encouraged me, or found out what I was hoping to do to her, what she once did to Catherine . . ."

"Whatever she finds out or suspects, she can do nothing at the moment. And I seek you out, Mistress, for the same reason that you delay your retirement until after the child's birth. I think there's a chance it may never be born. She nearly died before, and unless she was lying to the King, she's miscarried since. That's why I've come to you. If Anne is going to fall, I'd rather see a Howard in her place again when Catherine of Aragon dies."

"They say she's dying now," she whispered. "Of poison."

The Duke looked down at her.

"Better for all of us if she is," he said harshly. "The King intends forcing a bill for her impeachment on a charge of treason through the New Year Parliament. We've all argued with him —Cromwell, Suffolk and I—but he's adamant. It's the thought of this unborn son that's driving him. If he's got to kill Catherine to secure that son's succession and legalize his marriage to Anne, then he swears he'll do it.

"And the day Catherine enters the Tower, the whole of England will rise up against him. He'll lose his throne and we'll lose our heads. There'll be an imperial invasion from the Netherlands, and every peer in the country will raise his tenants and march on London."

"I never thought of that," Jane said. "God help her, I served her once; she was the only person at court who was kind to me."

He could just remember her then; plain and awkward and unattractive. He could imagine Catherine being kind . . .

"The Queen is lost, whatever happens; if she lives through her illness, she'll go to the scaffold—be sure the King will do that; even if the mob was storming the walls to save her, he'd throw them her head . . ."

"I know that," she answered. "As I told you, Uncle, I only want to be Queen. But I could repay her by being kind to the Princess Mary."

"That promise will gain you half the court," he said quickly. "I warn you, though, go carefully, especially if Master Cromwell's on the watch. He can change sides faster than Mercury can run!"

"I will," she promised. "But if things should alter suddenly —in my favor, I mean, can I count on you to help me?"

He watched her without answering for a moment, his head on one side. Jane, Queen of England. It sounded well enough, but two women had to be removed to make it possible. Catherine —Catherine was halfway gone, vomiting her life away, from an illness no one could identify . . . No bill would go through Parliament, there'd be no trial, and no popular revolt. Someone had taken the necessary step. Perhaps the King had guessed they would, when he threatened to bring her to open trial . . . No one would ever know, and Norfolk would never, in his life, try to find out.

And that left Anne. Anne, who had insulted and defied him, had his wife banished for a time, and refused to serve his interests and defer to him as soon as she had got what she wanted. Anne was in the way, with her unborn brat . . .

"If I give you my support," he said slowly, "don't ever try to get above yourself with me. Don't try to copy Madame Anne."

248

She shook her head, and in the shadows he thought he saw her smile.

"Dear Uncle, have no fear of that. I never want to see the day when you agree to turn on me, as you now turn on her."

She curtsied low to him, and glided out of the chapel, pausing to genuflect and cross herself before the door closed behind her.

On the seventh of January, Catherine, Queen of England lay dying in her room at Kimbolton Castle. The hangings were drawn back from the bed and she was propped up on a heap of cushions, with an old fur wrap drawn round her shoulders. She was too weak to sit up, or to raise her gray head from the cushions; she lay quiet at last, worn out in body and mind by mysterious vomiting and bouts of excruciating internal pain.

No one had been able to diagnose the illness, though the verdict of poison was on every tongue. Even her jailer, Sir Henry Bedingfield, watched the paroxysms of his prisoner with pity, and wondered whether what he heard was true. And if it were, which of the men and women sent by the Council to attend her had that terrible mark on their soul . . .

No one knew, and very soon it wouldn't matter. She was at the end of her strength when the King allowed Chapuys to see her; it could do no harm, Bedingfield thought unhappily, and allowed the imperial Ambassador and his suite more facilities than he need have done. And for a day she showed improvement; she slept, and seemed refreshed and strong enough to talk to her own countryman for almost two hours. She had a lot to say, and such a little time to say it. That thought was in her mind, as she struggled to tell Charles' envoy everything. In spite of her religious faith, human weakness made her upbraid her nephew for not coming to her assistance long ago, for leaving her daughter Mary helpless and motherless now, at the mercy of her father and that creature . . . The tears ran down her sunken cheeks at the mention of Mary. She would die without seeing her, for that anguished plea had been refused.

The Bishop of Landaff was called to her, and he celebrated Mass in her sickroom, and gave her the Communion. She lay so quietly with her eyes closed that her doctor, De Lasco, bent over her, thinking she was dead, but she was only praying, and then she asked for pens and paper and began her last letter to the King, her husband.

Her voice fell to a whisper, so that De Lasco had to lean over her with his pen poised, trying to hear for she was far too weak to write herself. She had written Henry many letters in the last ten years; letters pleading to be restored to her right place, or arguing obstinately against this or that attempt to make her change her mind. She had written angrily and in the bitterest sorrow and resentment, and lately she had not approached him at all, until she begged to see her daughter before she died. Now she was incapable of bitterness.

Her mind was strangely tranquil; even the agony of her anxiety for her daughter had faded before that pervading, deathly calm. She possessed only a few trinkets and a little money which she begged the King to give to the persons she named in her remembrance. De Lasco waited, watching her lips move, until the sound came again.

She pardoned him everything, and asked that God might do the same. There was another pause. De Lasco coughed, but she had turned her head away from him, and made a gesture with her hand for him to wait.

She had nothing more to say now, no reproaches or requests. She had forgiven him for everything, even for her death, she murmured, if her sickness came from human agency. She forgave, as she hoped to be forgiven. Even the woman who had begun it all, with her youth and her beauty and her terrible fascination. Anne was unhappy, so they said, and frightened now, suffering the humiliation Catherine remembered so well, as the King's fancy lighted on one woman after another. She could remember her own jealousy and pain, and thanking God for the rigid upbringing which helped her to disguise it, to keep the women among her maids and speak to them at court. . . . And in her heart she made excuses for him; he was young and vigorous and handsome, while she was staid and unable to keep up . . . She had loved him always, no matter what he did. Until the last year she had still looked on him as being led by others, influenced by the woman and her friends, ready to make excuses for him in her heart, because she still thought of him as the younger man that she had married, boyish and high-spirited, almost like a magnificent son. . . . When he sent the gentle Carthusian monks to their atrocious deaths, that image vanished. And when word reached her that her enemy was suffering just as she had done, neglected and trembling for her position, Henry the King achieved his full stature in Catherine's mind. In all victories, there is the germ of defeat. Her mother Isabella of Castile used to say that, and she who had achieved as much as any man should surely know.

With a great effort, the Queen said a short prayer for Anne Boleyn. It was the last time that image would torment her, either with jealousy or hate. Only the King remained, moving before her closing eyes, as near and real as if he stood at the foot of her bed. Her husband for twenty-six years. She could think of nothing in those moments but the good things of their life together; the laughter and generosity, the pleasure of making him gifts and opening his, of riding with him through the narrow London streets, or sailing down the Thames, with the infant Princess Mary on her knee. Christmas and Easter at Greenwich, the State balls when they led out the dancing, in those times when she wasn't pregnant and full of hope for a living son. . . . His kindness when she was ill, and their children died. . . .

"Madame, the letter . . . have you finished?"

She turned to De Lasco.

"I will finish it now. Write this, my friend! 'Lastly I do vow that mine eyes desire you above all things.' Now give it to me, with the pen."

She signed it, "Catherine, Queen of England," and a blot ran from the signature as the pen slipped out of her fingers. She lay back exhausted, and at two o'clock that afternoon she died.

The day after Catherine's death was a Sunday; when the news reached the court at Greenwich no one knew whether to show sorrow or jubilation. They only had the report of the King's reaction to guide them, and it was cryptic. "Thank God we are free from the threat of war."

There was a general feeling of relief; few had realized how near the Emperor Charles had been to taking up arms on his aunt's behalf, for Henry to say that.

The Emperor was now more powerful than ever before; having beaten the Turks at Tunis, he was the acknowledged savior of Europe, and the King of France had revised his policy accordingly. Friendship with England had brought him nothing, while he had been ruthlessly used for Henry's purpose. Because of it he was in danger of incurring Charles's enmity so now the alliance with England was to be broken. If the Emperor decided to invade England on behalf of his aunt and his Cousin Mary, it wouldn't be wise to be Henry's ally at that moment.

The time had come when England was alone, and if the Emperor attacked Henry, could expect no help from France or anywhere else. Catherine had died just in time. Cromwell said so to the Duke of Norfolk when both men met in the gallery, waiting to attend the King at his public Mass. Cromwell was dressed in black; he was lucky, the Duke thought angrily; he always dressed for a funeral, and if the King appeared in mourning for his dead wife, Cromwell would be correct. If he didn't, he wouldn't be noticed anyway. Norfolk had worried over what to wear; God knew what Henry's reaction might suddenly be to what had happened at Kimbolton. He was capable of turning his coat so violently that he caught everyone off guard; the man or woman who showed gaiety that day might find those terrible little eyes fixed on them in anger, and God, how that anger was dreaded! . . . Or if they chose mourning colors and put on long faces, they might find they'd been expected to rejoice. The Duke cursed and chose doublet and hose of a very dark red, with a black feather in his cap, and hoped for the best.

"She did indeed die just in time," he answered Cromwell. "His Grace was losing patience fast . . ."

The Secretary nodded. "He was indeed, my Lord, and who could blame him? Now your niece can feel that she is truly Queen at last."

The Duke stared at him, his good eye searching the flat face for some expression, and found nothing. Cromwell might have been wearing a mask. Yet he knew about Jane Seymour, knew that she had been aiming at the crown, that a large and powerful section of the court supported her in secret, himself among them —Norfolk didn't underestimate the Secretary's spy system—he knew even that the King himself had been considering it. He decided to clarify his own position, without committing himself too far.

"Anne will never feel truly Queen until she bears a son," he answered. "Nor will she be accepted by the adherents of the Princess Mary."

"The Lady Mary," Cromwell corrected gently. "I've caught myself using that title to His Grace and had to bite it off my tongue. . . . But I'll admit, my Lord, I still think of her as Princess, and the King's eldest born. As you say, the son is a most urgent matter. His Grace's heart is set on a boy to follow him, though he likes the Princess Elizabeth well enough. I pray that Queen Anne gives birth to a Prince this time, for her own sake as well as the sake of the kingdom."

The Duke of Norfolk leaned against the wall and slowly rocked backward and forward. There was no need to reveal himself to Cromwell; Cromwell already knew the direction he'd chosen; now it was Cromwell's turn to signpost his intentions.

"And if Her Grace doesn't bear a Prince, what then?" he asked.

"The King may replace her with someone who will. Now that Catherine of Aragon is dead, the Emperor has no excuse for war, and the Papal sympathizers would gladly see another woman take the place of someone they hate so bitterly. Someone who wouldn't press for the death of Princess Mary. It could mean many things, if she fails the King a second time."

There was no time to answer, for a blast of trumpets announced the arrival of the King. For a moment, Cromwell and Norfolk exchanged glances, and then slowly the Duke smiled. The Secretary bowed as they turned to face the doorway, and saw the King towering over his gentlemen, shaking the floor under his tread. Norfolk forgot the precautionary black feather in his cap, and thanked God that he had chosen red. The King was dressed from head to foot in brilliant yellow.

That Sunday was the gayest the court had spent for months. After the Mass the King visited Anne and her women; they too were dressed in the bright spring color, a color which didn't enhance the pallid looks of Mistress Seymour. The Queen's musicians played for them, and Anne sat beside the King and held on to his arm, while her lute player Mark Smeaton performed for them at her command. He played well, she said happily; no one at court could match him—except the King, of course, she added; and he grunted and moved his hand in time to the gay melody, and called out a coarse joke to her ladies, who shrieked with laughter.

She had to ask him, though she knew the answer; the answer was in that outrageous dress, in the music and dancing and stewards passing up and down with pitchers of wine. But she still asked, holding on to his sleeve because he had made a movement to get up and go to the group where Jane Seymour was sitting.

"Are you glad, Harry? Really glad?"

"Glad of what, Nan?"

He turned to her with the remains of a smile on his mouth, but it had left his eyes and they were cold and wary.

"Glad that she is out of our way at last."

His head turned away from her, and the hand which had been beating time to the music stayed still on his knee.

"I've thanked God on my knees this morning. So long as she lived, my son's legitimacy would have been disputed, and without her, Mary will submit and take the Oath."

He left her then, and she heard him laughing in the middle of the group of women; a shadow fell beside her and she glanced up. It was Smeaton the lute player, who had finished his playing.

"Madame, may I sit by you?"

He was always asking that, looking up at her with those

254

large soft eyes that reminded her of the spaniels she kept which never seemed to live for long. He was very handsome and young; she's heard gossip about his gallantry with the serving women, and once laughingly teased him, asking how many hearts he'd broken. He'd blushed, to the delight of her ladies, who missed the hurt expression on his face and the suspicion of tears. They also missed the mumbled answer:

"How could I break hearts, Madame, when I've lost my own to the Queen of all men's hearts . . ."

She had nearly dismissed him then and there; she knew she should have done it, that it was impertinent and perhaps even dangerous for a servant to entertain such thoughts, much less dare to hint at them. But he was young and foolish and meant no harm; and it was a long time since any man had said a tender word to her.

"What do you want?" she asked sharply.

"Only to sit by you, Madame, and play to you if you like. I thought you looked disconsolate . . ."

"It's not for you to notice how I look or don't look," she said angrily under her breath. The reckless fool, to come and moon round her in the King's presence . . . he really ought to be sent away. But perhaps if she warned him severely enough this time, he might keep his place.

"You play the lute, Master Smeaton, and God knows you play it well. But don't mistake your betters when they make much of you; one more liberty with your Queen, and you'll be treated as the inferior person that you are. Go back to your place with the other players immediately."

She could have struck him for the way he walked, with his curly black head hanging like a whipped child, and sat dangling his lute between his knees, and staring at the ground.

Henry had noticed it, and was frowning, puzzled. Some of her ladies were giggling openly at the young man's discomfiture; most of them spoiled him like a puppy, and some of them flirted . . .

Then she forgot Smeaton and his foolish conduct, and the color drained out of her cheeks, and her heart began jumping as

255

it did since she became pregnant, if anything upset or excited her. The musicians had begun a lively jig, and some of the courtiers had received Henry's permission to make sets to it. But the King did not dance; he sat with his back to her, leaning forward, talking to Jane Seymour.

She felt the tears filling her eyes, and knew that in a moment they would spill onto her face; he mustn't see her crying again, it would only irritate him and remind him that he had to be careful, to keep away from his fancies and not upset her while she was carrying the child.

She knew how the restraint annoyed him, and how he broke it time after time, in spite of Butts and the rest of the doctors. He was glad about the child, but he resented her weakness; he wanted his son and his pleasures and he had begun to hate her because she indirectly made demands. And during the hours she lay awake at night, thinking endlessly over the past, she knew his hatred dated from that night at Winchester.

He had behaved like an animal or a madman; he had used her as if she were an enemy. There was nothing in him but lust and the striving for something he had never attained, something the dance had promised him again and forced him to admit he wanted. And at the end, when he got up and left her, and she saw him looking down at her where she lay, she knew that it had still escaped him, and that he was aware of it and felt naked in her sight, as well as his own. His hatred for her had been born that night, the night she conceived, and it only waited, poised, to see if a son would restore his self-respect.

With an effort she got up from her chair and sent Meg Shelton over to the King to tell him she had gone to see Elizabeth, and begged to be excused. When she left the room with her attendants, she turned off down the corridor to the royal nursery, where the two-year-old Princess was lodged for a few weeks, and shut herself up with the child for the rest of the morning.

The King had arranged a joust for the afternoon of January twenty-fourth, and entered the lists himself. He was just finishing his meal, dining privately with Weston and Sir Nicholas Carew and Sir Edward Seymour, the brother of his gentle Jane, when the Queen sent a message asking if she might see him.

Henry paused, avoiding the eyes of Seymour and Carew; only Weston remained true to Anne; if he could find a good word in her favor, he risked annoying the King by saying it. At that moment he half rose from his chair.

"Shall I carry your answer back to Her Grace, Sire?"

"Sit down, Francis. The page who brought the request can return the reply," Henry said abruptly.

"You haven't much time, Sire," Carew reminded him quickly. "The joust is due to begin less than an hour . . ."

Edward Seymour said nothing; he stared at his plate. Henry knew that he would tell his sister that Henry was on good terms with his wife, had granted her an audience and kept the court waiting at the jousting field. And Jane would be shyer and more distant when he saw her next. Where Anne would have accused and stormed, the quiet, unfathomable woman merely stepped a little further out of reach. And she was already too far for his happiness, Henry thought irritably. She had all the qualities he now desired in a woman; she was gentle, obedient, modest . . . everything the fierce passionate creature he had married was not and never would be.

But for that night at Winchester, that damnable night when she used little less than witchcraft to seduce him back again, he might have been free to carry out his wish, to rid himself of her and all she represented and begin afresh with Jane.

"What will you tell Her Grace?"

That was Weston again, always trying to promote her interests. He was too partisan to her, too much her friend where he had once been Henry's. The King scowled. She wanted to see him; she wasn't well enough to go to the jousting, she was in the fourth month and Butts had been mumbling about her health again. The fortunetellers were obliging him with the same prophecies that this time it would be a son. It might well be; the hope softened some of his impatience with her, and when he thought of having a Prince to show the world, even the charms of Jane receded.

He turned to the page, waiting beside his chair.

"Tell the Queen I shall attend on her within a few minutes."

When he had gone, Sir Francis Weston glanced from Carew to Seymour, and made a little mocking bow to each of them.

"Since I hadn't the pleasure of giving the Queen a message, gentlemen, may I carry one to Mistress Seymour; I fear the King may keep her waiting . . ."

Anne had sent all her ladies away and was sitting alone sewing, her back to the window. She sewed beautifully, her needle darting through the linen in its square frame, but the fingers guiding it were trembling. Margaret Wyatt had repeated a rumor that the imperial Ambassador Chapuiys was making friendly overtures to the King on behalf of the Emperor, and that there was a move to get the Princess Mary declared legitimate by Act of Parliament, in case Anne was delivered of another girl.

Margaret had been white and anxious when she told her, dreading the effect of the news on her mistress at this time, yet more afraid of the success of the intrigue unless Anne made a move to stop it. And she had made that move by sending for the King. Sitting alone in the sunny room, she had rehearsed exactly what to say to him, and her fear was a wise counselor for once. Anger or accusations would not help her; gentleness might; some spark of his old tenderness might reawaken when she asked him to protect her and reminded him about the child. The child was his one weakness, the only weapon left to her with which to fight his love for someone else and the machinations of the men, both great and small, who were trying to anticipate her ruin.

He came in unannounced. She started at the sound of the door opening, and saw him swinging his feathered cap, carrying his gloves, obviously on his way to the joust and impatient to be gone.

"You sent for me," he said. "But I haven't much time, Nan. The lists will be open in a short while, and I don't want to delay too long. What is it?"

"I'm sorry, I'd forgotten you were holding the joust so early. But I had to send for you and have a word with you, Harry. I'm very troubled. Please, won't you come into the room and sit with me, just for a few minutes?"

He sighed and pulled out a chair and fell into it, his legs thrust out before him, the cap still swinging, swinging, so that she could hardly take her eyes off it.

"If it's a complaint, I beg of you, make it another time," he said. "I'm in a happy mood today, and I don't want it spoiled."

She flushed and folded the linen around the frame and put it down beside her chair.

"I don't want to spoil anything for you; I fear I've done too much of that already."

He said nothing, but his narrow lips compressed. So it was a complaint, or worse still, an emotional scene. If he was forced to endure one more, to hear her voice raised once again, he'd bundle her off to Windsor for the rest of the nine months.

"Meg Wyatt told me something today," she began, and saw him stiffen, thinking she was going to mention Jane.

"I haven't time for women's gossip," he retorted.

"I only hope to God that's all it is," she said. "She told me that serpent Chapuiys is hoping for an alliance with you and the Emperor."

His eyebrows raised. "And if he were? What's it to you."

"My ruin," she answered slowly, "and you know it. So do I. I've lived in the midst of politics long enough to know that I'm regarded as the obstacle to peace between England and Spain. Now *she's* dead, they want to make your daughter Mary legitimate in the hope that it's not a son I'm carrying. Isn't that true? Isn't it true that if I weren't with child, that Spanish dog would be suggesting a divorce as a means of making peace with Charles?"

"You know too much for your own good," he said at last. "You've always stuck your finger into men's affairs and it isn't fitting in a woman."

She smiled in irony.

"What would you have me do? Sit back with my sewing and my women's tittle-tattle, while the ground is being cut from under me? Would you let them cut it, Harry? Will you listen

259

to Chapuiys, who hates you and supports the Pope, and sacrifice me when he asks? Will you deprive Elizabeth of her birthright and restore Mary to the Succession?"

He looked at her as she had seen him look at others, and she knew the answer even before he gave it.

"I should do whatever I think is right. As for the matter of legitimatizing Mary, give me a son, Madame, and there'll be no need."

He moved as if to leave, and she sprang up and threw herself down by the chair, clutching his sleeve.

"Will you abandon me, Harry? Is it in your mind while you sit there, knowing I'm carrying your child, probably the son you've prayed for all these years . . . Give me one word of hope; oh, God, I need it, I need it now more than ever in my life . . . Tell me that in spite of all our differences, in spite of everything I've said and done that's turned you from me, there's some mite of love for me left in your heart."

He had never seen her like this, weeping at his feet, and all he could see was the incongruity, the lines under her eyes, already wet with tears, and the ugly, pained shape of her mouth as she struggled not to cry. She bent her head and hid her face against his arm.

"I've always been too proud to do this, though I've wanted to for months. Though I've quarreled with you and screamed at you and gone away and wept until I thought my heart would break, all the time I wanted to do this; just to get near you, to feel there was something left of what we had together."

She raised her head and stared at him imploringly, until he looked away in sudden embarrassment. This wasn't what he wanted, this miserable submission at the end, when he had neither love nor pity left; it didn't gratify him, it only somehow put him in the wrong. There was nothing he could answer.

Slowly she pulled herself up and stood half turned away from him, wiping her eyes. Then she went back to her chair and sat down.

"I needn't ask again," she said dully. "Very well, I'll ask you something easier instead. If I have a son for you, will you protect me from my enemies?"

He rose, and pulled the cap on his head, pushing the drooping feather back.

"What's done is done, Nan," he said heavily. "And no one regrets it more than I, but I promise you this at least: Give me a Prince for England, and you shall have nothing to fear from anyone, neither abroad nor at court."

The jousting field was crowded with spectators; in spite of the time of year, the weather was crisp and sunny, and the King's courtiers sat in the stands wrapped in their cloaks, the woman's jeweled headdresses flashing in the light. It was a colorful, brilliant scene, charged with the excitement which reached its peak as the massive figure of the King moved from among the group of challengers, his armor gleaming. He mounted, took the long pointed lance from his squire, and waved toward the stand where the ladies were sitting. Jane Seymour's kerchief fluttered from his helmet. He saluted, snapped down the visor, and settled the lance in its cradle, at the ready. His opponent was Sir William Brereton, who waited at the end of the jousting field, a rather small figure in his heavy armor, balancing the cumbersome lance, his horse moving restlessly.

There was a burst of cheering for the royal challenger; he had unseated three men already that afternoon, and though Will Brereton was popular, he had become too closely associated with the Queen. The Seymours, the Norfolks, the Exeters and half the great nobles either watching or taking part in the tournament would be glad to see him fall to the lance of Mistress Seymour's champion. Brereton knew it. He sensed the hostility as he waited, watching the huge armored figure holding the heavy lance as lightly as if it were matchwood, and he tensed, sighting his opponent through the slits in his visor. They wanted him to fall, not just because it was politic for the King to win, but because they felt it would be an ill omen for the Queen they hated. "Damn them," Brereton said under his breath, not knowing why he resented her unpopularity so much, except that all his life he had sided with the loser. He liked her better now in her adversity than he had ever done in the high summer of her beauty and her favor with the King. She represented the Protestant faith he believed in, the faith which had begun to flourish quietly under her protection.

He saw the signal given to begin; there was a split second's silence, then he drove his spurs into his horse and charged toward the galloping figure of the King.

A woman screamed first when Henry fell. The scream was lost in a pandemonium of shouts as the crowd leaped to their feet, and the stewards came running across the ground toward that figure lying sprawled upon the ground, anchored by the massive armor.

Brereton's splintered lance was flung aside; men were holding his horse's head and helping him to slide off its back. He pushed back his visor. The King was surrounded now, but he could see that he still lay there without moving.

The Duke of Norfolk was among the first to reach him; he had leaped over the low parapet of the stand and had run; he saw them lift the King's helmet off and bellowed at them not to move him, but to send for Dr. Butts. He knelt beside Henry, staring at the closed eyes and the failing pallor; his breathing was heavy and uneven.

Thank God the lance had not struck his head. Though the deadly steel point was masked for safety, a direct blow might have broken his neck.

There was a deep dent in the breastplate; Brereton had caught him squarely on and sent him flying with such force that God knew what injuries he'd suffered. Kneeling there, waiting for the physicians, Norfolk trembled. He looked up at the white, frightened faces round him and saw the dread in Suffolk's eyes and knew what he was thinking, what they all were thinking. If the King died, Anne would be Regent for her daughter; worse still, for a son if she had one. And Anne would show as little mercy as she had received. If Henry died . . .

"Where's Butts?" he snarled. "In God's name where is he?"

"Here, my Lord, here . . . Let me through and get back, please."

Butts ordered the crowd back and went on his knees beside the King. He unbuckled the heavy gauntlet and drew off the wristpiece and for a moment that seemed to Norfolk and the watchers like a hundred years, he felt for Henry's pulse.

"I can't tell his injuries," he said under his breath to the Duke. "But there's no danger of immediate death. Bring up a litter and we'll move him now."

Norfolk stood up stiffly; Suffolk was shouting for a litter and the stewards and gentlemen were pressing round again, trying to remove as much of the armor as they could.

There was no immediate danger of death. Butts never failed; he knew the King was injured, but not dying. For a moment the Duke closed his eyes, slowly he wiped the sweat off his face. In that moment the idea came to him. An idea so monstrous, so opportune that he sucked in his breath. It came like lightning, and it illumined the dark places of his mind in a piercing flash, touching his hatred, his grievances, his insatiable ambitions for personal power. This was the opportunity, the chance on which his plans for using yet another niece depended. This was the fulfillment of his obstinate hope that something, somehow would cheat Henry of his son, and Anne of her reprieve from the doom of that other Queen, less than a month dead. The idea came, and the risk followed, the risk of failure, the risk of being called to account afterward . . . Nothing risked, said the Duke, nothing won, and stepped back unnoticed. It was worth trying, anything was worth trying. Anything! He turned and raced towards the palace buildings.

She heard his feet pounding down the corridor, and let her sewing slip off her lap, half rising from her chair. The door crashed open and she sank back when she saw him, hatless and wild, glaring at her in the doorway like some demon in a masque, with one eye twisted almost out of sight and the other blazing at her. She was alone except for Lady Winfield, who was nearly eighty years of age and partly deaf.

"Uncle, what is it? What is it?" she gasped at him. The answer came at her like a blow, delivered at the top of his voice.

"The King! He fell at the jousting! The King is dead!"

Her mouth opened, but no sound came; he saw the shock dilate her eyes and her hands pushing, struggling to force her body out of the chair.

"Dead!" He repeated.

Then she screamed, a high pitiful shriek of terror, and fell on her face at his feet. The old woman stumbled toward her, muttering; he heard her ask his help and saw her try to lift the limp unconscious body. Then he turned and walked out, closing the door of her room behind him.

The King had multiple bruises and a joint of his armor had opened an ugly wound in his leg; he was shaken and bad-tempered, but he sent for Brereton and forgave him publicly for having nearly killed him. Then he remembered to send a message to Anne that he was well and unhurt except for a few scratches.

But the message came too late; before the week was out, Anne's pregnancy ended at four o'clock one morning. After a night of agony, she was miscarried of a son.

14

THEY HAD LIFTED HER UP ON THE CUSHIONS AND MADE SOME attempt to comb back her hair and arrange the bedclothes when word reached them that the King was coming. Anne let her women do what they could, but when Margaret Wyatt brought a pot of rouge and a mirror, she waved her wearily away.

"I know what I look like, Meg. Nothing can help me now . . ."

She was the color of wax, and her eyes were opened wide in an unnatural stare; her body was rigid and her hands opened and closed on the coverlets every few seconds. She was weak from loss of blood, and she had been terribly, convulsively sick when she heard someone whisper, "God have mercy on us . . . it was a boy . . ."

She should have fallen into a merciful sleep, but her whole being was stretched as taut as a bowstring, waiting for him to come. And Henry came.

The room was almost as full as it had been when Elizabeth was born, two and a half years earlier; she heard the same murmur of anticipation in the anterooms and the heavy tread as he approached. Then he was in the room itself, standing astride like a great red-necked bull, his fists on his hips, his eyes two green points of fury in his scarlet face.

Inch by inch she raised herself till she sat up, and her teeth nipped her lower lip to stop its involuntary trembling. He said nothing till he moved round to the side of the bed, and the ladies shrank back against the wall. Out of the corner of her eye she saw old Butts mustering his courage and moving forward to interfere on behalf of his patient.

The King's roar shook the window frames.

"None of your damned excuses this time! Get out of my way—all of you!"

They held each other's gaze like two animals at bay, while the women slipped past him and moved to the further end of the room; and finally they were isolated and out of earshot.

She knew what was coming; she knew the depth and insanity of his hatred as he looked down at her, struggling for words bitter enough to upbraid and wound in retaliation for what she had lost. And in her desperate defeat and vulnerability her courage faltered for a moment.

"Harry," her voice quavered, "Harry, I was frightened. . . . Norfolk did it . . ."

"Norfolk!" He snorted the word; his voice was shaking with rage. "Norfolk! You lying strumpet, hold your vile tongue!"

"Norfolk," she repeated. "Norfolk who burst in on me and told me you were dead."

"You lie," he roared. "God took my son to punish me for having married you! God's shown me the truth at last."

Something snapped in her then, something the years of pitiless anxiety and bitter disillusion had strained to the utmost; in that second all hope fled, and with it all fear for herself or the consequen-

265

ces. She dragged herself up on the pillows, so weak that the effort exhausted her, and then gathered what was left of her strength, blinded by pain to anything but the sight of his face, convulsed with hatred as he glared down at her, seeing his fury that he hadn't found her dead. And for the last time her fatal temper blazed.

"God shows you nothing!" She panted, "You come here and accuse me, you who never spared me anything to try to keep the child. So God's cast a blight on me now, as He cast one on Catherine? Oh, how convenient for you! What a good friend you've made of the Almighty that He always bears responsibility for everything you fail to do yourself. I lost the son you wanted; what a fine excuse you have at last for turning on me . . . you can run to the Seymour bitch with a clear conscience now and yelp that God's abandoned you because of me, just as He did when you were tired of *her!* Congratulations, Sire. Congratulations! What God takes from His faithful servant Henry Tudor with one hand, He gives with the other!" She stopped, gasping for breath.

She saw his hand come up, clenched into a fist to strike her, and for one wild moment hoped he would, and that the force of his blow would break her neck.

"Kill me," she said. "I'd like nothing better."

"Nor would I," he snarled. "Why didn't you die, when you spewed out my son from your miserable body? How dare you live and look at me and open your mouth with abuse and excuses. God, you talk of God! I doubt there is one, when I see such as you! You babble of Norfolk to me . . . you babble of my failure, you, who couldn't do what any woman worthy of the name could do—keep a child in your belly and deliver it alive!"

"Give me the chance!" she shouted wildly. "Come to my bed and play the man for a change! You stand there cursing me because you hate me—not for the child but because I've seen you as the others haven't. Mistress Seymour doesn't know you, does she? She only knows what I knew before I came into your bed and found a feeble pig's bladder instead of a man!"

"Hold your tongue, God's curse on you!" he choked, "God's curse on you, I say. You black whore. I plunged my arms in blood up to the elbow just to have you, just to have the son you promised me! And all I have is this . . . I let you hound Wolsey to his grave, I sent my wretched wife away and let her die alone because of you . . . my *wife*, do you hear! More wife than you are, better than you, royal born, worthy of the crown I took from her and put in the gutter when I put it on your head! More, who was my friend, died because of you . . . Fisher and the others. Good men, true men, when they denounced you. I killed and imprisoned and exiled those I loved because the Devil whispered in my ear through your mouth. By the living Christ, I might have harmed my own poor daughter Mary if I hadn't seen through you in time! May God forgive me! May God forgive the lives I've taken and the sins on my soul—all put there through you and for you. You lie there, daring to defy me still, you who've humbled my manhood by your own inadequacy, and stained my justice! You've said your last poisoned words to me this day."

He turned away from her, and his eye caught the sight of basins and something bundled into a tiny towel. Tears came into his eyes; they hid the yawning cleft she had made in his pride, his self-esteem; he wept for the dead infant in the eyes of his terrified court. In his heart he wept for his own guilt and his own failure and for the echo of her words, which he would spend the rest of his life trying to refute.

Then he turned and looked at her, weeping, once again, and this time they all heard what he said.

"Look to yourself! You'll get no more sons by me!"

When he had gone she collapsed; her strength ebbed out of her, leaving her too weak to speak or even cry. She lay with her eyes closed, drifting in the limbo of semi-consciousness, struggling for oblivion, and held back by the wordless repetition in her mind of one half sentence, spoken long ago by a voice that she loved . . . If you value your life, never say one word . . . if you value your life . . .

"Thomas, I am accursed."

Cromwell sat on his low chair in front of the King, his hands clasped on his knees, and watched him without answering.

"Accursed," Henry repeated. They were alone in the royal apartments at Greenwich; it was late at night and the King was in his night robe. He sat before a blazing fire, with a ewer full of posset beside him, and opened his heart to his secretary, Cromwell.

Cromwell had been in bed when the summons came, but he had dressed with lightning speed and presented himself at the private door into the sovereign's bedroom, where he found the King already prepared for bed, sitting alone, with his head in his hands.

The picture of regal despair, Henry could have been sculpted in that posture, Cromwell thought as he moved soundlessly to his place. The secretary was the audience for the play which was about to take place; he was not deceived; he knew it was a play. Over the years of his long climb to power on Henry's shoulders he had discovered that in all personal matters, the King lied and postured while he conveyed his wishes. The wise man obeyed the wish and ignored the hypocrisy.

He had heard of the scene in the Queen's room, and that sentence pronounced on her before witnesses, the sentence which everyone knew meant her divorce, and he had been expecting to be summoned.

Cromwell had helped Henry to marry her; now he would have to help Henry put her away. The King raised his head and stared at him with bloodshot eyes.

"It is a week today since God took my son," he said.

"I know, Sire. All England grieves with you."

"No," Henry shook his head. "No, all England rejoices. The world rejoices. Henry of England has no son!"

"No one who loves you is glad," Cromwell said gently, "Only your enemies. And they are nothing compared to your friends. *You* are not hated, Sire, believe me."

"While she is, eh? You tell the truth, Thomas; my people hate her and always have. They will never wish me well through her. Out of evil, good does not come . . . God's proved that once again. She is evil, and I am still in mortal sin; the good I want for my kingdom will never come through her, I know that now."

"What will you do?" Cromwell asked him. He was going to get rid of her, and Cromwell knew it without doubt. All the reasons had been put before him; the anger of God, the hatred of the people, the evil in the woman. All the reasons Henry was putting forward to himself as well as to him, reasons which would have to be accepted while the real one remained a mystery. What was it, he wondered for a second . . . The King was tired of her and wanted someone else . . . was it as simple as that? . . . Was it political as well? . . . No one would ever know. And it was not important.

"I want to take a true wife, Thomas; I want to purge myself of this sin I've committed. I won't suffer for the Queen's ill-doings, and I won't let England suffer."

"Cranmer can look into the marriage," he suggested quietly. "If your Grace's conscience is uneasy . . ." He let the sentence die away.

Henry leaned back, his eyes fixed on the fire; the muscles worked in his heavy jaw.

"Another divorce, Thomas . . . another Queen in exile, with a daughter to make claims for . . . a rallying point for malcontents, like Catherine for the last six years. Is that what you suggest?"

For one moment the Secretary couldn't find an answer. His lids lifted a hair's-breadth, showing the dull unfeeling eyes, with a gleam of astonishment in them like the vague stirring in the center of a muddy pond.

Then the expression vanished. Henry did not intend divorce. He did not want to send her away, or imprison her as he had done with Catherine. He wanted her death.

Cromwell moistened his suddenly dry lips and decided to make sure.

"This makes me wish she had died when the child miscarried," he murmured. "Death would resolve this problem."

The King did not look at him, but something flickered across his face, something gratified, which meant he knew his wishes had been understood.

"She urged the execution of Catherine and my daughter Mary

often enough," he said, as if he were speaking to himself. But Cromwell heard. "She showed no pity for any man or woman either. Urging me to be merciless, when I wanted to show mercy. Her crimes are worthy of nothing less than what she brought on others."

"Then she should pay for them," Cromwell suggested. "And for any others she may have committed—perhaps unknown to Your Grace."

"God knows," Henry said harshly. "God knows, I don't."

"It might be possible to find out," the Secretary suggested, "if you will trust in me and give me time."

"I trust you, Thomas," he said quickly. "No one knows my mind but you. Pray for me, friend, I'm grievously tormented . . ."

"I'll pray, Sire. Only have patience. It may take a little time."

"How much time?" the King demanded suddenly. "How long must I bear with this, and keep a virtuous and honorable lady waiting . . ."

"It's early February now, Sire," Cromwell promised him. "You shall be free before the spring."

In that first week in February Anne had seen no one but the women who attended her. When Henry left her room that day, everyone fled. Nobody came to visit her; her father shadowed the King as ostentatiously as he dared, to show where his sympathies lay, and went out of his way to express them in Cromwell's hearing. Even her maids of honor absented themselves, with the exception of Margaret Wyatt, who twice slipped into the room to try to comfort her.

But she found Anne beyond comfort. The tireless spirit was quenched as she lay in bed with her head turned to the wall, weeping or else in silence for hours at a time, while the isolation spread from her room to her entire quarters in the palace. The anterooms were empty, no one moved through the passages but servants; no voices, no laughter, no sign of life. The King had abandoned her, and from that moment she was alone. Cromwell, whose spies were everywhere, heard what had happened, and remembered his judgment of her true position, made long before the marriage. She stood in the jungle surrounded by enemies who were only waiting for the lion who sheltered her to move away.

The lion had moved at last, and they were preparing to advance on her for the kill. Cromwell had never imagined then that he would be the one to lead them.

He had decided what to do; the only thing he dared do which would make sure that the King would be free and revenged at the same time. Because Cromwell knew that Henry wanted a revenge, that the love he had once borne her had turned to the cruelest hatred. When he spoke of the executions of men he had sent to their death without a qualm and blamed Anne for them, Cromwell understood the direction that vengeance was to take. They might have poisoned her; he'd thought of that once, but Europe was ringing with the accusation that Catherine had been done to death at Kimbolton by that means; even Henry might be forced off his throne if the murder of a young and healthy woman was laid to his charge so soon.

Poison was not the way, but Cromwell knew the way, the way no Queen of England had ever trodden throughout history. There was only one charge which would ensure that she took it, and that her name was blackened for all time to come. Two of her chamberwomen were in his pay, so was her page and her steward of the household. He sent for them all and told them what to watch for as soon as she was out of bed.

"George."

Anne's brother turned impatiently to find his wife standing in the doorway. He had just returned to Greenwich from a mission, and the news of Anne's illness and disgrace had come to him from Wiltshire himself. One of the worst quarrels father and son ever had took place that day, when he told George that his sister was doomed, and the only way to avoid falling with her was to abandon her openly before the King. Something other than selfish fear had made Wiltshire offer such advice to his son; something that was trying to save him at the last moment, and it was rejected with such bitterness that even he recoiled. He

271

could desert his own daughter like the unnatural dog he was, George Rochford shouted, but if Anne was in trouble he was going to her then and there! He had been about to do so when his wife Jane came into the room.

"I've just seen Father, who told me you were here."

"Oh, did he!" Rochford snapped. "I hope he told you what a worthy homecoming I had, in that case."

Jane closed the door and came toward him slowly.

"He seemed very angry," she said, "but I didn't ask what was the matter; I only wanted to see you."

He ignored the last remark.

"Not another word will I speak to him as long as I live. God is my witness! Of all the vile, sneaking fiends, to stand there, telling me to leave her . . . leave her lying there ill and in terrible trouble and not go to see her! God's blood, I wouldn't have believed it possible!"

He didn't see the shadow cross her face, or hear the altered tone when she spoke again.

"You mean the Queen?"

"I mean my sister! He's not been near her since the miscarriage, do you hear that?"

"Nobody has," Jane answered slowly. "Nobody has dared, after what happened with the King. Are you going, George?"

He looked at her contemptuously.

"Nothing in heaven or earth would keep me away."

"I wanted to speak to you," she murmured. She had come close to him, and her pale face was turned up to his; her hands reached out uncertainly and touched the breast of his blue doublet.

"I've wanted to speak to you for a long time, George."

"What about?" Her touch repelled him, making him want to move away.

"About ourselves. I don't know how to begin to say it . . ."

"In that case why not wait till later?" he suggested. "I'll talk as much as you wish, Jane; it's high time we settled things between ourselves anyway, but I'm pressed now and I can't wait."

"You must wait," she said to him; her eyes had opened wide and were fixed on his face. "I beg of you, hear me."

He hesitated, fighting his impatience and his dislike of her nearness, trying not to be unkind.

"I love you," she whispered. "George, do you hear, I love you and I want you to love me."

She reached up and caught him round the neck, and the next moment her mouth was pressed on his, her body flattened against his. He had never enjoyed her as a woman; in the beginning he had found her cold and sneering, and then demanding and hysterical when he accepted her rebuffs. The practice of love had stopped between them a long time ago and the attempt to revive it was suddenly horrifying to him; the white face and hooded eyes, that bitter, hungry mouth filled him with blind horror. He felt as if he were holding a snake . . .

"Stop it, for God's sake!"

Embarrassed and sickened, he pulled her arms from round his neck and held her off.

"This is no time for that," he said awkwardly.

"Because you're worried about Anne?"

To his astonishment he saw that she was smiling.

"I am, and because we've left off all such things for God knows how long. You said you wanted to talk, Jane, but if that's what you wanted, you picked a poor time."

"I always pick a poor time," she said lightly. "Always. You're always about to see your sister or do something for her, when I come near."

He looked at her and his mouth hardened.

"We've had this bickering before. Don't waste my time and your own with it now. Nan has nothing to do with us and never has."

"She turned you against me," Jane said. "You love her best. That's why you don't love me. That's why you push me off when I come to you like any wife, after you've been away . . . because you'd rather go to her."

"God knows what you mean, I don't! You come to me like any wife . . . Jane, how can you talk such lunacy! You've never loved me and I suppose I've not loved you, if it comes to that." He gestured wearily. "Be honest, we married as little more than

273

children, and never were happy. Never. I'm sorry, Janey, I've said so before, but it was nobody's fault we didn't mix as well as marry. And don't let's quarrel now, when we're in trouble!"

She laughed at him.

"I'm not in trouble, dear husband. *She* is. The King's found her out at last."

"Hold your tongue."

"He's found her out," she went on. "She'll soon be gone, George, she'll soon be divorced and sent away somewhere, perhaps shut up, like Catherine. If you go to her, George, you'll be ruined too. She told me that herself last year. She told me other things too; she said the King was impotent, that it was *his* fault there weren't any children, not hers . . ."

"I don't believe you," he shouted and knew that he was changing color.

"Ah," said his wife. "I see she told you too . . . yes, she told me. She was overwrought—you know how she becomes at times—saying many things she tried to take back afterward. And when she thought I'd tell the King, she threatened me with you, George. She said, if I fall, George falls with me. That's why I kept quiet; I didn't want anything to happen to you. And I still don't! Don't go to her, don't go, I beg you!"

She rushed at him and clung on to his arm, pulling him back from the door.

"I love you, I love you . . . leave her alone," she shrieked. "Let her stay there . . . let her die! Stay with me, take me in your arms . . . I want you, George, I love you. This is your last chance . . ."

"I wouldn't touch you if you were the last woman in the world!" He wrenched his arm free, and she stumbled to her knees.

"You love me . . . ugh! I could vomit my heart up at the thought of you. And I'll never forgive you for what you've wished on Nan. Keep out of my sight from this day forward. I'm done with speaking to you as I've done with living with you!"

He slammed the door behind him, and she crouched on her knees, listening as his footsteps died away down the passage, hurrying footsteps, running to Anne. Slowly, she raised herself and automatically straightened her jeweled cap. Then she opened the door and went out to follow him.

George could hardly believe it when he saw her first; she looked so small lying in the bed, and the face which turned slowly toward him was yellow and haggard, the brilliant eyes were dull and sunken; even her magnificent hair hung down her shoulders in two lifeless plaits.

"Nan! Oh, Nan, Nan, what have they done to you!"

An elderly lady in waiting was moving about in a corner of the room, but he didn't even look at her; he ran to the bed and caught her in his arms.

"George . . ." It was a shaking whisper. He felt how thin she was, and then she began to tremble helplessly as he held her, rocking her back and forth in his arms as if she had been a child, murmuring that he was there, and she was safe now . . .

"Oh, God, I needed you so much . . . It's been so dreadful; the baby died and it was a boy, and he came and stood here and cursed me, George; he cursed me . . . I tried to tell him Norfolk frightened me, I tried to tell him, but he wouldn't listen . . . he raved at me . . . oh, oh, my brother, help me, what am I going to do . . ."

"Hush," he begged her. "Hush and be calm, I can't understand you, Nan, try not to talk so fast. . . . Who cursed you?"

"Henry," she sobbed. "And I cursed him back. I said everything to him . . . things I shouldn't have said. I must have been mad; but when I saw him look at me . . . hating me and so cruel. Jesus, I couldn't help myself! And now it's over, George. He's done with me."

"Of course he hasn't," he lied. "Don't be so foolish." Over her shoulder he closed his eyes for a moment. Dear God, she couldn't have said that to him . . . about his failure as a lover . . . she couldn't . . .

"What did you say to him, Nan? Try to think clearly."

He laid her back against the pillows, and wiped her wet face with his own handkerchief. "Try to tell me calmly."

"I told him it was his fault," she whispered. "I told him he

275

wasn't a man . . . that no one knew him as I did. I insulted him. . . . Oh, God, you know my tongue, George . . . I've always had a gift for the right words!"

"You have indeed," he answered ruefully. "What then?"

"He accused me of causing all those deaths . . . he said God was punishing him for marrying me. And he said I'd have no more sons by him! I tell you, he's finished with me!"

"Well," he said at last, "if he's finished with you, he's finished. There are worse fates. You'll have to retire to the country, Nan, and say farewell to all this for the rest of your life."

She looked up at him and tried to smile.

"You're right; there's no worse fate than this, living like this in his hatred, waiting to be flung aside like an old shoe that pinches. I'm weary of life, George. Whatever prison he chooses for me, I only care about one thing. I hope it isn't Kimbolton."

"Prison? Nonsense, Nan, you're letting your illness make you morbid. Why should he imprison you? You've committed no crime!"

"I've lost his Prince," she reminded him, and immediately the tears began to flow again at the mention of the subject. She took the handkerchief and choked into it for a moment; then she composed herself and went on.

"And I did what you warned me not to; I exposed him to himself. I know him, George, and he hates me now. He won't let me live in the country; he'll divorce me and then you'll see what he'll do. He'll treat me as he treated Catherine . . . God forgive me," she said shakily. "I never stopped encouraging him, I hated her so much. I thought if she were dead I'd be secure with him. I miscarried on the very day she was buried, did you know that?"

He shook his head.

"What does that matter? You're all that matters now, Nan. Something must be done; you've got to reach him, apologize, placate him in some way; you always could."

"No longer," she answered. "Not for nearly three years. No, there's nothing to be done. I've lain here for the past week, seeing no one but the women who waited on me, and poor old

Butts . . . He was kind, George." She began to weep again, but the trembling had passed.

"And I've had time to think of him, myself, and what's happened to us, the love we had. But never at the same time, brother; I only discovered my love when his was dead. . . . Now that's gone too; it went when he stood over me, with his fist raised to strike me, and asked me why I hadn't died. . . . Thank God, I'm free of that at least!"

She sighed, and held on to his hand.

"You shouldn't have come here, George; nobody's dared to visit me. That's a good measure of his anger, isn't it? I don't want you in his disfavor too."

"May God blight him and his anger," he answered harshly, "when I see what he's done to you . . . I'd like to kill him!"

"Don't, don't," she begged. "It isn't worth it now. Nothing's worth it. I'd be truly glad to die."

"You'll do no such thing," he said fiercely. "You'll prove yourself my brave sister and leave this sickroom as soon as you're well. You'll wear your finest dress and all your jewels and walk down among those cowardly scum like the Queen you are! And we'll just see how many dare do anything but bow the knee to you! I'll be behind you, and the first one I see lacking in respect will come out into the grounds and taste the edge of my sword!"

She smiled at him and moved up on the pillows.

"You almost give me courage," she said gently. "Courage at least to face them all; I've been afraid of that."

"Face them," he urged. "And face him too; you'll never mend anything lying rotting here. And remember this: We've always been together, even as children. If anything frightened you you used to run to me, Nan."

"And you went out to defend me," she finished. "I remember."

"That hasn't changed. I stand with you, Nan, whatever happens. We're truly alone, I think, from what I've seen and heard, but at least we're alone together. We'll fight together and get the best terms from him we can, if what you think is true. I'm not altogether without friends and influences, nor are you. I have money and tenants I can raise, and every Protestant in England thinks of you as their patroness. We won't be so easy to dislodge and mistreat as some people seem to think."

"I won't have you in danger," she said steadily. "I've brought enough suffering on others. I won't risk anything happening to you."

"Nothing will happen to me," he promised. "And remember, Nan, brother and sister we stand together, now as all through our lives. To the death."

She squeezed his hand and nodded.

"And you'll take heart and get strong and well enough to come out quickly? You promise me that?"

"I promise," she said.

"Keep a good heart, then," he said gently, "and be as brave as you've always been."

He kissed her thin cheek and waved to the waiting woman, old Lady Wingfield, who was dozing in a chair by the fireplace. He left her and walked slowly away down the corridor, without seeing the figure of his wife disappear through a doorway. She had been waiting, watching that closed door, until he came out.

Anne had kept her promise to her brother, and as soon as she was strong enough, she dressed and appeared in public. The ordeal was eased for her by his presence; he gave her his arm and supported her down the corridors from her apartments to the crowded gallery. A hush had fallen on the courtiers when they saw her in the doorway. The laughter and talk died away, leaving an awkward silence. Slowly she walked forward, her fingers digging into George's arm, and still no one moved or spoke.

It was Norreys who came to her first; she saw a figure detach itself from a small crowd round one of the window seats and recognized him; her heart jumped, and the hand he seized and kissed was shaking.

"Welcome back, Madame. The court's a brighter place for your presence."

She thanked him and saw the look in his blue eyes that had betrayed him on the day Sir Thomas More was executed, when the King laid the blame on her. She saw the look which said he

278

loved her, though he had denied it out of fear on that occasion, and she thanked him for that and his courageous act with a quick pressure of his hand. After that, several of the ladies curtsied and the men bowed; light-hearted Francis Weston saluted her, and a general polite murmur ran through the gallery. The King was not there to give the lead and it was safer not to be too hostile. Only Sir Edward Seymour turned his head and stared in the opposite direction as she passed.

As George said afterward, there was no better way to find their friends. She had nodded, already tired out, thinking of Norreys again and wanting to burst into tears because she was less deserted than she had imagined. He had been brave to do that; no one appreciated what it might mean to him better than she did, should the King hear the story and decide to punish him.

If she got the chance to speak to Henry, she would try to soften the account. But no action was taken against Norreys; he remained in the King's circle of intimates, his favor apparently unimpaired. And Anne never managed to speak to the King on that or any other subject.

Two days later they dined together in public, according to custom; Anne sat on his right hand and received his ceremonial kiss of welcome as she took her place, aware that hundreds of eyes were staring at her, and feeling only the freezing glance of his eyes as they rested for a moment on her face. No word passed between them during the meal. The King spoke to his neighbors and leaned across her to speak to the Duke of Suffolk, but he said nothing to her. She sat through the meal, trying to eat; she even tried to talk to Suffolk in her desperation, but the Duke bent over his plate and grunted. He was grinning at her discomfiture; he could have reminded her under his breath of those other times when she had snubbed and contradicted him and mocked him; he had always sworn to be revenged and now he was. The vengeance was sweet; he glanced up at her white face and settled back to enjoy himself.

When dinner was over the King turned to her.

"I trust you are recovered fully, Madame, and can fulfill your official duties, as I intend to fulfill mine."

Then he left the table, followed by Suffolk, who pushed against her deliberately, and said something and laughed to Sir Edward Seymour as he passed.

That was the pattern of her future. She was to continue in her official capacity as Consort, to appear at court ceremonies, to eat with the King in public, to be present on any State occasion he deemed her presence necessary. But he would neither speak to her nor see her privately, and he had made it plain that she could be insulted with impunity. Jane Seymour's brother was made a gentleman of his privy chamber and installed in rooms communicating with his own, so that Henry could see his favorite when he wanted to; everyone knew the extent of those visits; they took place every single day, and they were marked by an ominous decorum.

The King had such respect for the iron virtue of Mistress Seymour that he undertook never to speak to her alone. Someone was always present in that little chamber, while he wooed the impenetrable woman; someone watched when he held her hand and ventured to press it to his lips. Never did he hold her as he had Anne; the crudities which had attracted him to Anne originally were forbidden now, eschewed by his own wish. There should be nothing in this relationship to remind him of his feelings for that other . . . Nothing to recall the shameful heat, the bitter disillusion, the recurring sense of guilt which seeped into him after his failures. She had befouled passion, he thought violently; only in the cool purity of this unusual woman he had found, could he find peace and cleanliness again.

And Cromwell had promised him that he should find it by the spring.

The King bore with the sight of Anne; he tortured himself unmercifully by having her in his presence and at his table, when her scent or the sound of her voice taunted him with memories of that day in January when she showed him an image of himself that he must banish out of his mind one day or else go mad . . . He punished himself ruthlessly for having loved her, and he drew some comfort from her agony. She was in agony and he knew it; indeed, now that he was fortified by Cromwell's promise, it gave him the keenest satisfaction of his life to imagine her suspense and to keep her in it. He knew her eagle fierceness and guessed that she longed for an excuse to bring him within reach, down to the level of their old intimacy, where she had an equal chance. He never gave it to her; coldness and silence were breaking that strong spirit, as violence never could. He had found her weakness and probed it without pity, as she had probed his.

He watched her grow thinner and detected an odd air of uncertainty in the way she spoke and moved, noticing how low her pride was falling by the way she clung to the few men and women who still sought her out. Norreys was one of them, and Weston; the serious Brereton too, who had so nearly killed him at the joust. All good friends of his before she seduced them away, spoiling that intimacy as she had spoiled everything he loved.

They should pay for that desertion. These defectors should pay for every hour they spent with her and her treacherous brother, for every moment of laughter or relief they gave her. Without them she might have suffered more. They were giving her counsel and strength; he noticed with fury that by April she had adapted herself outwardly at least, that the signs of physical distress were balanced by a new dignity, a strange determined calm that threatened to place her out of reach of pain or insult. He sent for Cromwell and asked him one question only:

"How much longer?"

The Secretary held his gaze.

"I have studied the reports received by loyal members of the Queen's household. I fear they lead to a grave suspicion. It is too vile to be mentioned to you until proved. By May Day I shall have that proof."

Smeaton the lute player was in high spirits that morning of April 30th. The last three months had been the happiest of his life, for he had been in daily attendance on the Queen. The Queen was sick at first and needed cheering; he sang and played the gayest tunes he knew, and hung around her rooms every day in the hope of a summons which usually came. He was gentle and romantic-minded; the attention of some of the less discreet court ladies had

281

made him aware of his good looks and encouraged dangerous fantasies regarding the one who never looked at him at all. His vanity had given him the courage to pay her compliments and to disregard the rebuffs he received. She liked his playing, and he was certain she liked him. He bent over his lute and imagined coming close to her as he had done to others, touching her neck and her hair, and bending down to reach her mouth. The image made him blush and kept him awake at night, reliving the moments when the little group who spent so much time with her were silent, and her attention was given to him and his music.

He was popular with them all except Sir Henry Norreys; Norreys was arrogant. And he had seen Norreys looking at her when he thought it safe to do so. Norreys wasn't snubbed and put in his place, because he was a great noble. . . . Smeaton hated Norreys.

She was writing when he approached her that morning, and he waited in the doorway till she looked up.

"What is it, Mark?"

She laid down her pen, putting aside an appeal from a poor clergyman who had been deprived of his benefice because he was suspected of Lutheran sympathies. Many similar petitions came to her, begging her to use her influence on their behalf—small hope of that—she thought bitterly; or asking for money and protection, seeking her recommendation to a better living. What she had begun out of policy, to win as many of the Reforming clergy to her side as she could, had become a charity which cost her hundreds of pounds in alms. She had nothing now but money to give anyone who appealed to her, and all her life Anne had been generous with whatever she had.

In return these people prayed for her and somehow the thought of their good wishes comforted her. They addressed her as their sweet patroness, and she tasted the pleasure of good works which used to seem so dull and hypocritical when she was young, with both hands grasping for the things of this world. She had gained exactly what she sought; but the jewels had turned to stones, the prominence placed her now on a high platform of humiliation, and the downfall of her enemies gave little satisfaction; more grew in their place, like the dragon's teeth in the fable. Her hands were empty after all, and they were beginning to clutch at other consolations.

She noticed Smeaton coloring as he approached her; he always reddened if she spoke to him or paid him any attention; even if she were angry, he bore it better than being ignored or treated according to his place. He was spoiled and foolish, and lately she and George and all her small circle of friends had indulged him far too much.

"I'd like your permission to go out this afternoon, Madame," he said.

"You know you can go where you please," she reminded him. "There's no need to interrupt me on trivialities, Mark. You know that quite well!"

"Yes, Madame." He looked down. "But Master Secretary Cromwell has invited me to dinner at Stepney today, and I thought if you wanted me to play to you, you might be angry if I wasn't here. If you do want me, Madame, I'd gladly stay . . ."

"Cromwell . . ." She frowned. "Cromwell's invited you, you say?"

He smiled delightedly. He had been bursting with pride over the invitation since a page handed it to him that morning.

"Yes, Madame. I imagine he wants to hear me play, but he's asked me to dine with him just the same!"

She shrugged. "In that case, go. Make much of the opportunity, Mark, for he has the favor of the King!"

"I want no one's favor," the boy boasted, "as long as I have yours! I live and die your servant, Madame. Your humble servant," he added quickly. He hurried away, humming, and went to change into his best doublet. An invitation to the Secretary's house at Stepney was a great honor.

The cellar walls were thick; there was a sheen of damp on them, for they were below the level of the riverbank. No one could hear anything; Cromwell leaned forward in his chair.

"Give the cord another turn," he said.

"Aaah . . . aaah . . . !"

The scream rose to a deafening pitch, beating against the dark walls of the cellar at Stepney, and died away, choking in Smeaton's throat.

He was bound to a chair, and two of the Secretary's servants were standing over him, tightening a rough cord around his forehead with a stick. The skin had broken, and the blood was making a hideous pattern down his face. Cromwell watched him impassively as he sank back, writhing with pain and only signaled to the torturers to keep the stick tight.

"What you feel now, Master Smeaton, is a caress compared to the next time they twist it. You'll find your eyeballs on your cheeks. Answer me, before I give the word again. You are in love with the Queen, aren't you?"

"Yes," the voice sobbed.

That was the truth, and Cromwell knew it; the spying chamberwomen hadn't lied when they said that.

"And you've committed adultery with her, haven't you?" There was a pause, and Cromwell made a quick gesture.

The shriek was inhuman that time. It was such a simple method, and so seldom used, considering its efficacy. The only difficulty was that if the victim held out too long, he fainted. Smeaton vomited instead.

"You have committed adultery with her, haven't you?"

He couldn't answer at first; the Secretary knew the signs too well to mistake them for obstinacy.

"Haven't you?" he asked again.

It was only a whisper.

"Yes."

"And you weren't the only one. Who else?"

"I don't know . . . ah! No, no, no! Norreys . . . Norreys had her!"

Cromwell was busy writing. At last he looked up.

"Loose him, and throw him in the corner as he is. Then he can go to the Tower."

As he climbed the steps to the ground floor of the house, Cromwell could hear the sound of anguished, crazy sobbing coming from the cellar. No doubt Smeaton was finding the realization of what he'd done worse than the last half an hour of simple torture, Cromwell thought dispassionately. He drafted an order for the arrest of Sir Henry Norreys, and asked for an emergency meeting with the Dukes of Norfolk and Suffolk, on a matter closely concerning the honor and well-being of the King's Grace.

"Gentlemen," Cromwell said, "the thing is so vile I hardly know how to begin."

They were shut up in his closet at Greenwich; both Norfolk and Suffolk were half a head taller than the Secretary, and he stood looking up at them. They had refused his offer to sit down.

"Our ears can bear it," Suffolk said roughly. "Come, let's hear it; the whole court is buzzing with rumors like a beehive!"

"It concerns my niece the Queen," Norfolk said. "I knew it when I heard her musician had been sent to the Tower."

"It does," Cromwell agreed. "Gentlemen, I suggest once more that we sit down; this may take longer than you think. And I'm tired; I had an exhausting afternoon."

He pulled up a chair to his writing table and laid his finger on a roll of parchment.

"I shan't waste time reading this to you; I'll tell you the contents. It's the confession of Mark Smeaton, the Queen's lute player, made in my presence today. He confesses to adultery with her."

"What!"

The word escaped Suffolk like an oath. He stared at Cromwell, his thick brows beetling in disbelief.

"Smeaton! That sniveling boy . . . impossible! She wouldn't . . ."

"She would, and has," Cromwell interrupted. "There is no question about it, my Lord," he said gently. "No question at all."

Slowly the Duke sat back in his chair, and Cromwell smiled faintly at him.

"It may seem difficult to believe," he continued. "But His Grace will be convinced when he hears the evidence."

"If His Grace is convinced, so are we," Norfolk spoke for the first time.

Suffolk nodded. He understood at last; Smeaton . . . that wretched pretty youth with less spine than a woman. Cromwell

285

must have had him tortured. Adultery—he said the word to himself. Adultery would mean death. He looked at the ugly little Secretary with new eyes.

"This is painful for you, my Lord," Cromwell said to Norfolk. "The Queen is your own blood . . ."

"If she were my own daughter," the Duke answered shortly, "I should feel nothing but loathing for her crime."

"Crimes," the Secretary corrected. "Smeaton was not the only one. He named Sir Henry Norreys. You see, the affair will have terrible consequences, now that one of the King's intimate friends is involved. And as a powerful member of the Queen's faction at court, he will be arrested. There will be a great outcry among his friends and hers."

Norfolk leaned forward.

"The Queen is the figurehead of that faction," he said. "Are you suggesting that they will oppose his arrest . . . and hers?"

"I think it very likely," Cromwell answered. "That's why I've sent for you, my Lords. The King will need the support of all his loyal subjects, if this stain on his honor is to be wiped away. More than partisanship for the Queen is involved in this, for her friends have a political and religious interest at stake. If she falls, however justly, those interests will suffer. If this faction is destroyed, not only the King's welfare, but the welfare of England will be safeguarded."

"In other words, Anne is an adulteress, and her friends are traitors, isn't that it?" Suffolk said impatiently. He had no time for hypocrisy; the charge had been trumped up against her, that was obvious. As her bitter enemy, he would prosecute it with the utmost vigor and send her to her death if he could, but he refused to sit there play-acting with Cromwell.

"Come into the open, for God's sake," he said. "We haven't time to waste on a lot of niceties. Anne stands for the Protestant party, and against an alliance with the Emperor. She has dug her own grave; now you want a means of sending the rest of her supporters into it with her!"

"Politically she has become a disaster to the country," Cromwell explained. "The imperial Ambassador made it plain to me a little while ago that as long as she remained Queen, the Emperor would not mend his quarrel with England. And we need to mend that quarrel. We need to hold the balance against France, who has left us to side with Rome. We must have the alliance, my Lords, and we must protect the interests of the Princess Mary, until a son is born to the King. And no son will be born of *her* now.

"All this you know; I'm repeating it because this is the only time these added reasons for her complete destruction can be put forward. The Queen must die, and all those who might be tempted to rise in her defense must be struck down before they have the chance to move. You asked for plain words, now you have them. The onus will fall on the King's Council, of which you are leading members. The jury who will try her will be headed by you, especially you, my Lord Norfolk. His Grace will not tolerate an acquittal of any of the persons who may be charged in this."

"Then the King knows," Norfolk said softly.

"He knows," came the answer. "He knows everything and has left the conduct of it to me. He will not be officially informed until tomorrow at the joust."

"We have only her, and the lute player, and Norreys," Suffolk said. "What about her father? And her brother? Above all, her brother!"

"Lord Wiltshire will make no move to save her; he has withdrawn his support in public for the last four months. Wiltshire will follow the King, which is lucky; if a father abandons his own daughter, who would question her guilt?"

There was no pretense between them now.

"George will," Norfolk retorted. "George Boleyn will fight for her to the last drop of his blood. You'll have to arrest him the moment hands are laid on her."

The Secretary looked from one to the other before answering.

"I have already the means to do that," he said quietly. "He too has been accused."

"Of complicity?" Suffolk stared. "By God, you must have worried Master Lute Player with sharp teeth!"

"Smeaton never mentioned him. An hour ago his wife, Lady Rochford, came to see me. She had heard of the musician's arrest and suspected some trouble for the Queen." He paused; he had hardly been able to credit his good fortune at the time. It was still almost unreal.

"Jane accused him of complicity?" Norfolk exclaimed.

"Of incest."

For a moment there was silence. It was Norfolk who broke it.

"Great God!" he said at last. "And you'll charge him with it?"

"He shall go to the Tower when she does," Cromwell answered, "and he will also be tried by you."

"When will the arrests be made?" Suffolk asked.

"Tomorrow evening, after the joust. That is the King's wish."

"The lute player, Norreys, and her brother," Suffolk said again. "That's three at least."

"She shall be kept in the Tower for a few days," Cromwell said, "and questioned. At the end of that time we may have more. . . . Now, my Lords, have I made the situation clear?"

"Perfectly," Norfolk answered, rising, "perfectly clear. His Grace can rely on his loyal peers to see that these foul crimes are properly expiated."

"I shall convey that to him." Cromwell smiled. "And in return, my Lord, pay my respects to your niece, Mistress Seymour. I hope to prove myself her faithful servant."

15

THE JOUST AND THE HOURS THAT FOLLOWED SEEMED LIKE A nightmare to Anne; the events of that first day in May had an air of unreality, as if she moved and spoke in a waking dream. A formal message requested her presence at the jousting field, and for the first part of the afternoon, she sat in her place by the King's side, unwanted and ignored, like Catherine of Aragon at the bear-baiting all those years ago, trying to watch the tournament. The atmosphere had been oppressive, as if some violent storm were about to break, though the sky over their heads was blue and cloudless. She hardly saw the bouts, or noticed who won or who was vanquished, aware only of that immovable figure by her side, his gaze directed straight ahead. She remembered starting when he suddenly moved beside her. Someone had passed him a message; the paper was screwed up in his hand as he turned to look at her for a long moment, before he quitted his seat abruptly, taking half his gentlemen with him, and left the jousting field without a word of explanation.

She would never forget that look, never forget the small eyes blazing with hatred and something that was much like triumph as they met her own.

She knew, as he turned his back on her without a word, that at last the end had come.

The whispers rose around her all that evening. The King had gone straight to Westminster from Greenwich, to York Place, where they had spent so many days together after Wolsey's death, where he had met her after her progress through the City, with his arms outstretched, hoping she was pleased, hoping that the child she was visibly carrying was going to be a son.

She was left alone in the half empty palace for the rest of the day, for most of the courtiers had followed him to Westminster.

When one of her women left her rooms that evening to see if her brother George was among them, she ran back screaming to the Queen that guards were posted round the door.

That night was passed as a semi-prisoner, isolated from help as completely as if she were in the Tower. No one replied to her frantic questions or came in answer to her repeated summons. All was silence till the next morning—May second. And then she was told to attend before the Council.

She saw her Uncle Norfolk sitting at the long table in the Council Chamber with Suffolk and Sir William Paulet. Paulet stayed in her memory of that nightmare ordeal; he had not shouted and accused her like the others. He had not roared at her that she had lain with Smeaton and Norreys like a common whore . . . that she was going to be burned . . . Norfolk had said that.

When she denied the charges, Suffolk bellowed at her not to lie. The two men had confessed, he said. They had all had the satisfaction of seeing her break down and weep; that was when Paulet suggested that the Queen might be given a chair.

She had been too dazed to realize what had happened; when they brought her back to her apartments she stood rooted in the middle of the floor, the words chasing each other around her whirling brain. Adultery . . . she was under arrest on a charge of adultery with Smeaton . . . SMEATON . . . she cried the name aloud to her terrified women . . . Smeaton . . . and Norreys. They had confessed; confessed what, she demanded, rounding on Margaret Wyatt like a madwoman. What had those fiends been saying to her, trying to make her admit . . . What was this all about?

No one could answer; they begged her not to rage, to calm herself, and she could see the fear in their faces while they tried to comfort her. The blow had been struck so suddenly that she was breaking, and in terror she realized it; she was giving way, she thought hysterically. The agony of that night, lying half awake, half in tormented sleep, knowing that she was threatened by some unknown danger, that the King had gone to York Place, leaving her under a guard, that no one was able to reach her or tell her what had happened . . . She was breaking down before they ever dragged her in to the Council and bullied and threatened her with burning at the stake.

When Norfolk and her chamberlain came with an escort that afternoon, she had to be supported down the stairs and out into the gardens; when she saw the barge waiting at the jetty, she faltered and stopped.

"Where are you taking me . . . Uncle, for God's sake . . ."

"To the Tower, where you belong! Delay any more and I'll have you carried!"

Four women surrounded her in the boat; her aunt, Lady Boleyn, who was a stanch Catholic and friend of the Princess Mary, Mrs. Stonor, Mrs. Cosyns and one other. They were all enemies, she thought wildly, looking around for Margaret, or Meg Shelton or anyone she knew who should have come with her . . . Her protests died away as the barge began to move up the river, in the direction of the Tower.

Norfolk watched her from time to time; he saw that she swayed in her seat and that her eyes were closed. The parapet was lined with crowds who stretched and pointed at the soldiers on guard in the barge, and the woman sitting in cruel prominence. It was the Queen, they shouted. The Queen, under arrest! Nan Bullen, going to the Tower!

"They've seen you, Madame," Norfolk taunted grimly. "Open your eyes and take a last look at your subjects!"

She obeyed him, clinging to the shreds of her self-control, and saw the curiosity and hatred of the people who watched her sailing slowly past. Some of them cheered ironically, and waved, shouting insults. It was just three years since she'd sailed in Catherine's barge along the same route, to lodge in the palace buildings at the Tower before her coronation.

They were delighted, rejoicing. . . . She swallowed, fighting back more tears, helpless, foolish tears because the rabble were against her too.

"When my brother hears how I've been treated," she said shakily to Norfolk's back, "when he hears of this he'll make you pay . . ." The Duke glanced over his shoulder at her and laughed. Panic seized her.

"Where is he? Where is George?"

"At York Place," Norfolk snapped. "Now hold your tongue!"

The walls and turrets of the Tower were white in the late spring sunshine; she watched it growing larger as the barge approached, and unconsciously her hands gripped the edges of her seat. The landing stage was farther down the wall; the royal landing stage where she had disembarked that other May, with the Lord Mayor and the Tower Governor and dignitaries drawn up to meet her.

The barge was turning in against the tide; above her head the portcullis of Traitor's Gate stood out like black teeth in a gaping maw. The barge slid under it, into the gloom, beneath the stone archway. Ahead lay the wet steps leading up to the Tower and at the top of them she saw the Governor, Sir William Kingston. Kingston, who had always hated her and favored Catherine in the old days. Kingston, who had taken Wolsey on the last stages of his fatal journey. Now Kingston was waiting to take her into his custody.

Two of the women helped her disembark. A company of yeomen were drawn up with the Governor, waiting to close in on her. She mounted the steps up from Traitor's Gate, stepping with care, the woman Cosyns' hand under her elbow. And then she came face to face with Kingston.

"She is in your charge," Norfolk said. "Keep her strictly."

Anne stood there, aware of the women at her side and behind her, fighting a rising impulse to shriek with terror, feeling the high gray walls closing in on her and the ground moving under her feet. Then the threat of collapse receded; Kingston's face swam into focus, bearded and sharp-eyed, pitiless as stone. Her Uncle Norfolk had re-entered the barge and was leaving her. It was impossible, she said to herself firmly, quite impossible. She had been at Greenwich Palace less than two hours before; she could not possibly be standing in the precincts of the Tower . . . The Tower. Smeaton was in the Tower. And Norreys.

"Come, Madame."

She stared at the Governor, her lips quivering.

"Master Kingston, shall I go into a dungeon?"

If Henry did that to her she would go mad; she knew it. She would lose her mind if they shut her in one of those rat-infested holes, where no daylight ever penetrated . . .

"No, Madame, you shall go into the lodgings you lay in at your coronation."

"It is too good for me . . . Jesus, have mercy on me . . ."

To his astonishment she burst out laughing. She stood there with her hand to her throat and shook with laughter, while the tears ran down her face. Kingston was at a loss. He looked at her aunt, Lady Boleyn, for some assistance, and that determined lady took Anne's wrist in a firm grip, and began to lead her forward. The company of yeomen fell in on either side of her and Kingston offered her his arm, a courtesy he had not intended showing her, but the wretched woman looked as if she were about to fall. The fit of hysteria passed as they moved out toward the incline leading to the royal apartments on Tower Green.

Henry had not sent her to a dungeon. Henry had allowed her to rest in rooms she knew. Another fear returned, nagging at her.

"Have you seen my brother, Lord Rochford?"

He avoided the wide eyes, bright with terror, and said shortly: "I saw him at York Place this morning, Madame."

He could not bring himself to tell her that her brother had entered the Tower a few hours before.

"Why don't you admit it?" Lady Boleyn asked. "Lying won't save you, or them. Confession might!"

"I have nothing to confess! I'm innocent!"

"Smeaton told everything," Mrs. Cosyns reminded her. "So did that fine courtier . . . they've already given you away."

"They lie! They lie, there's nothing to confess against me . . . I've done nothing!"

"Weeping won't move the jury when you come to trial," said Lady Boleyn. "We pity you, in spite of what you've done. But they won't. And the more you persist in denying, the less hope you have. Come, calm yourself and think. Smeaton and Norreys weren't the only ones, were they? There were other men; you weren't content with only two . . . who else were your lovers?"

"No one! Oh, merciful God, You know that's true . . . I had no lovers . . ."

"But men were in love with you," said Mrs. Cosyns. "You can't deny that!"

"That's not my fault . . . It's not a crime . . . If Norreys loved me, they can't kill him and me for that!"

"How do you know he loved you?" That was Mrs. Stonor's gentle voice. "How can anyone believe anything you say . . ."

"Because I know it! I said it to him once, I said, 'You look to have me . . .'"

"The Queen is becoming hysterical again," Lady Boleyn said. "Fetch her some water. Now, Madame, drink this. And what did Norreys say?"

"He denied it . . . He was afraid. Everyone was afraid toward the end . . . Only Francis; Francis used to laugh and try to cheer me . . . Francis never cared for anything."

"Which Francis was this? I'll take the cup—which Francis?"

"Weston . . . Francis Weston. Why do you keep questioning me? For God's sake have pity and leave me alone. . . . Get out of my room and leave me alone!"

"You know that's not allowed," Cosyns admonished. "We have our orders, Madame, and you're not to be left alone even for a minute. Tell us about Weston. He's that handsome young knight who was always with you, isn't he? Was he in love with you too?"

"I don't know . . . no, I don't think so . . . he was always joking . . ."

"Did he say he loved you as a jest? It must have been a jest, Madame; he knew you wouldn't have him near you otherwise."

"Of course he knew! He knew I'd never be unfaithful to the King . . ."

"Try not to mumble so, it's difficult to hear," said Mrs. Stonor. "Speak up, Madame. Your handkerchief's in your sleeve . . . there, in the left one. What did you say to him?"

"I told him he ought to love his wife better than he did. . . . Ah, by God, I'd learned to pity wives whose husbands looked at other women by that time! He was always hanging after Meg Shelton. I reproved him, do you hear! I told him he had no right to love anyone but his wife . . ."

"Let her calm down a little," Lady Boleyn whispered quickly. "She can have all the fits of hysteria she wants when we've got this out of her . . ." She raised her voice.

"Don't distress yourself, Madame. You did quite right to rebuke him, quite right. And what did he say to that?"

"He only laughed. He was never serious . . . he said he loved someone better than Meg or his wife."

"And that was yourself, of course," said Mrs. Stonor.

"That's what he said. He laughed and said, 'Yourself.' I remember how angry I was with him . . ."

"Naturally," Mrs. Stonor soothed, "naturally. It was a terrible thing to say."

"It was a joke! Only a joke! The wretch wanted to wriggle out of what I'd said to him . . . he was always like that. We both laughed over it together afterward; he even promised me not to seduce Meg."

"He was a seducer, then?" Lady Boleyn queried.

"No, no, not in that way . . . Francis wasn't wicked; you know what I mean, you know what young men are with women . . ."

"No woman is safe from their lusts," Mrs. Cosyns said. "We know, Madame, we know how difficult it was for you . . ."

"Difficult? What do you mean, difficult . . . I did nothing . . . Francis only said . . . oh, Mother of Jesus, what are you doing to me? What am I saying? Stop it . . . stop it . . ."

"Shut the window," Lady Boleyn ordered quickly, "or we'll have Kingston up here if he hears her shriek like this. We'd better leave her alone now."

"Master Cromwell said we were to get everything out of her," Cosyns insisted stubbornly. "Now is the best time; she's apt to say anything. If you can't stand the crying out, my Lady, Stonor and I can continue without you."

"You know why this is? You know the real reason why I'm here? I lost the King's son!"

"Don't clutch at me like that, Madame, you'll tear my dress," Mrs. Stonor said. "That was the time His Grace fell at the joust, wasn't it?"

"Norfolk did it, Norfolk, my own uncle! He said the King was dead, and I miscarried . . . Stonor, he frightened me till I lost the child . . . I tried to tell the King, I tried . . ."

"Of course you were frightened . . . thinking His Grace was dead. . . . Sir William Brereton must have struck him very hard to give him such a fall. But he didn't do it purposely, Madame, nobody thinks that . . ."

"Brereton . . . Brereton? Didn't do what purposely?"

"Try to kill the King."

"Kill the King! Oh, God above, Will wouldn't touch a hair of anyone's head, however much he sympathized with me! Will wasn't like Norreys, Will was always gentle . . ."

"Norreys was more violent, then," the quiet voice prodded. "If the King had died, would he have married you, do you think, Madame? Would Norreys have married you? No one could blame him for wanting the Queen for his wife . . ."

"How could he, Stonor? How could he think of filling dead men's shoes? Nothing could happen to the King . . . Oh, how my head aches . . . Stonor, Stonor, when will I ever sleep again, when will I ever get some rest . . . Stonor! Where is my brother?"

"Lie back and calm yourself. No no, Madame, lie back! Your brother's well enough."

"Where is he? Why haven't I had word from him? Don't lie to me, for the love of God! Tell me what's happened to him . . . I know something's happened to him . . ."

The two women looked at each other. The senior, Mrs. Cosyns, nodded. Their work was done; there was no point in holding back the truth any longer. Her strength was at an end; when she found out, it was unlikely they'd get anything coherent from her for some time . . .

"Lord Rochford's in the Tower."

"What did you say? Stonor, what did you say?"

"He's in the Tower, Madame. He's been here for the last two days."

"In the Tower? All this time? No wonder he didn't send word. . . . But he's close to me. I'm glad he's close to me."

"Fetch Lady Boleyn, Cosyns. Tell her the Queen's fainted!"

"I forbid you to tell me anything about her, Thomas!" Henry cut the Secretary short in the middle of a sentence. They were at York Place, standing together in the room which had been Anne's privy chamber, the fine room facing the gardens at the back.

"I want no account of her tears or lying protests," the King repeated. "Just report on the charges and the prisoners."

"Weston and Brereton are in the Tower, Your Grace," Cromwell explained. "Sent there by her confessions to the ladies guarding her. So are two more: her cousin, Thomas Wyatt, and Sir Richard Page, another gentleman of your chamber."

"Why those two?" Henry asked, frowning. He was fond of

296

Page; Page had been friendly enough with her in the old days, but the friendship had cooled when Henry's favor was withdrawn. Page was innocent. He did not want anything to happen to Page. He would have Page released anyway.

"What is the charge against Wyatt?"

"Infidelity with the Queen before marriage, Sire. It was common gossip through the court for years."

"So common that even I heard it," Henry retorted sharply. "Is there evidence against him since?"

"Why, no," Cromwell shook his head, "but surely the fact that before she was Queen he had . . ."

"If we were to behead every man who knew her before I did, there'd be no heads left in England! Don't let your zeal carry you away, friend. Wyatt was my rival in the past; he had as much right to her then as I had, may God forgive us both. Would you have me pointed out as taking revenge for that old rivalry, now, after all these years? Be careful, Thomas, lest you hurt my dignity!"

Cromwell managed a nervous smile. He had begun to sweat as Henry talked. It was becoming more difficult to fathom the workings of that mind, and more dangerous to make even small mistakes. He had thought Henry would be gratified to hear of Anne's disintegration in the Tower, to know that whatever his private grudge against her was, it was being amply satisfied. Kingston wrote, faithfully reporting everything she said and did, and that guard of watchful harridans had twisted her inside out with their trap questions and their mental torturing. Far more effective than the rack; she'd appear at her trial without a bruise on her body, convicted out of her own mouth. . . . He had been taken by surprise when the King stopped his recital of her raving and distress and heaved an inward sigh. The mood had changed. The mood of frantic spite was masked under an air of false impartiality; even of pained disgust. To Cromwell, of all men, he was insisting that he believed the charges.

Now he objected to two of the victims, two legitimate victims, in the Secretary's opinion. Both Protestants, both friends of Anne, one indeed her cousin and former lover . . .

"Have Page and Wyatt released," the King ordered. "No man

shall point at my justice. Only the guilty are to suffer, Thomas. I say these two are innocent."

"As you command, Sire."

"When will the trials begin?"

"The four commoners stand trial at Westminster on the twelfth. The Queen and her brother will come before their judges at the Tower on the fifteenth. My Lord Norfolk will preside over a panel of twenty-six peers. It was thought expedient to exempt her father from this duty . . . if Your Grace agrees."

"No man shall point me out for cruelty, either," Henry answered. "Wiltshire is excused. Anything else? No further evidence or suspects?"

"None, Sire."

"Excellent, Thomas. You may go now."

When Cromwell left him, Henry went to the window and stood looking out over the formal gardens; they were green and colorful in the May sunshine and a small fountain in the paved court in the center scattered water like a shower of diamonds. Wolsey had taken pride in those gardens, long before the King had enlarged and improved them, as he did with Hampton when he took it from his Minister. Wolsey had loved gardens, as he loved architecture. Henry used to see him poring over the builder's plans, making suggestions, and going out to supervise the gardeners' work.

Wolsey, he had been fond of Wolsey once. He could remember their long talks together, the jokes they shared, the enthusiasms, the plans to advance England at the expense of France . . . Wolsey had always distrusted the French, and he was right. They had abandoned their alliance . . .

He could remember the wars, when the priest plotted and directed the campaigns with the skill of any general in the field.

He could remember many things, standing in the house which had once been Wolsey's, in the room where *she* had sat by the fireplace, forcing an account of the Cardinal's death out of Northumberland and Kingston.

It was fitting that Kingston should be her jailer and ironic too, like some punishment devised by the ancient gods. It proved yet again that she was responsible for the harsh end of his old friend and faithful servant. Wolsey had not betrayed his interests; he had only fought hers, seeing, most likely, what Henry himself saw now. That she was evil and unworthy . . . that the union would never be blessed by God.

His fists clenched slowly; he stared out over the pleasant vista from the window and saw nothing but her face, gazing up at him from the pillow, with the disappointment lurking in her eyes . . . her face set in anger, in pleading, in pain . . . Her face, covered by a false mask of desire with her anxiety showing through it, the face he had thought the most beautiful in the world, and come to hate until he longed to disfigure it with blows . . .

She had made him cruel to Catherine too; though oddly, he had less regret for her than for Sir Thomas More . . . Catherine had deserved her fate.

Women, he thought viciously, women, women, always women in the way. Women offering him what he partly wanted and somehow hated; women hanging onto his arm, dragging at him with cries and claims. Wives and mistresses; jealous and petty and totally inferior. Yet they held the secret of life; only a woman could give him what he wanted more than anything else in the world; the son to follow him. However much he hated women, he raged inwardly, he had to have one to achieve his purpose.

But not one like her, not a fierce, strong, passionate woman, who dared to judge him and pass that judgment in words. No woman should be like her! No ordinary woman was, he muttered; she had bewitched him. How often he had told her that, making a compliment out of his own servitude . . . how often he had made a horrible truth into a pretty speech . . . Bewitched. Goaded to bloodshed and cruelty, brought by her influence to the frame of mind where he had even threatened the life of his own daughter Mary. He sighed, and the tension in him eased.

He had an affection for Mary; there was less need to deny it now, to others or himself. Mary was his daughter; she didn't come within the category of the rest . . . Jane Seymour praised her to him, showing a courage he admired, because in his heart he wanted a wife who would make peace between them. One thing was certain; he'd have the marriage annulled and bastardize *her* brat. Jane's boy should have no rivals.

Jane had gone to Sir Nicholas Carew's house as soon as Anne had been arrested. There she waited with her usual patience, until the thing was done. . . . And it would be done. They would find her guilty, Norfolk, Suffolk and the rest; even Northumberland, who had once loved her many years ago. She would pay for the enemies she had made in the heyday of her pride, when she stood helpless in front of them, with her life in their hands.

She would die. He said the sentence aloud to himself. She would die and he would be free of her forever. Free of the thought of her —free of her scorching wit, her subtle scent, her empty grace . . . Free with brutal finality. Never until that moment had he appreciated the subtlety of death, the tremendous power vested in his right hand when it traced his signature. The power to wipe out an enemy, to destroy a memory . . . to send an unwanted image out of the sight of all men forever. To send her into oblivion, and with her, everything she represented.

He need never bear with anyone again, he thought calmly; he need never to endure an uncomfortable situation or tolerate an enemy; he need never be balked of anything he wanted. He could do to anyone what he was going to do to Anne, his wife. The precedent was set. When a Queen died, no man was safe . . .

And he would blot her out of his mind, now, before the thing was done. She would be already dead, as far as his actions were concerned.

He would go down to Hampton Court and take Jane with him, and he would enjoy himself like any eager bridegroom.

The Queen left her prison for the first time in a fortnight when she crossed Tower Green to go to the great hall to stand her trial.

It was a lovely day, and Anne walked slowly, preceded by Kingston, with her hated attendants on each side, and the small escort of yeomen. The air was warm, and birds were twittering in the trees. They had brought the clothes she asked for, and some of her jewels, and she had chosen her dress as carefully as if she were

300

going to a State occasion. She knew it angered them when she dressed in black; dead-black satin, with trimmings of royal ermine, and a rich headdress of diamonds and pearls.

She was prejudged, for they had told her that the others accused with her had been found guilty and condemned. Only her brother and herself were left. And at last, by the mercy of the God she had invoked so desperately, her courage had returned.

For days she had been calm, almost indifferent. The women probed and threatened in vain for they had no weapons left after they told her that George was taken too. Even when they told her what he was charged with, she only paled and turned away in sick contempt. It was all over; the tears and trembling and hysterics, the battle she had fought for ten long years was lost and at the same time, won. If the King hoped she'd plead for mercy in front of his judges, he was going to be disappointed.

After the bright sunshine outside, she blinked in the dim light of the hall and nearly stumbled on the steps; Kingston caught her arm and steadied her.

She smiled at him. The hall was packed with people; they were crowded behind barriers, and the smell told her they were ordinary citizens of London, come to see their Queen condemned to death, and their King's action vindicated. The smile remained on her pale lips. He had arranged everything very cleverly, but he might regret that audience before the day was done.

The twenty-six peers chosen to try her sat in two rows on the dais; the Duke of Norfolk was in the middle of them, wearing his robe as Lord High Steward of England, balancing a quill pen in his fingers. Suffolk was close beside him in the front rank. And there, surely that was Henry Percy . . . A hush had fallen; one of the yeomen stationed in the body of the hall moved his pike, and the haft clanked on the stone floor. They had built a low platform in front of the dais, and there she saw her brother standing between two guards.

At the bottom step, she paused, and for a moment they looked at each other. He was white from his imprisonment, but he held himself as proudly as ever, one hand on his hip, his handsome face set in a defiant sneer. They had not tortured him or questioned him; he had admitted nothing. Nor had Norreys, Brereton, nor Weston, as everyone knew now. But that had not saved them. They were all in the Tower, awaiting execution.

For a long moment brother and sister looked at each other, close enough to reach out, but separated by the line of yeomen.

"My brave Nan," he said huskily, and his face twisted suddenly.

"God bless you, my brother . . ."

Then they had moved her up onto the platform, and placed a chair for her to sit in.

"You know the charges of which you are accused," the Duke of Norfolk said.

"I would like to hear them. There may be some I'm not aware of; they've increased in number since I was first arrested, I believe."

He was unprepared for that, or for the firmness of her voice. He glanced up quickly, and frowned when she met his eye. He knew that look; she was going to fight back. Much good would it do her . . .

"You are charged with adultery with the prisoners Smeaton, Weston, Brereton, Norreys and your own brother George Rochford. You are charged with conspiring the King's death, with speaking disrespectfully and disloyally about his person, and with planning to marry one of your lovers after His Grace had come to harm. Those prosecuting may put their case."

The King's prosecutors rose to read the list of accusations. For the first time Anne saw that one of them was Thomas Cromwell. She sat very still and listened, memorizing the dates given. She noticed the Lord Mayor of London and representatives of the powerful City Guilds sitting in special seats. The voices droned on, taking it in turn. Cromwell read the most serious charges, his back half turned toward her. She had given herself to the three gentlemen and the bastard lute player on numerous occasions since October 1533 till April, when she was arrested. She had discussed the King's death, telling Norreys that he hoped for dead men's shoes. . . . The phrase returned to her, torn out of context, twisted from her babblings in the Tower, when her sanity was wavering . . . dead men's shoes.

She had made fun of the King with her brother, decrying his literary and musical talents, his dress . . . she had hoped to place a bastard on the throne of England, indulging in vile relations with the said brother for that purpose, having kept him in her room for more than an hour, while she was known to be in bed . . .

The case was proved, Cromwell stated flatly. The criminal Smeaton had confessed, though the others had persisted in their denial of the truth, but all had been found guilty on the evidence given. The same verdict must be given against the Queen.

Cromwell bowed to the judges and sat down, his back turned to Anne. Norfolk looked up. It was difficult to judge the reaction of the crowd; almost too many crimes had been alleged, and the foulest, concerning Rochford, sounded miserably flimsy when put into words. He didn't want to ask the question, but he had to, for form's sake.

"What have you to say to these things, Madame? Do you admit your guilt?"

She stood up, one hand resting on the arm of the chair, and looked from the peers to the Lord Mayor, and then around the people, packed tight to the walls.

"Before God, I deny every word. You ask me if I have anything to say, my Uncle. Very well, you shall hear my defense."

She paused; the hall was completely quiet, the attention of every man and woman in it was riveted on that upright figure, in deep black, standing alone on the platform.

"I am accused of adultery with Mark Smeaton. I lack words to express my contempt of such a charge. To all who know me, and they sit there in judgment, I say this: Am I a woman who'd degrade herself with a base-born servant, a woman without pride or dignity? . . . How often have I been criticized for too much pride, rather than too little, for seeking to rise above my station rather than sink below it? No, my lords, and you, good people. Pity the wretch who dishonored himself and me because he wasn't man enough to bear the torture. But look on me, and don't believe him! I am an English gentlewoman born, not a Princess of France!"

The reference to the King's great-grandmother and the Welsh clerk of the wardrobe drew a gasp.

"Stop her," Suffolk snapped under his breath. "Broken in spirit, was she . . . wait till I lay hands on Master Cromwell . . ."

"As for the others," Anne's voice rang out clearly. "I hear that they maintained the truth, as I shall. My accusers mention dates. They say I betrayed the King in October, 1533. That was the year of my marriage, the year of my daughter Elizabeth's birth. You must remember that birth, my Lords, for many of you were present at it. It was not an easy travail . . . it nearly cost my life. Yet I am supposed to have recovered my health so quickly that within one month I went lusting after one of the King's gentlemen! My traducers should have been more careful when they made the time October. . . . And again in December, when I was three months gone with child . . . the child I knew my life and future depended on safely bringing to bed. I lost that child, as all of you know . . . God help me, that's why I stand here now . . . but not through betraying the King its father . . . virtue apart, only a madwoman would have taken such a risk!"

"You forget your own admissions," Norfolk cut in quickly. "You forget the confessions made to those who guarded you! And the reports of those in your household who saw these abominations!"

"Servants," she said scornfully. "Always servants . . . scullions and chamberwomen, ready to lie from fear or greed. Couldn't you find any other to bear false witness for you? My confessions in the Tower! Ah, God forgive those who took advantage of my agony, and my fear, to twist my words for their own purpose. My fear, my Lords and people! I don't deny it; for which of you women standing here today, would not have been afraid, if you'd been lying there, where I was, alone except for spies and enemies, trembling for my friends and those I loved! I was afraid, and I babbled through my tears, as prisoners do. You've taken a word here and a phrase there and turned the meaning round, putting things into my mouth which never came out of it! I deny what is charged against me. I deny it as a Queen and a woman, before the God who judges us all."

"Do you deny the testament of your own sister-in-law, Lady

Rochford, when she accuses you of the foulest crime known to mankind?"

That was her old enemy, Lord Exeter.

She faced him directly, and for the first time, the tears came into her eyes, and her voice quivered.

"I did not know *she* was responsible for that. May God forgive her; I tremble for her soul. And for yours, because you don't believe it, even as you ask that question. It *is* the foulest crime known to mankind, and it's laid to my brother's charge and mine. Those of you who hate me, and would believe any vileness of me, believe what you wish concerning the rest; but think of my brother as you know him, and you must refute this. You do refute it, in your hearts . . ."

"She's gone a good way to saving *him*, at least," the Duke of Norfolk said under his breath. At that moment he felt a curious pride in her; she was doomed and he hated her and had been anxious to bring that doom about, but he saw her then as a Howard, as part of his own proud, ancient line, nobler than any King of England, and was glad that she had acquitted herself well.

"You've made your defense, Madame," he said. "And you've had a fair hearing."

It was a pity that such a large crowd had heard Anne already; the Duke could tell by the changed atmosphere in the hall that she, who had always been so hated by the common people, had gained a lot of sympathy. Cromwell and the King had insisted on making the trial public, sure of popular support for the unprecedented thing they were about to do. That was a mistake. She had aroused sympathy among her judges too; Norfolk could see that. Many were looking uncomfortable and whispering among themselves; only Suffolk and Exeter and Lord Dacre preserved their hostility intact.

"The evidence against you has been heard, your defense has been weighed. I call now upon my fellow judges to record their verdict."

For a moment uncle and niece looked at each other.

"For myself, I find you guilty on all counts."

She stood very still, her face unchanging as, one after the other, the judges echoed Norfolk's words. She saw Northumberland hesitating when his turn came; he was staring at her, terribly pale, his features working. She would never know what he was thinking, whether he remembered their long dead love, the kisses and vows and hopes exchanged between them so many years ago, in that moment when he had to send her to her death.

"Guilty."

It was a croak, and he dropped the pen when his turn came to sign the declaration.

The Duke of Norfolk's voice echoed through the silent hall.

"You are found guilty of the charges laid against you. According to the law I hereby sentence you to suffer death. You shall be burned alive or beheaded, at the pleasure of our Sovereign Lord the King."

Lady Boleyn made a move toward her from the back of the platform, thinking she might falter, but Anne stopped her with a gesture.

"I welcome death, whatever form it takes." Her voice was clear and steady.

"I have only one regret; that four innocent men, loyal to their King, are to die through me, and only one request; that I be allowed a little time to make my soul."

She turned then and descended the short steps from the platform to the ground. Not once had she ever looked at Thomas Cromwell. She stopped, searching for George, hoping for one last word before they passed out of sight of each other forever. But he had been moved to the other side of the platform, to avoid a second meeting. She would not see him before he took his place before the judges. The throng of people parted as she passed between her guards, walking through them with her head up and her eyes fixed ahead. As she went by in her disgrace, some of the citizens who'd spat and jeered at her on her way up the Thames to her imprisonment in the Tower took off their caps and bowed.

306

16

GEORGE, VISCOUNT ROCHFORD, DIED ON THE SCAFFOLD ON MAY seventeenth and with him perished the three noblemen and the humble musician who had loved his sister. They died well, even Smeaton, who had been kept in chains in a dungeon because of his low birth.

George died when he might have escaped, thanks to his defense and the change in public sympathy; he was about to be acquitted when Cromwell handed him a paper with his wife's accusation that Anne had said the King was impotent and asked for a plain answer, forbidding the contents to be read aloud. The charge had been withheld from Anne's trial for fear that she might reveal the nature of it and expose Henry to doubt and ridicule.

At the top of his voice, Anne's brother read the charge touching the King's impotence and failure to have children, to an audience of two thousand of the King's subjects. Anne was to die, and he gladly took the one revenge upon her murderer he could, knowing his own life was forfeit when he did so.

He was beheaded within sight of her window, on Tower Green, but the window was tight shut, and no one heard her screams when her jailers told her what was happening and suggested that she might be made to watch. . . . She clung to the bedpost, shaking with violent hysterics, and Kingston ordered her tormenters away. Harsh and prejudiced though he was, he balked at that last savagery. By nightfall the scaffold was taken down, and all through the morning and day of May eighteenth she heard the sound of hammering as a new one was erected, a low one, invisible from outside the Tower, for public feeling was running high in her favor, and Cromwell thought it unwise to let the common people see her die.

On her last night on earth she slept deeply, worn out in mind and body, her shattered nerves at peace. She had received the Sacrament, and the courage which had sustained her through her trial returned, as all hope and grief subsided before approaching death.

She had wakened at dawn on the nineteenth and dressed in a robe of gray damask, with a crimson petticoat, and elegant red shoes, and dressed her hair high on her head, leaving the delicate neck bare. Then she turned to the women who had guarded her night and day, who had seen her wild with terror and distress like a trapped animal, and ordered them out of the room. And though Cranmer had pronounced her marriage to the King invalid and stripped her of titles, they looked at her uneasily, curtsied and went out.

She was kneeling by the window, staring unseeing at the lightening sky over the gray Tower rooftops; her hands were clasped in prayer but she was done with praying. Her peace was made with God, and the one thing which troubled her most had been put right as far as it was possible.

It was strange how the thought of Mary Tudor tormented her. Of all the mistakes and sins of her short life, she regretted her treatment of Mary most, seeing that pale face under the old-fashioned headdress and hearing the harsh, strained voice defending her mother's rights through choking tears. . . . She had never known such love from her own child. There had not been time. She had sent a message to her stepdaughter, asking her forgiveness, but she would never know if it were granted, or the message even conveyed.

Now, in the last hour that remained to her, she knelt in the attitude of prayer, with a line from Wyatt's old love poem running through her head:

> "Noli me tangere
> For Caesar's I am"

He had escaped; he had not paid for what had happened in the past, like those others who were not even guilty. The words written to her in that fine summer of their love would live, but the love had quickly died. Almost as quickly as that other love . . .

"Caesar's I am"

Henry had written verse to her too; he had written letters such as few women had inspired, offering his heart, his services, his life . . . offering his throne. He had loved her for seven years, and tired in seven months. He had hunted the sweet hart of Hever and caught her, and at eight o'clock that morning, the pursuit would end with a kill, as all hunts did. She suddenly began to tremble; she clenched her hands and struggled for control, her lips moving in a desperate plea for courage, that when they told him, he should hear she had died bravely. . . .

Slowly the spasm passed. He was at Hampton Court, waiting for her to die before he married Jane, and he was very merry while he waited. The time was passed with hunting parties, and balls and masques in the evening; he was gay and active, with that cold woman by his side, meek and unobtrusive, with her eyes cast down. When she heard that he was never idle or alone, she smiled, puzzling her enemies, who hoped to hurt her. Never alone, never alone with his thoughts and his memories, laying the ghost of their past at Hampton with the fierce callousness she knew so well. Let him make merry now, and in the years to come. Let him deface the lovers' knot with their initials on the walls of the palace, and give her rooms to her rival. He would never be free of her; he would hear her voice in every song and her touch when a lute was played; her laughter would mock him in the mirth of others, and her step echo down the corridors they trod together, her black eyes would watch him from the shadows, and stare out of his daughter Elizabeth's face. And he would find her in his bed, no matter whom he put there . . .

His love was dead, but he would never be free, and she knew it at that moment; he would never escape her as she had never escaped him; for good or evil, Fate had joined them, and the sword of the headsman from Calais wouldn't sever that bond. . . .

"For Caesar's I am."

She said the words aloud, and as they died away she heard the sound of footsteps and the opening of the door in the next room.

The sun was up, and it was a lovely cloudless morning. For a moment she waited, savoring one last extension of her time before they came. When the door opened she had risen.

Kingston addressed her.

"Madame, the time has come."

A slow flush rose in her cheeks, and the beauty tears and agony had ravaged lighted her face for the last time.

"Thank you, Master Kingston. I am ready. And may God receive my soul."